Additional Praise for *The Warren Buffett Way*

"*The Warren Buffett Way* outlines his career and presents examples of how his investment techniques and methods evolved and the important individuals in that process. It also details the key investment decisions that produced his unmatched record of performance. Finally the book contains the thinking and the philosophy of an investor that consistently made money using the tools available to every citizen no matter their level of wealth."

from the foreword by Peter Lynch

"The book's popularity is a testimony to the accuracy of its analysis and the value of its advice. The enduring value of Hagstrom's work is due to this clear focus – although the book talks about investment techniques, it is fundamentally about principles. And principles do not change."

from the foreword by Bill Miller

"Warren Buffett is focused, disciplined, and purposeful; he's hard working; highly numerate and logical; he's a voracious collector of information. The attributes listed are rare, but not unique. It's just that few people are able to demonstrate all of them in action. It's the combination of all of them that has enabled Warren to succeed so exceptionally by applying *The Warren Buffett Way*."

from the foreword by Howard Marks

"In simple language, this book tells the rules by which the most successful stock investor of modern times got that way. It could be a godsend to the legion of unhappy investors who keep floundering because they ignore the basics of major investment success."

Phil Fisher, Author, *Common Stocks and Uncommon Profits*

"Robert Hagstrom presents an in-depth examination of Warren Buffett's strategies, and the 'how and why' behind his selection of each of the major securities that have contributed to his remarkable record of success. His 'homespun' wisdom and philosophy are also part of this comprehensive, interesting, and readable book."
John C. Bogle, Chairman, The Vanguard Group

"Warren Buffett is surely the Greatest Investor of this century – not so much because he built a great fortune with a free market as because he shared his important thinking with us and openly demonstrated the sagacity and courage so vital to success. Berkshire Hathaway has been my largest, longest investment. Warren has been my best teacher."
Charles D. Ellis, Managing Partner, Greenwich Associates

"By placing Buffett's approach into a broader context, Robert Hagstrom captures not just the key ideas of this century's investing giants, from Ben Graham to Phil Fisher, but also lucidly explains the theoretical foundation of their insights. This is not an investing book, it's an investing library."
Chris Davis, Davis Advisors

"Warren Buffett is often characterized simply as a 'value investor" or a Ben Graham disciple. Hagstrom fills in the rest of the story with some immensely practical pointers on prospering in the market."
Martin S. Fridson, Author, *Financial theory, reporting, and history*

"Thank you, Robert Hagstrom, for the finely honed thinking, the clear writing, and the simple strategies that help all of us be more successful at one of the life's most intriguing and intimidating tasks; investing our money."
Janet Lowe, Bestselling author, *Warren Buffett Speaks*

THE WARREN BUFFETT WAY

30TH ANNIVERSARY EDITION

INTRODUCING WILEY INVESTMENT CLASSICS

There are certain books that have redefined the way we see the worlds of finance and investing—books that deserve a place on every investor's shelf. *Wiley Investment Classics* will introduce you to these memorable books, which are just as relevant and vital today as when they were first published. Open a *Wiley Investment Classic* and rediscover the proven strategies, market philosophies, and definitive techniques that continue to stand the test of time.

Books in the series include:
Only Yesterday: An Informal History of the 1920's by Frederick Lewis Allen
Lombard Street: A Description of the Money Market by Walter Bagehot
The Go-Go Years: The Drama and Crashing Finale of Wall Street's Bullish 60s by John Brooks
Fifty Years in Wall Street by Henry Clews
Value Averaging: The Safe and Easy Strategy for Higher Investment Returns by Michael E. Edleson
Common Stocks and Uncommon Profits and Other Writings by Philip A. Fisher
Paths to Wealth through Common Stocks by Philip A. Fisher
Extraordinary Popular Delusions and the Madness of Crowds by Charles Mackay and Confusion de Confusiones by Joseph de la Vega by Martin S. Fridson, Ed.
Where the Money Grows and Anatomy of the Bubble by Garet Garrett
The Stock Market Barometer by William Peter Hamilton
Manias, Panics, and Crashes: A History of Financial Crises by Charles P. Kindleberger and Robert Aliber
Reminiscences of a Stock Operator by Edwin Lefevre
The Battle for Investment Survival by Gerald M. Loeb
A Fool and His Money: The Odyssey of an Average Investor by John Rothchild
The Common Sense of Money and Investments by Merryle Stanley Rukeyser
Where Are the Customers' Yachts? Or A Good Hard Look at Wall Street by Fred Schwed, Jr.
The Alchemy of Finance by George Soros
The Aggressive Conservative Investor by Martin J. Whitman and Martin Shubik
Supermoney by Adam Smith
Bogle on Mutual Funds: New Perspectives for the Intelligent Investor by John C. Bogle
John Bogle on Investing: The First 50 Years by John C. Bogle

THE
WARREN BUFFETT WAY

30TH ANNIVERSARY EDITION

ROBERT G. HAGSTROM

WILEY

Copyright © 2024 by Robert G. Hagstrom. All rights reserved.

Published by John Wiley & Sons, Inc., Hoboken, New Jersey.
Published simultaneously in Canada.

No part of this publication may be reproduced, stored in a retrieval system, or transmitted in any form or by any means, electronic, mechanical, photocopying, recording, scanning, or otherwise, except as permitted under Section 107 or 108 of the 1976 United States Copyright Act, without either the prior written permission of the Publisher, or authorization through payment of the appropriate per-copy fee to the Copyright Clearance Center, Inc., 222 Rosewood Drive, Danvers, MA 01923, (978) 750-8400, fax (978) 750-4470, or on the web at www.copyright.com. Requests to the Publisher for permission should be addressed to the Permissions Department, John Wiley & Sons, Inc., 111 River Street, Hoboken, NJ 07030, (201) 748-6011, fax (201) 748-6008, or online at http://www.wiley.com/go/permission.

Trademarks: Wiley and the Wiley logo are trademarks or registered trademarks of John Wiley & Sons, Inc. and/or its affiliates in the United States and other countries and may not be used without written permission. All other trademarks are the property of their respective owners. John Wiley & Sons, Inc. is not associated with any product or vendor mentioned in this book.

Limit of Liability/Disclaimer of Warranty: While the publisher and author have used their best efforts in preparing this book, they make no representations or warranties with respect to the accuracy or completeness of the contents of this book and specifically disclaim any implied warranties of merchantability or fitness for a particular purpose. No warranty may be created or extended by sales representatives or written sales materials. The advice and strategies contained herein may not be suitable for your situation. You should consult with a professional where appropriate. Further, readers should be aware that websites listed in this work may have changed or disappeared between when this work was written and when it is read. Neither the publisher nor authors shall be liable for any loss of profit or any other commercial damages, including but not limited to special, incidental, consequential, or other damages.

For general information on our other products and services or for technical support, please contact our Customer Care Department within the United States at (800) 762-2974, outside the United States at (317) 572-3993 or fax (317) 572-4002.

Wiley also publishes its books in a variety of electronic formats. Some content that appears in print may not be available in electronic formats. For more information about Wiley products, visit our web site at www.wiley.com.

Library of Congress Cataloging-in-Publication Data Is Available:

ISBN 9781394239849 (Cloth)
ISBN 9781394239863 (ePDF)
ISBN 9781394239856 (ePub)

Cover Design: Wiley
Cover Image: © Michael Prince/The Forbes Collection/Contributor/Corbis via Getty Image

SKY10068656_030524

Contents

Foreword to the First Edition		ix
Foreword to the Second Edition		xv
Foreword to the Third Edition		xvii
Preface		xxvii

Chapter One	**World's Greatest Investor**	**1**
	Understanding Patterns	3
	The Making of an Entrepreneur	4
	Buffett Limited Partnership	16
	Berkshire Hathaway: Compounding Conglomerate	20
Chapter Two	**The Education of Warren Buffett**	**25**
	Howard Homan Buffett: Earliest Influence	26
	Benjamin Graham: Developing an Investment Methodology	33
	Philip Fisher: Discerning a Good Business	41
	Charlie Munger: An Intellectual Perspective	50
Chapter Three	**Business-Driven Investing**	**65**
	Business Tenets	68
	Management Tenets	71
	Financial Tenets	79
	Value Tenets	85
	An Intelligent Investor	91
Chapter Four	**Common Stock Purchases**	**93**
	The Washington Post Company	96
	GEICO Corporation	107

	Capital Cities/ABC	120
	The Coca-Cola Company	130
	Apple, Inc.	140
	The Value of Retained Earnings	159
Chapter Five	**Managing a Portfolio of Businesses**	**163**
	Portfolio Management Today: A Choice of Two	164
	A Third Choice: Focus Investing	166
	The Superinvestors of Buffettville	170
	Three Thousand Focus Investors	181
	A Better Way to Measure Performance	185
	High Active-Share Investing	200
Chapter Six	**It's Not That Active Management Doesn't Work**	**203**
	High Priests of Modern Finance	204
	Efficient Market Hypothesis	218
	Investment and Speculation: Understanding the Difference	225
	Investing in a Parallel Universe	230
Chapter Seven	**Money Mind**	**235**
	Sportsman, Teacher, Artist	238
	Berkshire Hathaway: An American Institution	245

Appendix A

Berkshire's Performance versus S&P 500 Index (1965–2022) 251

Appendix B

Berkshire's Common Stock Portfolios (1977–2021) 253

Notes 279

Acknowledgments 293

About the Author 297

Index 299

Foreword to the First Edition

One weekday evening early in 1989, I was home when the telephone rang. Our middle daughter, Annie, then 11, was first to the phone. She told me that Warren Buffett was calling. I was convinced this had to be a prank. The caller started by saying, "This is Warren Buffett from Omaha [as if I might confuse him with some other Warren Buffett]. I just finished your book, I loved it, and I would like to quote one of your sentences in the Berkshire annual report. I have always wanted to do a book, but I never have gotten around to it." He spoke very rapidly with lots of enthusiasm and must have said 40 words in 15 or 20 seconds, including a couple of laughs and chuckles. I instantly agreed to his request and I think we talked for 5 or 10 minutes. I remember he closed by saying, "If you ever visit Omaha and don't come by and see me, your name will be mud in Nebraska."

Clearly not wanting my name to be mud in Nebraska, I took him up on his offer about six months later. Warren Buffett gave me a personal tour of every square foot of the office (which did not take long, as the whole operation could fit inside less than half of a tennis court), and I said hello to all 11 employees. There was not a computer or a stock quotation machine to be found.

After about an hour we went to a local restaurant where I followed his lead and had a terrific steak and my first Cherry Coke in 30 years. We talked about jobs we had as children, baseball, and bridge, and exchanged stories about companies in which we had held investments in the past. Warren discussed or answered questions about each stock and operation that Berkshire (he never called his company Berkshire Hathaway) owned.

Why has Warren Buffett been the best investor in history? What is he like as an individual, a shareholder, a manager, and an owner of entire companies? What is so unique about the Berkshire Hathaway annual report, why does he donate so much effort to it, and what can someone learn from it? To attempt to answer those questions, I talked with him directly, and reread the last five annual reports and his earliest reports as chairman (the 1971 and 1972 reports each had only two pages of text). In addition, I had discussions with nine individuals who have been actively involved with Warren Buffett in varied relationships and from different viewpoints during the past four to over 30 years: Jack Byrne, Robert Denham, Don Keough, Carol Loomis, Charlie Munger, Tom Murphy, Carl Reichardt, Frank Rooney, and Seth Schofield.

In terms of his personal qualities, the responses were quite consistent. Warren Buffett is, first of all, very content. He loves everything he does, dealing with people and reading mass quantities of annual and quarterly reports and numerous newspapers and periodicals. As an investor he has discipline, patience, flexibility, courage, confidence, and decisiveness. He is always searching for investments where risk is eliminated or minimized. In addition, he is very adept at probability and as an oddsmaker. I believe this ability comes from an inherent love of simple math computations, his devotion and active participation in the game of bridge, and his long experience in underwriting and accepting high levels of risk in insurance and in reinsurance. He is willing to take risks where the odds of total loss are low and upside rewards are substantial. He lists his failures and mistakes and does not apologize. He enjoys kidding himself and compliments his associates in objective terms.

Warren Buffett is a great student of business and a wonderful listener, and he is able to determine the key elements of a company or a complex issue with high speed and precision. He can make a decision not to invest in something in as little as two minutes and conclude that it is time to make a major purchase in just a few days of research. He is always prepared, for as he has said in an annual report, "Noah did not start building the ark when it was raining."

As a manager he almost never calls a division head or the chief executive of a company but is delighted at any time of the day or night for them to call him to report something or to seek counsel. After investing in a stock or purchasing an entire operation, he becomes a cheerleader and sounding board: "At Berkshire we don't tell .400 hitters how to swing," using an analogy to baseball management.

Two examples of Warren Buffett's willingness to learn and adapt himself are public speaking and computer usage. In the 1950s Warren invested $100 in a Dale Carnegie course "not to prevent my knees from knocking when public speaking but to do public speaking while my knees are knocking." At the Berkshire annual meeting in front of more than 2,000 people, Warren Buffett sits on a stage with Charlie Munger, and, without notes, lectures and responds to questions in a fashion that would please Will Rogers, Ben Graham, King Solomon, Phil Fisher, David Letterman, and Billy Crystal. To be able to play more bridge, early in 1994 Warren learned how to use a computer so he could join a network where you can play with other individuals from their locations all over the country. Perhaps in the near future he will begin to use some of the hundreds of data retrieval and information services on companies that are available on computers today for investment research.

Warren Buffett stresses that the critical investment factor is determining the intrinsic value of a business and paying a fair or bargain price. He doesn't care what the general stock market has done recently or will do in the future. He purchased over $1 billion of Coca-Cola in 1988 and 1989 after the stock had risen over fivefold the prior six years and over five-hundredfold the previous 60 years. He made four times his money in three years and plans to make a lot more the next 5, 10, and 20 years with Coke. In 1976 he purchased a very major position in GEICO when the stock had declined from $61 to $2 and the general perception was that the stock was definitely going to zero.

How can the average investor employ Warren Buffett's methods? Warren Buffett never invests in businesses he cannot understand or that are outside his "circle of competence." All investors can, over time, obtain and intensify their circle of competence in an industry where they are professionally involved or in some sector of business they enjoy researching. One does not have to be correct very many times in a lifetime, as Warren states that 12 investment decisions in his 40-year career have made all the difference.

Risk can be reduced greatly by concentrating on only a few holdings if it forces investors to be more careful and thorough in their research. Normally more than 75 percent of Berkshire's common stock holdings are represented by only five different securities. One of the principles demonstrated clearly several times in this book is to buy great businesses when they are having a temporary problem or when the stock market declines and creates bargain prices for outstanding franchises. Stop trying to predict the direction of the stock market, the economy, interest rates, or elections, and stop wasting money on individuals who do this for a living. Study the facts and the financial condition, value the company's future outlook, and purchase when everything is in your favor. Many people invest in a way similar to playing poker all night without ever looking at their cards.

Very few investors would have had the knowledge and courage to purchase GEICO at $2 or Wells Fargo or General Dynamics when they were depressed, as there were numerous learned people saying those companies were in substantial trouble. However, Warren Buffett also purchased stock of Capital Cities/ABC, Gillette, Washington Post, Affiliated Publications, Freddie Mac, or Coca-Cola (which have produced over $6 billion of profits for Berkshire Hathaway, or 60 percent of the $10 billion of shareholders' equity); these were all well-run companies with strong histories of profitability, and they were dominant business franchises.

In addition to his own shareholders, Warren Buffett uses the Berkshire annual report to help the general public become better investors. On both sides of his family he is descended from newspaper editors, and his Aunt Alice was a public school teacher for more than 30 years. Warren Buffett enjoys both teaching and writing about business in general and investing in particular. He taught on a volunteer basis when he was 21 at the University of Nebraska in Omaha. In 1955, when he was working in New York City, he taught an adult education course on the stock market at Scarsdale High School. For 10 years in the late 1960s and 1970s he gave a free lecture course at Creighton University. In 1977 he served on a committee headed by Al Sommer Jr., to advise the Securities and Exchange Commission on corporate disclosure. After that involvement, the scale of the Berkshire annual report changed dramatically with the 1977 report written in late 1977 and early 1978. The format became more similar to the partnership reports he had produced from 1956 to 1969.

Since the early 1980s, the Berkshire annual reports have informed shareholders of the performance of the holdings of the company and new investments, have updated the status of the insurance and the reinsurance industry, and (since 1982) have listed acquisition criteria about businesses Berkshire would like to purchase. The report is generously laced with examples, analogies, stories, and metaphors containing the dos and don'ts of proper investing in stocks.

Warren Buffett has established a high standard for the future performance of Berkshire by setting an objective of growing intrinsic value by 15 percent a year over the long term, something few people, and no one from 1956 to 1993 besides himself, have ever done. He has stated it will be a difficult standard to maintain due to the much larger size of the company, but there are always opportunities around and Berkshire keeps lots of cash ready to invest, and it grows every year. His confidence is somewhat underlined by the final nine words of the June 1993 annual report on page 60: "Berkshire has not declared a cash dividend since 1967."

Warren Buffett has stated that he has always wanted to write a book on investing. Hopefully that will happen someday. However, until that event, his annual reports are filling that function in a fashion somewhat similar to the 19th-century authors who wrote in serial form: Edgar Allan Poe, William Makepeace Thackeray, and Charles Dickens. The Berkshire Hathaway annual reports from 1977 through 1993 are 17 chapters of that book. And also in the interim we now have *The Warren Buffett Way*, in which Robert

Hagstrom outlines Buffett's career and presents examples of how his investment technique and methods evolved as well as the important individuals in that process. The book also details the key investment decisions that produced Buffett's unmatched record of performance. Finally, it contains the thinking and the philosophy of an investor who has consistently made money using the tools available to every citizen no matter one's level of wealth.

PETER S. LYNCH
OCTOBER 1994

Foreword to the Second Edition

When Robert Hagstrom first published *The Warren Buffett Way* in 1994, it quickly became a phenomenon. To date [2004], more than 1.2 million copies have been sold. The book's popularity is a testimony to the accuracy of its analysis and the value of its advice.

Any time the subject is Warren Buffett, it is easy to become overwhelmed by the sheer size of the numbers. Whereas most investors think in terms of hundreds or perhaps thousands, Buffett moves in a world of millions and billions. But that does not mean he has nothing to teach us. Quite the opposite. If we look at what he does and has done, and are able to discern the underlying thinking, we can model our decisions on his.

That is the profound contribution of Robert's book. He closely studied Warren Buffett's actions, words, and decisions for a number of years, and then he set about analyzing them for common threads. For this book, he distilled those common threads into 12 tenets, timeless principles that guide Buffett's investment philosophy through all circumstances and all markets. In just the same way, they can guide any investor.

The enduring value of Robert's work is due to this clear focus—although the book talks about investment techniques, it is fundamentally about investment principles. And principles do not change. I can almost hear Warren saying, with his wry smile, "That's why they call them principles."

The past 10 years have given us a vivid demonstration of that basic truth. In those 10 years, the trends of the stock market changed several times over. We witnessed a high-flying bubble that made many people rich, and then a steep crash into a protracted, painful bear market before the market finally hit bottom in the spring of 2003 and started to turn back up.

All along the way, Warren Buffett's investment approach never changed. He has continued to follow the same principles outlined in this book:

- Think of buying stocks as buying fractional interests in whole businesses.
- Construct a focused, low-turnover portfolio.
- Invest in only what you can understand and analyze.
- Demand a margin of safety between the purchase price and the company's long-term value.

Berkshire Hathaway investors, as usual, reap the benefits of that steady approach. Since the recovery began in 2003, Berkshire Hathaway stock is up about $20,000 per share, more than 30 percent, far surpassing the returns of the overall market over the comparable period.

There is a chain of thinking for value investors that begins with Benjamin Graham, through Warren Buffett and his contemporaries, to the next generation of practitioners such as Robert Hagstrom. Buffett, Graham's best-known disciple, frequently advises investors to study Graham's book *The Intelligent Investor*. I often make the same recommendation myself. And I am convinced that Robert's work shares with that classic book one critical quality: The advice may not make you rich, but it is highly unlikely to make you poor. If understood and intelligently implemented, the techniques and principles presented here should make you a better investor.

BILL MILLER
CHAIRMAN AND CHIEF INVESTMENT OFFICER, LMM, LLC
OCTOBER 2004

Foreword to the Third Edition

What accounts for Warren Buffett's exceptional investment success? That's one of the questions I'm asked most often. It's also the question I want to explore in this foreword.

When I studied for my MBA at the University of Chicago in the late 1960s, I was exposed to a new theory of finance that had been developed, largely there, in the preceding few years. One of the most important components of the "Chicago School" of thought was the Efficient Market Hypothesis. According to that hypothesis, the combined efforts of millions of intelligent, motivated, objective, and informed investors cause information to immediately be reflected in market prices such that assets will provide a fair risk-adjusted return, no more and no less. Prices are never so low or so high that they can be taken advantage of, and thus no investors can be capable of consistently identifying opportunities to benefit. It's this hypothesis that gives rise to the Chicago School's best-known dictum: You can't beat the market.

The Efficient Market Hypothesis supplies the intellectual basis for that conclusion, and there are lots of empirical data showing that, despite all their efforts, most investors don't beat the market. That's a pretty strong case for the inability to outperform.

It's not that no investors beat the market. Every once in a while some do, and just as many underperform; market efficiency isn't so strong a force that it's impossible for individual investors' returns to deviate from the market's return. It's merely asserted that no one can do it to a sufficient degree and consistently enough to disprove the Efficient Market Hypothesis. There are outliers, as in most processes, but their superior returns are described as being based on randomness and thus ephemeral. When I grew up, there was a saying that "if you put enough chimpanzees in a room with typewriters, eventually one of them will write the Bible." That is, when randomness is present, just about anything can happen once in a while. However, as my mother used to say, "It's the exception that proves the rule." A general rule may not hold 100 percent, but the fact that exceptions are so rare attests to its basic truth. Every day, millions of investors, amateur and professional alike, prove you can't beat the market.

And then there's Warren Buffett.

Warren and a few other legendary investors—including Ben Graham, Peter Lynch, Stan Druckenmiller, George Soros, and Julian Robertson—have performance records that fly in the face of the Chicago School. In short, they've outperformed by a big enough margin, for long enough periods of time, with large enough amounts of money, that the advocates of market efficiency are forced into the defensive. Their records show that exceptional investors can beat the market through skill, not chance.

Especially in Warren's case, it's hard to argue with the evidence. On his office wall, he displays a statement, typed by him, showing that he started The Buffett Partnership in 1956 with $105,000. Since then, he has attracted additional capital and earned returns on it such that Berkshire Hathaway now has investments totaling $143 billion and a net worth of $202 billion. He's kicked the hell out of the indices for many years. And in the process, he's become the second wealthiest man in America. This last achievement wasn't based on dynastic real estate assets or a unique technological invention, as with so many on Forbes's lists, but on applying hard work and skill in investment markets that are open to everyone.

What's responsible for Warren Buffett's singular accomplishments? In my view these are the keys:

- **He's super-smart.** One of the many bon mots attributed to Warren is the following: "If you have an IQ of 160, sell 30 points. You don't need them." As Malcolm Gladwell pointed out in the book *Outliers*, you don't have to be a genius to achieve great success, just smart enough. Beyond that, incremental intelligence doesn't necessarily add to your chances. In fact, there are people so smart that they can't get out of their own way or can't find the path to success (and happiness) in the real world. A high IQ isn't enough to make someone a great investor; if it were, college professors would probably be the richest people in America. It's important to also to be business-oriented and have "savvy" or "street smarts."

I have a sneaking suspicion that Warren's IQ is well above 130 . . . and that he hasn't made any effort to dispose of those "nonessential" extra points. His ability to cut to the core of a question, to reach a well-founded conclusion, and to hold that conclusion even if things initially go against him are all key elements in who he is and what he's accomplished. In short, he's fiercely analytical.

He's also incredibly quick. It doesn't take him weeks or months to reach a conclusion. He also doesn't need a cadre of analysts pushing numbers. He doesn't feel the need to know and consider every data point: just the ones that matter. And he has a great sense for which they are.

- **He's guided by an overarching philosophy.** Many investors think they're smart enough to master anything, or at least they act that way. Further, they believe the world is constantly changing, and you have to be eclectic and change your approach to adapt, racing to stay up with the latest wonder. The trouble with this is that no one really can know everything, it's hard to constantly retool and learn new tricks, and this mindset prevents the development of specialized expertise and helpful shortcuts.

  Warren, however, knows what he doesn't know, sticks to what he does know, and leaves the rest for others. This is essential, since as Mark Twain said, "It ain't what you don't know that gets you into trouble. It's what you know for sure that just ain't so." Warren only invests in industries he understands and feels comfortable with. He emphasizes fairly prosaic fields and avoids, for example, high-tech companies.

He famously passes on things that are outside his philosophy and ken. Importantly, he can live with the possibility that the things he passes on will make money for others and he'll be left looking on as they do. (Most people can't.)

- **He's mentally flexible.** The fact that it's important to have a guiding philosophy doesn't mean it's never good to change. It can be desirable to adapt to significantly changed circumstances. It's even possible to come across a better philosophy. The key lies in knowing when to change and when to hold fast.

    Early in his career, Warren adopted the approach of his great teacher, Ben Graham. It's called "deep value"—buying castoffs when they're being given away, especially when companies can be bought for less than their net cash. It has sometimes been derided as "picking up cigar butts." After a while, however, with urging from his partner, Charlie Munger, he switched to emphasizing high-quality companies with protective "moats" and pricing power, led by outstanding people, at reasonable (but not necessarily giveaway) prices.

    It was long an aspect of Warren's approach to eschew companies that were capital-intensive, but he was able to overcome that bias to buy the Burlington Northern Santa Fe railway and take advantage of its economic sensitivity coming out of the 2008 financial collapse, and the outlook for increasing rail carriage.

    A philosophy should supply guidance but not rigidity. This—like many other things in investing—is a tough dilemma to master. Warren doesn't shrink from the challenge, neither changing with every new fad nor letting his thinking get stuck in cement.

- **He's unemotional.** Many of the obstacles to investment success relate to human emotion; the main reason for the failure of the Efficient Market Hypothesis is that investors rarely satisfy the requirement of objectivity. Most become greedy, confident, and euphoric when prices are high, causing them to celebrate their winners and buy more rather than take profits. And they get depressed and fearful when prices are low, causing them to sell assets at bargain prices and invariably discouraging them from buying. And perhaps worst of all, they have a terrible tendency to judge how they're doing based on how others are doing, and to let envy of others' success force them to take additional risk for the simple reason that others are doing so. Envy is enough to make people follow the crowd, even into investments they know nothing about.

Warren appears absolutely immune to these emotional influences. He doesn't get overjoyed when things appreciate, or downcast when they don't, and for him success is clearly defined by himself, not the masses or the media. He doesn't care whether others think he's right, or whether his investment decisions promptly make him look right. (He was written off as "past his prime" early in 2000 because of his failure to participate in what turned out to be the tech bubble, but he never changed his spots.) He only cares what he (and Charlie Munger) thinks . . . and whether his shareholders make money.

- **He's contrarian and iconoclastic.** Whereas the typical investor thinks he should follow the herd, despite its susceptibility to the errors of emotion, the best investors behave in a contrarian fashion, diverging from the herd at the key moments. But it's not enough to do the opposite of what others are doing. You have to understand what they're doing, understand why it's wrong, know what to do instead, have the nerve to act in a contrary fashion (that is, to adopt and hold what Yale's David Swensen calls "uncomfortably idiosyncratic positions"), and be willing to look terribly wrong until the ship turns and you're proved right. That last element can feel like it's taking forever; as the old saying goes, "Being too far ahead of your time is indistinguishable from being wrong." Take it all together and it's clear that this isn't easy.

It's obvious that Warren is highly capable of contrarian behavior. In fact, he revels in it. He once wrote me that he had seen high-yield bonds when the market priced them like flowers and he had seen them when they were considered weeds. "I liked them better when they were weeds." The contrarian prefers to buy things when they're out of favor. Warren does it like no one else.

- **He's counter-cyclical.** Investing consists of dealing with the future, and yet many of the best investors accept that they can't predict what the macro future holds in terms of economic developments, interest rates, and market fluctuations. If we can't excel at the thing that most people want to hang their hat on, what can we do? In my view, there are great gains to be had from behaving counter-cyclically.

  It's emotionally easy to invest when the economy is improving, companies are reporting higher earnings, asset prices are rising, and risk bearing is being rewarded. But buying appreciated assets doesn't hold the key to superior investment results. Rather, the greatest bargains are accessed by buying when the economy and companies are suffering: that's more likely to be the climate in which asset prices understate their merits. However, this, too, is not easy.

  Warren has repeatedly demonstrated his ability—in fact, his preference—for investing at the bottom of the cycle, when optimism is in short supply. His investments of $5 billion each in 10 percent preferred stock of Goldman Sachs and General Electric at the depths of the 2008 financial crisis, and his purchase of economically sensitive Burlington Northern for $34 billion in 2009, are emblematic of this. The wisdom of these investments is obvious today in retrospect, but how many acted as boldly when fear of a financial collapse was rampant?

- **He has a long-term focus and is unconcerned with volatility.** Over my 45 years in the business, investors' time horizons have gotten shorter and shorter. This is likely the result of increased media attention to investment results (there was none in the 1960s), its contagion to investors and their clients, and the striving for yearly gains introduced by hedge funds' annual incentive fees. But as other people allow nonsensical biases to affect their thoughts and actions, we can profit from avoiding them. Thus, most investors' excessive concern with quarterly and annual results creates profit opportunities for those who think in terms of longer periods.

Warren has famously said that his "holding period is forever," and that he "prefers a lumpy 15 percent a year over a smooth 12 percent." This allows him to stick with great ideas for long periods of time, compounding his gains and allowing profits to build up untaxed, rather than turning over the portfolio every year and paying taxes at short-term rates. It also helps him avoid getting shaken out in times of volatility, and instead lets him take advantage of them. In fact, rather than insist on liquidity and take advantage of the ability to exit from investments, Warren's actions make clear that he is happy making investments he could never shed.

- **He's unafraid to bet big on his best ideas.** Diversification has long played a leading part in so-called prudent investment management. In short, it reduces the likelihood of large individual losses (and of being sued for having had too much in a losing position). But while it reduces the pain caused by losing investments, a high degree of diversification correspondingly reduces the potential gain from winners.

  As in many things, Warren takes a divergent view of diversification: "The strategy we've adopted precludes our following standard diversification dogma. Many pundits would therefore say the strategy must be riskier than that employed by more conventional investors. We believe that a policy of portfolio concentration may well decrease risk if it raises, as it should, both the intensity with which an investor thinks about a business and the comfort level he must feel with its economic characteristics before buying into it."

  Warren understands that great ideas come along only on rare occasion, so he keeps the bar high, only invests in great ideas, and bets big when he sees one. Thus, he commits significantly to the companies and people he believes in; he doesn't hold anything just because others do and he's worried it may perform well without his being represented; and he refuses to diversify into things he thinks less of just to mitigate the impact of errors—that is, to practice what he calls "de-worstification." It's obvious that all of these things are essential if you're to have a chance at great results. But that doesn't keep them from being the exception in portfolio management, not the rule.

- **He's willing to be inactive.** Too many investors act as if there's always something great to do. Or perhaps they think they have to give the impression that they're smart enough to always be able to find a brilliant investment. But great investment opportunities are exceptional . . . and by definition, that means they're not available every day.

  Warren is famously willing to be inactive for long periods of time, turning down deal after deal until the right one comes along. He's famous for his analogy to one of baseball's greatest hitters, Ted Williams, standing at the plate with his bat on his shoulder and waiting for the perfect pitch; it exemplifies his insistence on making investments only when they're compelling. Who would argue that the supply of good deals is steady, or that it's always an equally good time to invest?

- **Finally, he's not worried about losing his job.** Very few investors are able to take all the actions they think are right. Many are constrained in terms of their ability to buy assets that are illiquid, controversial, or unseemly; sell appreciating assets that "everyone" is sure will go further; and concentrate their portfolios in their few best ideas. Why? Because they fear the consequences of being wrong.

  "Agents" who manage money for others worry that acting boldly will expose them to the risk of being fired by their employers or terminated by their clients. Thus, they moderate their actions, doing only that which is considered prudent and uncontroversial. That's the tendency that caused John Maynard Keynes to observe, "Worldly wisdom teaches that it is better for reputation to fail conventionally than to succeed unconventionally." But that tendency introduces an important conundrum: if you're unwilling to take a position so bold that it can embarrass you if it fails, it's correspondingly impossible to take a position that can make a real difference if it works out well. Great investors are able to follow up their intellectual conclusions with action; in short, they dare to be great. Warren obviously doesn't have to worry about being let go by his employer. His position is as close to permanent as there is, as is his capital. There are no clients able to withdraw their capital, mandating the sale of assets at bargain prices as befalls the typical money manager during market crashes. This simple fact plays a significant part in any great investor's success, and I'm sure it's no coincidence that Warren set things up this way, transitioning from a hedge fund structure to Berkshire Hathaway's corporate form. He wouldn't have it any other way.

Of course, Warren Buffett shares many other attributes of outstanding investors. He's focused, disciplined, and purposeful; he's hard working; he's highly numerate and logical; he's a voracious collector of information, through both reading and networking with people he respects; and at this point, he invests because he enjoys solving the complex intellectual problem that it represents, not to gain fame or make money. Those latter things are the byproduct of his efforts, but not his goal, I'm sure.

In theory, many others could have done what Warren Buffett did over the last 60 years. The attributes listed are rare, but not unique. And each one makes compelling sense; who would take the other side of any of these propositions? It's just that few people are able to demonstrate all of them in action. It's the combination of all of them—and the addition of that intangible "something" that makes a special person special—that has enabled Warren to succeed so exceptionally by applying *The Warren Buffett Way*.

HOWARD MARKS
JULY 2013

Preface

I first met Warren Buffett 40 years ago. Not in person, but by reading his chairman's letter in the 1983 Berkshire Hathaway annual report. I was training to be a stockbroker with an aid-Atlantic brokerage firm. Part of my studies included analyzing Berkshire's annual reports. Like so many, I was instantly impressed with the clarity of Buffett's writing. Most important, I was struck with how sensibly he laid out the idea that owning a stock was equivalent to owning a business. As a liberal arts major in college, I didn't study accounting or finance, so trying to understand stocks only using rows of numbers in balance sheets and income statements did not come easily.

But when Warren Buffett introduced me to Rose Blumkin at Nebraska Furniture Mart, Stan Lipsey at Buffalo Evening News, Chuck Huggins at See's Candy Shops, and Jack Byrne at GEICO, I instantly connected to Buffett's persuading argument that the most intelligent way to think about stocks was from a businessperson's perspective. In buying a stock, I was in fact becoming an owner in a company. It now all made sense. In one epiphanic moment, Warren Buffett revealed the inner nature of investing. The balance sheet and income statements were still there, but those numerical skeletons had suddenly grown muscle, skin, and purpose. In a word, common stocks had come alive. Instead of seeing just numbers, I began to think about companies and the people who were running the businesses selling products and services that ultimately generated sales and earnings; the numbers, in turn, filled a spreadsheet.

When I earned my broker stripes and went into production I knew exactly what I was going to do. I would invest my client's money in good businesses. Put differently, I was going to heed Warren Buffett's advice and become a "business picker" not a "stock picker." And most of all, I was going to dedicate myself to continually studying the investment strategies of Warren Buffett. I wrote to the Securities and Exchange Commission for all the past Berkshire Hathaway annual reports and the annual reports of the public companies Berkshire owned. Over the years, I collected all the newspaper and magazine articles written about Warren Buffett and Berkshire. I was like a kid following a ballplayer.

Years later, Warren Buffett stated, "What we do is not beyond anybody else's competence. It's just not necessary to do extraordinary things to get extraordinary results." Now, I'm sure whoever read this chalked it up to Buffett's Midwestern humility. Buffett is not a braggart, but neither does he mislead. I was sure he would have not made this statement if he did not believe it to be true. And if it were true, as I believed it was, it meant there was the possibility of uncovering a road map or, better yet, a treasure map that would describe how Buffett thinks about investing in general and stock selection specifically. This was my motivation for writing *The Warren Buffett Way*.

The principal challenge I faced in writing the book was to actually prove Buffett's claim that what I do is not beyond anybody else's competence. Some critics argue that, despite his success, Warren Buffett's idiosyncrasies mean his investment approach cannot be widely adopted. I disagreed. Buffett is idiosyncratic—it is the source of his success—but his methodology, once understood, is applicable to individuals and institutions alike. The goal of this book is to help investors employ the strategies that made Warren Buffett successful.

To do this, I culled the best of Warren Buffett's writings from Berkshire's chairman's letters, countless magazine and newspaper articles, television interviews, and of course the annual shareholder meetings. No stone was left unturned. From this I gleaned how Buffett examines a company from a **business** perspective, **management** behavior, *financial* returns, and, lastly, how to *value* common stocks. These became the 12 Investment Tenets of *The Warren Buffett Way*. These core principles are called out, to detail and clarify Buffett's four-part investment strategy:

1. Analyze a stock as a business.
2. Demand a margin of safety for each purchase.

3. Manage a low-turnover, focused portfolio.
4. Protect yourself from the speculative and emotional forces of the market.

The Warren Buffett Way describes at its core a simple approach. There are no computer programs to learn, no two-inch-thick investment manuals to decipher. Whether you are financially able to purchase 10 percent of a company or a hundred shares of stock, this book can help you achieve profitable investment returns.

Still there are skeptics. The major pushback we received over the years is that reading a book about Warren Buffett will not ensure you will be able to generate the same investment returns that Buffett has achieved. First, I never insinuated that by reading the book an individual could achieve the same results as Buffett. Second, I was puzzled why anyone would think so. It seemed to me that if you bought a book about how to play golf like Tiger Woods, you shouldn't expect to become Tiger's equal on the golf course. You read the book because you believe there are some tips in the book that will help improve your game. The same is true of *The Warren Buffett Way*. If, by reading this book, you pick up some lessons that help improve your investment results, then the book is a success.

The buy-and-hold investment strategy that is at the core of Warren Buffett's approach appeals intuitively to people. The concept of buying and holding an investment for several years, thus achieving returns commensurate with the economics of the business, is simple and straightforward. Investors can easily understand the mechanics of this approach. Warren Buffett's attraction is twofold. One, he is the designated representative of the buy-and-hold approach and, two, in doing so he also became the world's greatest investor.

In the 30 years since I wrote *The Warren Buffett Way*, the noise in the stock market has continued to rise. And just when you think it can't get any louder, it turns into a deafening screech. Television commentators, financial writers, analysts, and market strategists are overtalking each other, all vying for investors' attention. The stock market appears to have become a cynical game for many who know the price of everything and the value of nothing.

Yet, despite an avalanche of information, investors continually struggle to earn a profit. Some are hard-pressed to even continue. Stock prices skyrocket for little reason, then plummet just as quickly. People who have turned to the stock market to invest for their children's education or even their own retirement are bewildered. There appears to be no rhyme or reason to the stock market, only folly.

But far above the market madness stands the wisdom and counsel of Warren Buffett. In an environment that seems to favor the speculator over the investor, Buffett's advice has proven, time and again, to be the safe harbor for millions of lost investors.

Long-term investing used to be a prudent course of action. Now when you tell someone you are a long-term investor, you are considered old-fashioned, out of step, clinging to a quaint idea for a time that has come and gone. The world is on the move, we are told. If you are not constantly buying and selling, you must be falling behind.

Being a business-driven investor in the stock market can sometime feel like you are a round block trying to fit into a square hole. But we have been educated by Warren Buffett and we have learned how to thoughtfully measure our progress without having to rely on the market's short-term prices to tell us whether or not we are doing a good job. The question is not whether business-driven investors can be successful operating in the stock market, rife with all its challenges. It is a question of whether we have acquired the right mindset—studying the lessons learned from the ultimate investor.

CHAPTER 1

World's Greatest Investor

We investors have a built-in need to understand the world, especially that sliver that has a direct impact on our financial well-being. And when the unexpected occurs, we seek answers.

That surely was the case in 1973, when stock prices started a brutal downhill slide that only got worse the following year. By the end of 1974, the overall stock market was down an agonizing 50 percent. Investors were left shaken, wondering what happened to their portfolio, their retirement savings. And they asked themselves, What should I have done differently?

As it happens, academicians at leading universities had been thinking about the stock market for some time. Working separately, they had developed and refined several ideas about the behavior of markets, particularly the core concept of risk and return.

One idea, with its roots in psychology, starts with the acknowledgment that most people get emotional when it comes to money. Specifically, most investors abhor the thought of losing money, which these financial scholars equated with price volatility. If investors don't have the emotional fortitude to remain calm when stock market prices start bouncing wildly, they are almost certain to panic and make bad decisions. Therefore, the ideal investment strategy must reflect their specific point on the risk/reward scale, which measures their ability to tolerate price volatility.

Another concept, closely tied to risk tolerance, is the notion of diversification. The core idea is that volatility can be better managed if a stock portfolio is diversified among different companies and industries. Thus, if any one particular area of the economy is hit by some disaster, a widely diversified portfolio has the built-in protection that works to mitigate price losses.

Over the years both these general theories—risk equals price and diversification tempers price volatility—have been debated, amended, expanded, published, footnoted, and debated again. Eventually, through a kind of cloistered evolution, those separate ideas coalesced into one overall concept that came to be known as *Modern Portfolio Theory*. But it remained quietly ensconced in academia until the dramatic stock market sell-off of 1973–1974. Those crushing losses sent investors and their advisors looking for answers.

That's when Modern Portfolio Theory was "discovered" in the ivory towers and brought down into the marketplace. Suddenly, or so it seemed at the time, everyone turned to Modern Portfolio Theory as the one approach that made the most sense for investors.

There's just one problem with Modern Portfolio Theory. His name is Warren Buffett.

Buffett does not equate risk with price volatility. He does not manage a broadly diversified portfolio of common stocks but rather a concentrated, low-turnover portfolio. Nonetheless, his performance through almost seven decades has led many to call him the world's greatest investor—or, in some cases, a five-sigma event, a statistical phenomenon so rare that it practically never occurs.[1]

Omaha-born and -raised, Warren Buffett graduated from the University of Nebraska, then went to Columbia University to study with Benjamin Graham and David Dodd, the coauthors of *Security Analysis*, the seminal book on value investing. Graham was also the author of *The Intelligent Investor*, which Buffett has called the most important investment book ever written. He has often declared that it had forever changed his thinking on how to invest in the stock market.

After Columbia, Buffett worked for a time at his mentor's company, the Graham-Newman Corporation, before returning to

Omaha and launching his own investment company, the Buffett Limited Partnership, in 1956. He set an ambitious goal for himself: to beat the Dow Jones Industrial Average by an average 10 percentage points per year. For the next 13 years (1957–1969), the partnership generated an average annual return of 31 percent, 22 points higher than the Dow's 9 percent average annual return. Even more amazing, Buffett beat the Dow every single one of those 13 years. In all that time, he never had a down year.

In 1962, the Buffett Partnership began buying shares in a Massachusetts textile manufacturer called Berkshire Hathaway. By 1965, Buffett was in effective control of the company. When the Buffett Partnership ceased operations at the end of 1969, he told his partners he was going to move his personal investments from the partnership into Berkshire Hathaway stock. That was the start of what became the Berkshire Hathaway of today: a conglomerate that owns both private companies and public securities. In its first 10 years with Buffett at the helm (1965–1974), which included the disastrous bear market of 1973–1974, a dollar invested in Berkshire Hathaway tripled. Over the same time frame, that same dollar in the S&P 500 Index with dividends reinvested returned 13 cents. And he was just getting started.

No professional investor has managed money longer than Warren Buffett.[2] Adjusting for the overlap between Buffett Partnership and Berkshire Hathaway, he has managed portfolios for 66 years. Separating Berkshire Hathaway's performance (1965–2022), Berkshire's overall gain for 58 years was 3,787,464 percent compared to the S&P 500 Index, which, with dividends included, returned 24,708 percent. That's a compounded annual gain of 19.8 percent for Buffett, versus the 9.9 percent for the S&P 500 Index. Put differently, one dollar invested in the S&P 500 Index in 1965 would be worth $248 at the end of 2022; invested in Berkshire, it was worth $37,875.

Understanding Patterns

The human mind craves patterns, for they suggest order that, in turn, enables us to make sense of the world.[3] Investors are no different.

They, too, are pattern-seeking animals. Unfortunately, most investors are looking for patterns in the wrong place. They are certain that there is some reliable pattern for predicting short-term price changes. But they are mistaken. There are no models that can consistently predict the direction of the stock market. Markets are too large, too complex, and are constantly evolving over time. The exact patterns to predicting markets do not repeat. Still, investors keep trying.

Warren Buffett also seeks patterns. But the patterns he looks for are not confined to the market but those found when analyzing businesses. Buffett has learned that inside each company there are recognizable patterns in three distinct areas: the nature of the business, financial returns, and management qualities. He firmly believes that these patterns will, at some point, reveal the future direction of the stock price. Of course, over the short run stock prices do not obligingly follow every change in a business. But if your time horizon is long enough, it is remarkable how stock prices eventually match up with the patterns revealed by the economics of the underlying businesses.

It's been said that some measure of luck is always part of a streak. There is no question Warren Buffett caught some lucky breaks over his career alongside his fair share of bad luck. But make no mistake, long streaks are imposed on great skill.[4] The objective of *The Warren Buffett Way* is to explore the skill set of the world's greatest investor.

The Making of an Entrepreneur

We can trace the Buffett clan all the way back to John Buffett, who married Hannah Titus on the north shore of Long Island, New York, in 1696. Fast-forward to 1867, when Sidney Homan Buffett, hearing the call of the West, left New York and took a job driving a stagecoach to Omaha. Once there, he decided to stay, and in 1869 he opened the S. H. Buffett Grocery, setting in motion the Buffett dynasty that remains in Omaha today.

By 1900, Omaha was sprinkled with tall buildings and cable cars. Its population had swelled to 140,000. Sidney Buffett expanded his grocery business, and soon his two sons joined him. The youngest, Ernest, left his father's bigger downtown location and established in the suburbs a new grocery store he grandly called Ernest Buffett, Grocer and Master Merchant. Ernest had four sons, one of whom, Howard, became the father of Warren Buffett.

Howard Buffett had little interest in the grocery business. He dreamed of becoming a journalist and at the University of Nebraska served as editor of the school newspaper, the *Daily Nebraskan*. Then, in his senior year a chance meeting with Leila Stahl, soon to be Mrs. Howard Buffett, changed his future. To win Leila's heart and her father's approval, Howard forsook a career in the news business and instead took a more dependable job selling insurance. He later parlayed that sales experience into a new job as a securities salesman, and that led to the formation of a new brokerage firm: Buffett, Skelincka & Company.

In his early years, young Warren took lessons from his grandfather, the grocery merchant. What we know is that before Warren Buffett became an investor, he became an entrepreneur: someone who starts a business to seek a profit. When Buffett was six years old, his beloved Aunt Alice sent him a present. On Christmas morning, he ripped off the wrapping paper and strapped to his belt what would become his most prized possession—a nickel-coated money changer. He quickly found many ways to put it to good use. Young Warren set up a table outside on the sidewalk and sold Chiclets to any who passed by. He went door-to-door selling packs of gum and soda pop. He bought six-packs of Coke at his grandfather's grocery store for 25 cents and sold the individual bottles for a nickel: a 20 percent return on investment.

Later, Buffett sold copies of the *Saturday Evening Post* and *Liberty* magazines. Each weekend he hawked popcorn and peanuts at local football games. In his spare time, he walked the nearby golf courses looking for lost balls, which he washed and cleaned and then resold for $6 a dozen. He attended horse races at the Ak-sar-ben Racetrack (Nebraska spelled backwards) looking for discarded tickets mistakenly thrown away that might have been worth something.

Later he published his own racer's tip sheet called the *Stable-Boy-Selections* for 25 cents, undercutting the price of the track's official *Blue Sheet*.

In 1942, when Buffett was 12, his father was elected to the US Congress and moved the family to Washington, DC. The change was hard on the young boy. Miserable and hopelessly homesick, he was allowed to return to Omaha to live with his grandfather and Aunt Alice. The following year, Buffett gave Washington another try and restarted his entrepreneurial adventures. He was soon working two paper routes delivering the *Washington Post* and the *Washington Times-Herald*.

At Woodrow Wilson High School, he made friends with Don Daly, who quickly became infected with Buffett's enthusiasm for making money. The two pooled their savings and bought a reconditioned pinball machine for $25. Buffett convinced a local barber to let them put a machine in this shop for half the profits. After the first day of operation, they returned to find $4 in nickels in their machine. The Wilson Coin-Operated Machine Company expanded to seven machines, and soon Buffett was taking home $50 a week. Next up, Buffett and Daly partnered on a 1934 Rolls Royce they purchased for $350 and rented out for $35 a day. At age 16, Buffett purchased a 40-acre Nebraska farm and leased it back to a farmer. By the time he graduated high school he had saved $6,000.

What accounted for Buffett's burning passion to make money? One dramatic, heartbreaking circumstance: the Great Depression. Although in some ways Buffett's younger years seem to reflect an idyllic childhood, all that changed when his father returned home one night and informed the family the bank where he worked had closed. His job was gone and their savings were lost. The Great Depression had finally made its way to Omaha. Buffett's grandfather could not afford to give his son a job but he did supply the family with food, on credit.

Warren Buffett was in every way a child of the Depression, and its effect, albeit brief, made a deep and profound impression on him. As Roger Lowenstein, author of *Buffett: The Making of an American Capitalist*, put it, "He emerged from those first hard years with an absolute drive to become very, very, very rich. He thought about it before he was five years old. And from that time on, he scarcely stopped thinking about it."[5] Buffett often visited the home of Carl Falk, then his father's business partner, to read Falk's investment books. One day Mrs. Falk, making lunch for young Warren, heard him declare that he "would be a millionaire before the age 30 and if not, I'm going to jump off the tallest building in Omaha." Mrs. Falk, horrified, asked Warren to never say that again. He just laughed. She pressed him: Why would he say such a thing? "It's not that I want money," he replied. "It's just the fun of making money and watching it grow."[6] In later years he added, "Money could make me independent. I could do what I wanted to do with my life. And the biggest thing I wanted was to work for myself. The idea of doing what I wanted and to do it every day was important to me."[7]

Chasing His Dreams: Early Influences

Many popular stories swirl around Warren Buffett that account for his success. But there is one story that is not widely known, and it is quite possibly the most significant of all.

In 1941, 11-year-old Warren, browsing in the Benson branch of the Omaha Public Library, came across a distinguished-looking book with a shiny silver cover, *One Thousand Ways to Make $1,000: Practical Suggestions, Based on Actual Experience, for Starting a Business of Your Own and Making Money in Your Spare Time* by F. C. Minaker, published by the Darnell Corporation in 1936. In the fashion of the time, Frances Mary Cowan Minaker used initials to disguise her gender.

Think about a young boy living in Omaha, Nebraska, in the 1940s. There were no televisions, no video games, no personal computers or smartphones. Yes, there were radio programs and a rare Saturday afternoon movie at the downtown cinema. But for most people, including Warren, entertainment was reading: newspapers, magazines, and books. Now imagine young Warren running home from the library, tightly clutching his new treasure, bursting into the house, plopping down in a chair, opening the book to page one and diving into a new world of how to make money—a world he had not yet fully understood or appreciated.

Minaker's book is long (408 pages) and comprehensive. In addition to hundreds of specific suggestions for new businesses, it offers clear, straightforward lessons on good salesmanship, advertising, merchandising, customer relations, and much more. It is filled with stories of people who turned a good idea into a good business, sometimes with stunning success.

There is the stirring story of James C. Penney, whose first job paid him a measly $2.27 a month. Penney combined his small grubstake with two other partners and opened the first J.C. Penney on April 14, 1902. That first year, store sales amounted to $28,891. James' share of the profits was a tad over $1,000.

Warren flipped another page and read the story of 23-year-old John Wanamaker, who persuaded his brother-in-law, Nathan Brown, to combine their piddling savings and open a gentleman's clothing store in their home town, Philadelphia. It was 1861. Before them lay the prospects of national civil war. Behind them were the remnants of the 1857 banking depression that caused massive unemployment and the almost complete ruination of manufacturers and wholesalers. Undeterred, they opened the doors on April 27, 1861. Eight years later Wanamaker & Brown was the largest men's retailer in the United States.

With daydreams mounting, Warren read on.

When he came to page 153, Warren must have broken out with huge grin. Chapter 6 is all about starting roadside businesses, something the young entrepreneur had already been doing for more than five years. Chapter 10 is filled with scores of ideas for service businesses, one of which involved placing coin-operated pool tables in local stores and taverns. From our present-day perspective, we can see a straight line from that story to Buffett's pinball business two years later. In the same Chapter 10, "Selling Your Services," we find another story, one that had an even greater influence on Warren's thinking.

In 1933, a man named Harry Larson was shopping in his local drugstore when someone (we don't know who exactly) asked him how much he weighed. Harry turned around and spied a coin-operated scale; he put in his penny and got his answer and then moved over to the cigar counter. During the few minutes he waited in line, seven other customers decided to try the penny scale. That caught Harry's attention, and he set out to learn more. The store owner explained that the machines were leased and that his 25 percent share of the profits was about $20 a month, leaving 75 percent for the company that owned the scale.

That, Harry told Minaker, was the start of everything. He took $175 from savings and bought three machines, and was soon earning a monthly profit of $98. But it was what Harry did next that intrigued Buffett. "I bought 70 machines altogether. . . . The other 67 were paid out of the pennies taken from the first three. . . . I've earned enough to pay for the scales, and make a good living besides."[8]

And that—one penny at a time—is the essence of compounding. We often think of compounding only as it applies to interest. You probably know Albert Einstein's famous quote, "Compound interest is the eighth wonder of the world. He who understands it, earns it. He who doesn't, pays it." But at its core the concept is broader and more powerful: Use profits to make further profits. Harry Larson instinctively understood it; so did a young Warren Buffett.

Many years later, Buffett used the penny-weight machines to describe his thinking. "The weighing machine was easy to understand. I'd buy a weighing machine and use the profits to buy more weighing machines. Pretty soon I'd have 20 weighing machines, and everybody would be weighing themselves 50 times a day. I thought—that is where the money is. The compounding of it—what could be better than that?"[9] It was the exact mental model that formed the outline, the architecture, of what became Berkshire Hathaway.

"The first step in starting a business of your own," Minaker writes, "is to know something about it. . . . So read everything published about the businesses you intend to start, to get the combined experience of others, and begin your plans where they left off." That means, she insists, learning all you can from both sides of the question: how to succeed *and* how not to fail. Reading about a business, she says, is like sitting down with a businessman in his parlor and talking about your problem. "Only those who think they know all there is to be known—and more besides—consider such an exchange of ideas foolish," she writes. What's really foolish is spending hundreds of dollars (in today's dollars probably hundreds of thousands, even millions) to discover that your idea won't work, when someone else who has already tried it and wrote about it can tell you "exactly *why* it is not a good idea."[10]

The lesson was not lost on Warren Buffett. At Berkshire Hathaway's headquarters, the largest room is not Buffet's office but the reference library down the hall. It is lined with row on row of filing cabinets, all filled with the stories of businesses. The cabinets contain every annual report, past and present, of all the major traded companies. Buffett has read them all. From them he has learned not only what worked and was profitable but, more important, what businesses failed and lost money.

The second lesson Buffett took from Minaker can be encapsulated in two words: Take action. Or, as Minaker so compellingly puts it, "The way to begin to make money, is to begin."[11] Hundreds of thousands have dreamed about starting their own business, she notes, but never did because they were stuck—waiting for business forecasts to improve, or perhaps waiting for their own prospects to get better, or just simply waiting for the right moment. They often delay getting started "because they cannot see clearly ahead." The caution here is, be aware that the perfect moment is never beforehand, and waiting for it is simply a way to hide in the safety of doing nothing.

Another manifestation of this phenomenon, Minaker points out, is that people become frozen because they spend too much time seeking counsel from others. "If you ask the advice of enough people, you are sure to almost end up doing nothing."[12] Those who have studied Warren Buffett easily recognize Minaker's counsel. Yes, Buffett discussed big ideas with his longtime business partner, Charlie Munger. But it is also true that if Buffett believes Berkshire is in line to make a good purchase he won't spend all day talking on the phone. He never holds off making a final decision because the stock market is up or down, or the economy is growing or contracting, or the forecast for interest rates is rising or falling. If it is a good business at a good price, Buffett takes action.

Along with her advice, Minaker also delivers compelling inspiration. "Leaving the harbor [with your new business] is like the captain of a ship at sea; you rely on your own judgment and ability." She calls it "the most satisfying part of a business life."[13]

It's easy to imagine the young Warren recognizing the truth to that. From the time he started selling candy and soda pop at age six, Buffett was his own boss. He was steadfastly confident and loved his independence. By the time he graduated from high school he was already the richest 16-year-old in Omaha. He may very well have been the world's richest self-made teenager. But he was not yet the millionaire he had once bragged about becoming. That required him to stay in school.

Getting an Education

As a boy, Warren Buffett was always fascinated with numbers and could easily do complex mathematical calculations in his head. At age eight, he began reading his father's books on the stock market; at age 11 he marked the board at the brokerage house where his father worked. That same year he bought his first shares of stock, Cities Services Preferred. As we have seen, his early years were enlivened with money-making entrepreneurial ventures and lessons about the stock market. Despite his father urging him toward higher education, young Warren believed he was already successful. He told his father he would rather skip college and go directly into business. Anyway, he argued, he had already read hundreds of books on business and investing, so what could college teach him? He was overruled.

Buffett was right. Although he enrolled at the Wharton School of Finance and Commerce at the University of Pennsylvania in 1947, after two unrewarding years there it was clear he knew more about accounting and business than his professors. He was spending more time at Philadelphia brokerages studying the stock market than studying for class. When the fall semester began in 1949, Buffett was nowhere to be found.

Back in Omaha, Buffett enrolled at the University of Nebraska and earned a bachelor's degree in one year, taking 14 courses over two semesters. All that year, and even after graduating, most days Buffett could be found in the library absorbing every book he could find on business and investing. Sometime in that summer of 1950 he found a copy of a new book by Benjamin Graham, *The Intelligent Investor*. The book that changed his life.

It led Buffett to start researching business school, and later that summer he discovered that Benjamin Graham and David Dodd, coauthors of the textbook *Security Analysis*, were listed as professors at Columbia University. "I figured they were long since dead," he said.[14] As it turns out, Graham and Dodd were not dead but actually teaching classes at Columbia. So he quickly submitted an application and was accepted. By September 1950, Buffett was 1,200 miles away from Omaha walking onto the New York City campus.

Buffett's first class was Finance 111–112, "Investment Management and Security Analysis," taught by David Dodd.[15] Before heading to New York, Buffett had grabbed a copy of *Security Analysis*. By the time he got to Columbia he had practically memorized it. "The truth was I knew the book. At the time, literally, almost in those seven or eight hundred pages, I knew every example. I just sopped it up."[16]

When the spring semester began Buffett could hardly contain himself. His next class, taught by Benjamin Graham, was a seminar of 20 students that combined the teachings in *Security Analysis* and the lessons from *The Intelligent Investor* linked to actual stocks that were trading in the market.

Graham's message was simple to understand but revolutionary in practice. Before *Security Analysis*, the common Wall Street approach to picking stocks was to begin with some overall opinion about a stock. Do you like it or not? Then try to figure out what other people might do with the stock: buy or sell it? The financial facts were largely overlooked. Ben Graham backed up the train.

Before you throw money at a stock based on nothing more than prevailing opinions, he argued, why not first figure out what it might be worth.

Graham's method was simple. First, add up the company's current assets (account receivables, cash, and current assets), then subtract all its liabilities. That gives you the company's net worth. Then, and only then, look at the stock price. If the price was below the net assets, it was a worthwhile and potentially profitable purchase. But if the stock price was higher than the company's net worth, it wasn't worth investing. The approach fit comfortably into Buffett's sense of numbers. Ben Graham had given him what he had been seeking for years—a systematic approach for investing: Buy a dollar's worth of securities for 50 cents.

Warren relished every moment of the Columbia experience. When not in class, he could be found in the university library reading old newspapers about the stock market going back 20 years. He never stopped, seven days a week from early in the morning to late in in the evening. Most wondered if he ever slept.

It was soon clear to everyone that Buffett was the brightest student. He often raised his hand to answer Graham's question before Graham had finished asking it. Bill Ruane, a classmate, recalled there was an instantaneous chemistry between Graham and Buffett, and the rest of the class was primarily an audience.[17] At the end of the semester, Buffett received an A+, the first time Graham had ever awarded that grade in his 22 years at Columbia University.

When school was over, Buffett asked Graham about working at Graham-Newman, the investment partnership Graham managed while teaching at Columbia. Graham turned him down. At first Buffett was stung by the rejection but later was told that the firm preferred to fill the slots at Graham-Newman with Jewish analysts who, it was perceived, were being treated unfairly on Wall Street. Buffett offered to work for free. Again, a polite no thank you. So Buffett returned to Omaha, determined to see what he could do on his own.

He was just turning 21 years old.

Investing Becomes the Focus

When Buffett arrived in Omaha in the summer of 1951, his mind and energy were singularly focused on investing. He was no longer interested in part-time jobs to make extra money. First Graham then Buffett's father—the two men Buffett respected over all others—cautioned him that now was not the time to invest in the stock market. Both men warned a correction was long overdue. Warren heard only Minaker. "The way to begin making money is to begin."

Buffett was offered a job at the Omaha National Bank but he turned it down, preferring the familiarity of his father's firm, Buffett-Falk & Company. The name of the firm had changed to reflect the contribution of its partner, Carl Falk. A friend of Howard Buffett asked if the name would soon be changed to Buffett & Son. Warren replied, "Maybe Buffett & Father."[18]

Buffett threw his heart and soul into Buffett-Falk & Company. He enrolled in the Dale Carnegie course for public speaking and began teaching "Investment Principles" at the University of Omaha; his lectures were based on Graham's book *The Intelligent Investor*. He wrote a column for *The Commercial and Financial Chronicle* under the headline "The Security I Like Best." In one of the columns Buffett touted Graham's favorite investment, a little-known insurance company called Government Employees Insurance Company (GEICO). Throughout this period, Warren maintained his relationship with Ben Graham and sent him stock ideas from time to time.

Then one day in 1954, Graham called his former student with a job offer. Buffett was on the next plane to New York.

During his tenure at Graham-Newman, Buffett became fully immersed in his mentor's investment approach. He was not alone. In addition to Buffett, Graham also hired Walter Schloss, Tom Knapp, and Buffett's classmate, Bill Ruane. Schloss went on to manage money at WSJ Limited Partners for 28 years. Knapp, a Princeton chemistry major, was a founding partner in Tweedy, Browne Partners. Ruane along with Rick Cuniff cofounded the famous Sequoia Fund. Each day the four analysts spent their time pouring over the Standard & Poor's *Stock Guide* and pitching ideas for the Graham-Newman mutual fund.

The two years that Buffett spent at Graham-Newman were exhilarating but also frustrating. Graham and his partner, Jerry Newman, batted down most of his recommendations. When the Dow Jones Industrial Average hit a record high 420 in 1955, the Graham-Newman mutual fund was sitting on $4 million in cash. No matter how compelling were Buffett's stock picks, the door at Graham-Newman was closed. Buffett concluded that the only place for his ideas was his own portfolio. The following year, Graham himself had enough. He retired and moved to Beverly Hills, California, where he continued to write and teach, this time at UCLA, until his death at age 82.

For Buffett, Graham was much more than a tutor. Roger Lowenstein describes it well: "It was Graham who provided the first reliable map to that wondrous and often forbidding city, the stock market. He laid out a methodological basis for picking stocks, previously a pseudoscience similar to gambling."[19] Since the days when 11-year-old Buffett first purchased Cities Service Preferred, he had spent half his life studying the mysteries of the stock market, including vast amounts of time deciphering technical analysis and chart reading. Now he had answers. Alice Schroeder, author of *The Snowball: Warren Buffett and the Business of Life*, adds a compelling analogy: "Warren's reaction was that of a man emerging from a cave in which he had been living all his life, blinking in the sunlight as he perceived reality for the first time. Buffett's original concept of a stock was derived from the patterns formed by prices at which pieces of paper were traded. Now he saw that those pieces of paper were simply symbols of an underlying truth."[20]

So Buffett returned to Omaha for the second time, far different from the young graduate five years earlier. He was now older, more experienced, certainly wiser about investing, and definitely a lot richer. Armed with the knowledge he acquired from Graham, and with the financial backing of family and friends, he began a limited investment partnership. Buffett was 25 years old, and he knew one thing for sure: He would never work for someone else again. He was ready to be his own captain.

Buffett Limited Partnership

Chapter 10 of Minaker's book, titled "Selling Your Services," begins by asking the reader to take a personal inventory. Figure out what you're good at, what you do better than anyone else. Then figure out who needs help and how best to reach them.

Through his teaching at the University of Omaha and his popular column on investing, Buffett had already begun to build his reputation in Omaha. The time spent at Graham-Newman only added to his credibility. So no sooner did he arrive back in Omaha than family and friends pounced, asking him to manage their money. His sister Doris and her husband, his loving Aunt Alice, his father-in-law, his ex-roommate Chuck Person, and a local Omaha attorney named Dan Monen all wanted in. Collectively, in the spring of 1956 they gave Buffett $105,000 to invest. Thus was born the Buffett Limited Partnership with 25-year-old Warren as general partner.

When everyone gathered for the kickoff meeting at a local Omaha dinner club, Buffett set the tone. He handed each person the formal partnership agreement, assuring them there was nothing nefarious about the legalistic look of the document. Then with complete disclosure he set the ground rules for the partnership.[21]

First, the financial terms. Limited partners would receive the first 6 percent return of the investment partnership. Thereafter, they would receive 75 percent of the profits, with the balance going to Buffett. Any annual deficiency in performance goals would be made up the next year. So if the limited partners didn't get their full 6 percent return in any one year, the following year the shortage would be added to that year's 6 percent. Buffett would not receive his performance bonus until his partners were made whole.

Buffett told his partners he could not promise results, but he did promise that the investments he made for the partnership would be based on the value principles he learned from Ben

Graham. He went on to describe how they should think about the yearly gains and losses. First, they should ignore the daily, weekly, and monthly gyrations of the stock market, which, in any event, were beyond his control. Furthermore, they should not put much emphasis on how well or poorly the investments performed in any one year. Better to judge results over at least three years, five years was even better.

Buffett promised his partners that our "investment results will be chosen on the basis of value not popularity" and that the partnership "will attempt to reduce permanent capital loss (not short-term quotational loss) to a minimum."[22] Last, Warren told his partners he was not in the business of forecasting the stock market or economic cycles. That meant he would not discuss or disclose what the partnership was buying, selling, or holding.

At dinner that night, everyone signed up for the partnership. Over the years, as more partners were added, they were given the same ground rules. Lest anyone forget, Buffett included the rules with performance results sent every year to each partner.

Growing the Partnership

Out of the gate, the Buffett partnership posted incredible numbers. In the first five years (1957–1961), a period when the Dow Jones Industrial Average was up 75 percent, the partnership gained 251 percent (181 percent for limited partners). Buffett was not beating the Dow by his original goal of 10 percentage points a year but by an average 35 percent.

As Buffett's reputation became more widely known, more people asked him to manage their money. At the end of 1961, the Buffett partnership had $7.2 million in capital, more than Graham-Newman managed at its peak. And $1 million of that belonged to Buffett. He had just turned 31.

Still more investors came in, more partnerships were formed, until by 1962 Buffett decided to reorganize everything into a single partnership. That year, he moved the partnership office from his home to Kiewit Plaza in Omaha, where his office remains today.

The following year, 1963, Buffett made one of his most famous investments, one that served to boost his already growing reputation.

One of the worst corporate scandals in the 1960s occurred when Tino De Angelis, CEO of the Allied Crude Vegetable Oil Company, discovered he could obtain loans based on the inventory of the company's salad oil. Using one simple fact, that oil floats on top of water, he rigged the game. He built a refinery in New Jersey, put in five-story storage tanks to hold soybean oil, then filled the tanks with water topped with just a few feet of salad oil. When inspectors arrived to confirm inventory, Allied employees would clamber up to the top of the tanks, dip in a measuring stick, and call out a false number to the inspectors on the ground. When the scandal broke, it was learned that Bank of America, Bank Lemumi, American Express, and other international trading companies had backed over $150 million in fraudulent loans.

American Express was one of the biggest casualties of what became known as the salad oil scandal. The company lost $58 million and its share price dropped by more than 50 percent. Buffett was certainly aware of the financial loss, but he did not know how customers of American Express viewed the scandal. So he hung out at the registers of Omaha restaurants and discovered there was no drop-off in the use of the famous American Express Green Card. He also visited several banks in the area and learned that the financial scandal was having no impact on the sale of American Express Travelers Cheques. Back in the office, Buffett promptly invested $13 million, a whopping 25 percent of the partnership assets, in shares of American Express. Over the next two years, the shares tripled and the partners netted $20 million in profit.

Beating the Dow

Buffett continued to soundly beat the Dow Jones Industrial Average. After 10 years, the Buffett Partnership's assets had grown to more than $53 million. Buffett's share was near $10 million. But even as the partnership was adding heroic returns, difficulties were mounting. Scouring the market, Buffett was having great difficulty finding stocks that met his definition of value. Since the first days of the partnership in 1956, the valuation strategy Buffett had learned from Ben Graham dominated the stock market. But by the mid-1960s, a new era was unfolding. It was called the "go-go" years(*go-go* meaning growth stocks). Greed began driving the market. Fast money was made and lost in the pursuit of high-flying performance stocks.[23]

Still, despite the underlying shift in market psychology, the Buffett Partnership continued to post outstanding results. By the end of 1966, the partnership had gained 1,156 percent (704 percent for partners), blitzing the Dow's gain of 123 percent over the same period. In 1968, the Buffett Partnership returned 59 percent compared to the Dow's 8 percent. It was the single best performance year of the partnership. Ever the realist, Buffett wrote to his partners that the results "should be treated as a freak—like picking up thirteen spades in a bridge game."[24]

Nevertheless, Buffett was becoming increasingly uneasy. The new drumbeat being played in the stock market made little sense to him. He found the market highly speculative and worthwhile values increasingly scarce. Finally, in 1969, at the height of his investment success, Buffett decided to end the investment partnership. He mailed a letter to his partners confessing that he was out of step with current market environment. "On one point, however, I am clear," he said. "I will not abandon a previous approach whose logic I understand, although I find it difficult to apply, even though it may mean forgoing large and apparently easy profits, to embrace an approach which I don't fully understand, have not practiced successfully, and which possibly could lead to substantial permanent capital loss."[25]

In shutting down the Buffett Partnership, Buffett took extra care to ensure all the partners clearly understood the next steps. He outlined three different options. For those who wished to remain in the stock market, Buffett recommended Bill Ruane, his former classmate and colleague from Graham-Newman. Twenty million dollars in the Buffett Partnership were transferred to Ruane, Cuniff, & Stires and thus was born the Sequoia Fund.

A second option for partners was to invest in municipal bonds. To Buffett's mind, the 10-year outlook for stocks was approximately the same as for municipal bonds, which by their nature are tax-free and less risky. The consummate educator, Buffett sent each partner a 100-page manifesto on the mechanics of buying tax-free bonds.[26] As a third option, partners could allocate their assets to one of the partnership's major holdings, the common shares of Berkshire Hathaway.

When Buffett disbanded the partnership, more than a few thought his best days were behind him. In reality, they were just beginning. Buffett was always upfront and plainspoken. He told his partners he was going to move his personal investment in the Buffett Partnership to Berkshire Hathaway. From its initial asset base of $105,000, the Buffett Partnership had grown to $104 million in assets under management; from this, Buffett earned $25 million. Now he was telling his partners he was moving this money to Berkshire Hathaway, giving him full control of the company. As Doc Angel, one of the early Buffett Partnership loyalists, said, "That's all anybody had to hear if they had any brains."[27]

Berkshire Hathaway: Compounding Conglomerate

The original company, Berkshire Cotton Manufacturing, was incorporated in 1889. Forty years later, Berkshire combined operations with several other textile mills, resulting in one of New England's largest industrial companies. During this period, Berkshire produced approximately 25 percent of the country's cotton needs and absorbed 1 percent of New England's electrical capacity. In 1955, Berkshire merged with Hathaway Manufacturing, and the name was changed to Berkshire Hathaway.

Early in the Buffett Partnership time line, Buffett began acquiring shares in Berkshire Hathaway. The stock was selling for $7.50 per share with working capital of $10.25 and a book value of $20.20. It was a classic Ben Graham stock.

Unfortunately the years following the merger between Berkshire and Hathaway were dismal. In less than 10 years, stockholder's equity dropped by half and losses from operations exceeded $10 million. Buffett was well aware of the difficulties US textile manufacturers faced in competing against much cheaper foreign imports. Even so, he couldn't resist the attractiveness of "picking up a discarded cigar butt that had one puff remaining in it."[28] The cigar butt theory is the name given to Graham's emphasis on buying hard assets on the cheap even though those assets had little economic vitality. With the cash and securities on the balance sheet along with even a limited potential for business profits going forward, Buffett figured there was not much downside to Berkshire Hathaway and a reasonable likelihood of making money.

By 1965, the Buffett Partnership owned 39 percent of the Berkshire Hathaway common shares outstanding. Buffett was then locked in a proxy battle with the board of directors to take over the company, fire the inept management, and replace them with people better at allocating capital. When the dust settled, Warren won the fight but in doing so found he had allocated 25 percent of the Buffett Partnership's assets to an economically sinking ship with no exit strategy. "I became the dog who caught the car."[29]

The journey from managing one of the greatest investment partnerships in history to then parlaying his net worth into owning a dying manufacturing business had all the markings of Greek tragedy. What was Buffett thinking?

It's clear what he was *not* thinking. Buffett had no clear plan to engineer a complete turnaround. And even though he had Graham whispering in his ear, he never intended to sell the company to a greater fool. Who would have wanted to buy a 75-year-old, low-margin, capital-intensive, labor-dependent, 19th-century New England maker of fabric liners for men's suits? No, Buffett was guided by a stronger principle, a principle that in fact lies at the heart of his investing philosophy—long-term compounding.

From an early age, Buffett was taught the benefits of compound interest. More important, he experienced the benefits of a compounding machine firsthand when he took the earnings from his various jobs and plowed them back into his young enterprise. If one paper route was a good job for making money, then having two paper routes meant more money. If owning one pinball machine added to his savings, then owning three was better. Even as a kid, Warren was not geared to spend the money he earned.

In many ways, Buffett's childhood enterprises were like a conglomerate, enabling him to transfer money unimpaired from one business to another or, better yet, to plow money back into the best business. And 20 years later, a conglomerate is what he had with Berkshire Hathaway, although few recognized it.

Most thought that Warren Buffett had rolled the dice on a beaten-down textile business, but what they missed is that in one bold step he now owned a corporate entity called Berkshire Hathaway that in turn owned a textile company. Buffett figured all he had to do was to wring out whatever cash was left from Berkshire Hathaway manufacturing and reallocate it to a better business. Fortunately, the textile group of manufacturers under the Berkshire name did hold enough cash and short-term securities on their balance sheet to allow Buffett to buy other businesses, which, as we will see, is a much brighter story. It wasn't long before the metamorphosis of Berkshire Hathaway was complete, from a single-line textile manufacturer to a conglomerate that owned a portfolio of diversified business interests.

In the 2014 Berkshire Hathaway Annual Report, Buffett gave shareholders a short tutorial on the advantages of owning a conglomerate. "If the conglomerate form is used judiciously, it is an ideal structure for maximizing long-term capital." A conglomerate is perfectly positioned to allocate capital rationally and at a minimal cost, he explained. Furthermore, a conglomerate that owns different businesses is in an ideal position: "Without incurring taxes or much in the way of other costs [it can] move huge sums from businesses that have limited opportunities for incremental investment to other sectors with greater promise."[30]

You have probably noticed that with his decision about Berkshire Hathaway, Buffett had pulled away from the stock-picking methods taught by Ben Graham. Maximizing long-term capital gain was not a Ben Graham strategy. His approach to buying stocks was to keenly focus on cheap stocks based on hard assets with limited downside price risk. Once the stock price reset back to fair value,

Graham would quickly sell and move on to the next investment. The idea of compounding an existing position over several years was not part of his calculation. In fact, the word *compound* appears nowhere in *Security Analysis* or *The Intelligent Investor*.

By contrast, even in the earliest years of his partnership Buffett was writing about the "Joys of Compounding."[31] In the 1963 Buffett Partnership letter to his partners, he relayed the story of Queen Isabella underwriting the voyage of Christopher Columbus for $30,000. He pointed out that if that investment compounded at 4 percent, it would have been worth $2 trillion 500 years later. Year after year, Buffett would school his partners on the wonders of compound interest, a mathematical concept discovered almost 300 years earlier (1683) by the Swiss mathematician Jacob Bernoulli. Buffett pointed out that a $100,000 investment compounded at 4 percent becomes $224,000 in 30 years but $8,484,940 when compounded at 16 percent. His advice: live a long life and compound money at a high rate.

However, we should not forget that the partnership years, and Graham's influence thereon, are critical to the story of Warren Buffett. He grew the Buffett Partnership assets by perfectly executing Graham's stock-picking methodology. Its success helped to build Buffett's net worth, and the yearly performance bonus added to his financial security. That enabled him to provide a solid financial foundation for his family. But once their financial future was secured, the question became, what next?

One option was to continue the partnership. Keep on buying and selling stocks each year, paying commissions and taxes along the way, always having to navigate the rocky shores of overpriced markets. The other was to change vessels and chart a new course.

In 2023 Berkshire Hathaway, once a modest New England textile manufacturer, had a market value of $744 billion. It was the ninth-largest company in the world. The original A shares, which Buffett purchased in 1962 at $7.50, trade for $517,917. What is spectacular about this achievement is that Berkshire Hathaway reached this milestone not by discovering a blockbuster drug or inventing a new technology but rather perfecting an older miracle—the 17th-century idea of financial compounding.

CHAPTER 2

The Education of Warren Buffett

Investing is a thinking game. It is not a physical challenge. It doesn't matter how strong you are or how fast and far you can run. But it does matter—a lot—how you conceptualize the investment world and your role in it.

Another name for that is your worldview. It is a complex, fascinating mix of your innate temperament, the experiences of your life and your reaction to them, and the ideas you absorbed along the way, from formal education, reading, and significant people in your life. All these elements go into shaping a mental mosaic that is your personal philosophy of life. But here we are concerned with just one dimension: your philosophy of investing and how it influences your decisions and then in turn is affected by them.

A good working definition of an investment philosophy is "a set of beliefs and insights about how financial markets work and what it takes to exploit those workings in the service of an investment objective."[1] Like all good definitions, it is compact and succinct; to get its full meaning, we need to break it open and look closely at its parts.

First, let's explore "a set of beliefs and insights." It asks, what is your personal set of beliefs, your overall view of how the financial markets operate? For his part, Buffett has a succinct answer. He tells us the stock market is frequently efficient in pricing securities, but not always. This is his *view* of financial markets.

Second, "what does it take to exploit the market?" This is a more complex question because it involves two separate considerations: methods and personal traits. Here, too, Buffett gives us guidance. He believes investors should manage a concentrated, low-turnover portfolio composed of common stocks based on business-driven principles and then value these stocks using the discounted present value of future free cash flow model. This is Buffett's process, the *methods* he uses to beat the market. For the second aspect, *personal traits*, Buffett speaks of the importance of what he calls the "temperament" of an investor, specifically, how someone thinks about the change in stock prices.

All of these separate components—your view of the market, your methods, and your temperament as an investor—reflect the totality of your philosophy of investing.

If we set out to understand Buffett's philosophy, we have no shortage of information to draw on. Even so, the tendency of most is to focus too much time on analyzing his methods and too little on appreciating the philosophical underpinnings, acquired over the years, that enabled him to successfully apply those methods. The goal of this chapter is to outline the methods Buffett learned through time and the philosophical constructs he acquired throughout his early life that strengthened his resolve while investing in the market.

We do that with a deep look at the significant influences that played a role in shaping his investment philosophy, starting with one influencer who has not been fully recognized and appreciated—his father. Once we understand just how much the father's influence affected the son, then we are able to better understand the earliest roots of Buffett's philosophy, which has guided not only his personal life but also his approach in the investment world.

Howard Homan Buffett: Earliest Influence

Warren Buffett is not shy about reminding everyone that a good deal of his success can be attributed to being born at the right time and in the right place. He calls it the *ovarian lottery*. "I've had it so good in the world. The odds were fifty-to-one against being born in the United States in 1930. I won the lottery the day I emerged from the womb by being in the United States instead of in some other country where my chances would have been way different."[2] To which I would add, he also won the Powerball by being born in Omaha, Nebraska, as a member of the Buffett clan.

In Chapter 1, I described Sidney Homan Buffett's adventurous job driving a stage coach from New York to Omaha and then settling down in 1867 to start a grocery. It was an opportune time. The town was bustling. A scant 15 years earlier, land speculators from nearby Council Bluffs, Iowa, had crossed the Missouri River at the Lone Tree Ferry (the exact spot where the Lewis and Clark Expedition had passed in 1804) to homestead the land, the beginnings of what we now recognize as Omaha's pioneer period. After a series of 26 separate treaties with the Native Americans, the land was ceded into what is today east-central Nebraska. Then, in 1862, President Abraham Lincoln designated Omaha as the eastern terminal of the Union Pacific Railroad connecting the transcontinental railway. In short order, the city became a new economic center for the continuing western expansion of the United States.

Most of us know the basic outlines of this phase of US history, but for our purposes here, we should take a minute to think about what life was like for these pioneers. Without pay or promise of employment, they left their homes for the unknown. Along the way they endured scorching heat, lashing rains, mud pits, and drownings. They lost loved ones in ferocious attacks from bears, wolf packs, and rattlesnakes. Countless number of pioneers succumbed to diseases for which there was no treatment.

Why did they do it? What drove them ever westward? Freedom, in all its facets, and not the least of those, the freedom to pursue their own business opportunities to better provide a secure future for their family.[3]

According to the National Bureau of Economic Research, the United States had 15 recessions between 1854 and 1913. That's one economic downturn every four years, many of them severe, including the 1873 recession that lasted until 1879. There was no shortage of explanations and plenty of blame to go around: the weather, uncertainty over how to plan for the future, innovations of modern society, manufacturing of new industrial equipment that displaced workers, the cyclicality of savings then massive overproduction, the failure of banks and the unethical behavior of corporate titans.[4] But all these excuses collapsed into one singular blame—the political establishment. In that viewpoint, Washington, DC, and by connection New York City, had for years mismanaged the US economy. The pioneers who headed west wanted a new start, unchained by the bad decisions of government they desperately wanted to leave behind.

Previously we took note of Howard Buffett's decision to bypass the grocery business run by his father, Ernest Buffett. Instead he took a job selling insurance, then securities, which led him to start his own brokerage firm. Howard Buffett worked hard for his family and was successful at business, but he was not driven to make more and more money. Instead, Howard Buffett's passions were politics and religion. He served on the Omaha school board and taught Sunday school classes. He was a man of unquestionable integrity and forthrightness. He did not drink or smoke. And when an investment turned out poorly for a customer he often felt so bad he repurchased it for his own account. He reminded his children, Warren and his two sisters, Doris and Bertie, that they had a duty to not only God but also to the community. "You are not required to carry the whole burden," he said, "nor are you permitted to put down your share."[5]

Political Roots

In 1942, Howard Buffett was the Republican candidate for Nebraska's second Congressional district. His political slogan was "Do you want your children to be FREE?" In newspaper ads featuring pictures of his wife and children, he promised, "If you're tired of the way selfish politicians are messing up our government—if you want to see politics removed from the war effort . . . then let's get together on it. You and I, as dyed-in-the-wool Americans, have it in our power to keep America free for our children."[6] Howard

Buffett was considered an underdog, but he was popular and his message of freedom resonated with Omaha's pioneer spirit. He won the 1942 election and was re-elected in 1944, 1946, and 1950.

Today, Howard Buffett is politically remembered as a libertarian, an "Old Right" member of the GOP. The Old Right was an informal designation of a branch of American conservatism that included both Republicans and Democrats united in their opposition to military intervention overseas, to the removal of the gold standard as a backstop for paper currency, and most especially to President Roosevelt's New Deal coalition. It was Howard Buffett's profound belief that government, particularly the policies of the Roosevelt administration, had shackled human ingenuity and were leading the country to ruin. He was a close friend of Murray Rothbard, a US economist who supported the development of modern libertarianism under the belief that all government services could be more efficiently provided by the private sector.

As a politician, Howard Buffett resurrected his dreams of being a journalist and became a prolific political writer. In one noted article written in 1944 for the *Omaha World-Herald* titled "Government Puts Handcuffs on Use of Human Energy," he pointed out it was "human energy that discovered electricity, invented the automobile, and created sulfa drugs and penicillin, and all other good things we enjoy today. Human history goes back about six thousand years. For over 5,800 of those years, governments blocked the free use of energy. Then came the American Revolution and human energy was turned loose for the first time in history. As a result, the day laborer has conveniences and comforts unknown even to a king one hundred years ago."

Libertarianism is a political philosophy that at its core upholds liberty—not only political freedom but also freedom of choice. At the heart of libertarianism is the celebration of "self"—the individual over the state, whose authority is met with skepticism. Here in the United States we can trace libertarianism to John Locke, whose 1689 *An Essay Concerning Human Understanding* established the basis of liberal political theory. Thomas Paine espoused libertarianism ideals in his political pamphlet *Common Sense* (1776), calling for the independence of the colonies. The poet and naturalist Henry David Thoreau was also an early influencer of libertarian ideals, reflected in his book *Walden* (1854), which advocated simple living and self-sufficiency. But there was no greater voice for the idea of libertarianism than the American philosopher, essayist, and poet Ralph Waldo Emerson. According to Harold Bloom, the famed literary critic, "the mind of Emerson is the mind of America."[7]

It was the financial journalist Roger Lowenstein who first made the connection between Ralph Waldo Emerson and Howard Buffett, and thence to Warren. "Buffett's trademark self-reliance," Lowenstein wrote in *Buffett: The Making of American Capitalist*, was connected to the "sweetness of Emersonian independence which Buffett learned from his father."[8]

Philosophical Roots

Emerson was a champion of individualism and a critic of society's countervailing forces against individual thought. "Self-Reliance," first published in 1841, is considered to be his most famous essay. In it he presents three major themes. First is *solitude and community*. Emerson warns us the community is a distraction to self-growth; he believes more time should be spent in quiet reflection. Second is the sense of *nonconformity*. "Whoso would be a man," he writes, "must be a nonconformist." He argues that an individual must do what is right no matter what others think. Last, the theme of *spirituality* is especially important. Emerson tells us truth is within oneself and warns that relying on institutional thought hinders an individual's ability to grow intellectually.

Those who have read "Self-Reliance" can easily spot the connections between Emerson's philosophy and Warren Buffett's investment behavior. Can we describe Buffett as a nonconformist? Put his widely known approach to investing in stocks side by side with the standard practices of Modern Portfolio Theory, which dominates today's money management industry, and you have your answer. Giving us another link, Emerson writes, "What I do is all that concerns me, not what the people think." Buffett has always been puzzled why people desperately seek conversations about the stock market. It is not that he doesn't think about stocks and pricing of the markets, but the need to be in constant communication with others baffles him. "I don't want to hear what a lot of other people think, I just want a lot of facts. I mean, in the end, I'm not handing my money over to anybody else."[9]

Emerson is careful to warn us that operating in solitude is a challenge: "It is harder because you will always find those who think they know what is your duty better than you know it. It is easy in the world to live after the world's opinion; it is easy in solitude to live after your own; but the great man is he who in the midst of the crowd keeps with perfect sweetness the independence of solitude."[10]

One of the more difficult challenges investors face is to maintain a level of independent solitude in a media environment that is constantly grabbing for their attention. But Warren Buffett learned early on how important it is to protect and maintain the "sweet independence" of solitary thinking.

Self-reliance, mirrored as self-confidence, is a robust trait of Buffett's thinking and it requires twin incubators of solitude and reflection. But that's not all. It is critical to understand that this mental strength of independent thought and action is what makes possible profitable investing in the stock market. You cannot walk lockstep with the market if you want to outperform it. Taking advantage of the market's mispricing, a prerequisite for outperforming the market, often requires the ability to act in conflict with the market.

And there lies the difficulty. Before executing an order to buy or sell a security, investors are alone with their final decision. Make no mistake—successful investing is about self-reliance. It lies at the core of Buffett's investment approach. Those who have self-reliance do well. Those who don't, suffer. Thus, Emerson travels through Howard Buffett onto his son Warren.

The close bond between Warren Buffett and his father is well known. During Warren's childhood, father and son were inseparable. Howard Buffett called his little boy *fireball,* and Warren wanted nothing more than to imitate his dad. Years later he confessed that if his father had been a shoe salesman "I might be a shoe salesman right now."[11] Warren Buffett has often said his dad was the number one teacher in his life, the person who introduced him to his love of books. We all know Buffett spends the greatest amount of time each day reading and learning in quiet solitude. I believe Emerson would approve.

Now take a moment to reflect on what it was like for young Warren to grow up in Omaha in a home with a father he adored. Day after day he listened to his dad discuss current events, always from a libertarian point of view. In the evenings, conversation at the dinner table often turned to politics, and the calculus was "will this add to, or subtract from, human liberty."[12]

Without a doubt, Warren Buffett inherited his sense of patriotism from his father. But he also learned the primacy of honesty, integrity, and virtuous behavior. "The best advice I've ever been given is by my father who told me it took 20 years to build a reputation and 20 minutes to lose it. And if you remember that you'll do things differently."[13]

Congressman Howard H. Buffett died on April 30, 1964. His last will and testament recorded an estate value of $563,292, of which $335,000 was invested in the Buffett Partnership. A trust was established for his wife, Leila, and daughters Doris and Bertie; Warren was named trustee. Aside from a few personal items of sentimental value, Howard Buffett made no bequeath for his son. He explained his reasoning: "I make no further provisions for my son, Warren, not out of any lack of love for him, but because he has a substantial estate in his own right and for further reason that he has advised me that I not make any further provision for him."[14]

Yet though the tangible inheritance items were small, there can be no doubt that the intangibles Warren Buffett received from his father were far more valuable. "Nothing can bring you peace but yourself," wrote Emerson. "Nothing can bring you peace but the triumph of principles." That was his father's ultimate gift to his son.

Warren Buffett was once asked whom he would choose if he could go back and speak to anyone in history. He didn't hesitate. "My father."[15]

Benjamin Graham: Developing an Investment Methodology

Benjamin Graham was born in London in 1894 to a Jewish family of merchants who imported china and bric-a-brac from Austria and Germany. In 1895, Graham's father moved his family to New York to open an American branch of the business. Soon after, Graham's father died at the young age of 35, leaving his penniless mother to raise him and his two brothers.

Despite the financial setback, Graham's mother held the family together. Ben Graham attended the prestigious Boys High School in Brooklyn, then enrolled at Columbia University. A brilliant scholar, he mastered the teachings of mathematics and philosophy all the while consuming the major classical works in Greek and Latin. His long-time friend Irving Kahn said that Graham's "speed of thought was so great that most people were puzzled at how he could resolve a complicated question directly after having heard it." Graham, Kahn continued, "had another extraordinary characteristic in the breadth and depth of his memory." He could read Greek, Latin, German, and Spanish. Without formally studying the language, Graham once translated "a Spanish novel into literary English so professionally that it was accepted by an American publisher."[16]

Graham graduated Columbia University second in his class and was immediately offered teaching jobs by the philosophy, mathematics, and English departments. Concerned about the low starting salaries in academia, he asked Columbia's dean, Frederick Keppel, for advice. Dean Keppel must have known his man, for he steered Graham to Wall Street, and in 1914, Benjamin Graham joined Newburger, Henderson, and Loeb as an assistant in the bond department.

Soon, though, he grew restless. He started as a clerk, then trained to be a salesman. But what he really wanted to do was write, not sell bonds. Despite lacking any formal training in economics or accounting, Graham began researching railroad companies, specifically railroad bonds, on his own and writing research reports.[17]

One of his reports, on the Missouri Pacific Railroad, caught the eye of a partner at J.S. Bache and Company, a respected New York Stock Exchange firm. He was quickly offered a job as a statistician with a 50 percent increase in salary. Graham let Newburger know that although he felt a sense of loyalty to the firm, he was not motivated to be a salesman. Newburger countered with its own pay raise. It was not quite 50 percent, but it included a sweetener: the opportunity for Graham to start his own statistical department. He decided to stay and pursue his writing at the same time.

In the early 1900s, serious investment capital was limited to buying bonds. Common stock investing was thought to be a speculative game played not on the basis of financial data but on insider information. Nonetheless, Graham began writing articles for *The Magazine of Wall Street*, a newsletter with investment tips for bonds as well as stocks. He soon developed a following. He next published a pamphlet called "Lessons for Investors" where he argued, "If the market value of a stock is substantially less than its intrinsic value, it should have excellent prospects for an advance in price." It was the first time the term *intrinsic value* appeared in the financial press.[18]

Early Years as an Investor

Graham left Newburger in 1923 to start his own investment firm. Two years later he hired Jerome Newman and formed the Graham-Newman Corporation, which lasted until 1956. Graham's early investment results were promising. Much of his portfolio was hedged or in arbitrage situations, which dampened the steep losses of the 1929 crash. But in 1930, Graham tiptoed back into the stock market—this time unhedged—believing stocks had hit bottom. When the market dropped again, Graham, for the second time in his life, was near financial ruin.

But all was not lost. In 1927, before the stock market crash, Graham had begun teaching a night class on investing at his alma mater. The Columbia University catalog promised that a Wall Street investment professional would be teaching advance security analysis on Monday evenings in room 305 of Schermerhorn Hall. The class description read "Investment Theories subjected to practical market tests. Origin and detection of discrepancies between price and value." It was in this class that Graham coined the term *security analysis* and replaced the Wall Street job title of statistician with a new name—security analyst.[19]

Graham had one stipulation in agreeing to teach the class: someone had to be assigned to take detailed notes. David Dodd, a young finance professor with recent degrees from the University of Pennsylvania (BS) and Columbia University (MS), volunteered. Dodd's notes formed the substance of their seminal book, *Security Analysis*. When it appeared in 1934, Louis Rich of the *New York Times* wrote, "It is a full-bodied, mature, meticulous, and wholly meritorious outgrowth of scholarly probing and practical sagacity. If this influence should ever exert itself, it will come about by causing the mind of the investor to dwell upon the securities rather than the market."[20]

Part of the enduring significance of *Security Analysis* was its timing. This book appeared just a few years after the 1929 stock market crash, a world-changing event that had a major impact on Graham and profoundly influenced his ideas. While other academicians sought to explain this economic phenomenon, Graham helped people regain their financial footing and proceed with a profitable course of action.

The danger of 1929, he explained, was not that speculation tried to masquerade as investing, but rather that investing fashioned itself into speculation. Graham noted that optimism based on history was rampant—and dangerous. Encouraged by the past, investors projected forward an era of continued growth and prosperity, and they began to lose their sense of proportion about price. Graham said people were paying prices for stocks without any sense of mathematical expectation; stocks were worth any price that the optimistic market quoted. At the height of this insanity, the line between investment and speculation had blurred.

Graham and Dodd attempted a precise definition of investing and speculation in *Security Analysis*. "An investment operation is one which, upon thorough analysis, promises safety of principal and a satisfactory return. Operations not meeting these requirements are speculative."[21]

Defining Investment

Despite the high regard for *Security Analysis*, Graham and Dodd's definition of investment and speculation left readers wanting more—a fact he confessed years later in *The Intelligent Investor*. "While we have clung tenaciously to this definition, it is worthwhile noting the radical changes that have occurred in the use of the term 'investor' during this period." He was concerned the term *investor* was being applied ubiquitously to anyone who participated in the stock market. "The newspapers employed the word 'investor' in these instances because, in the easy language of Wall Street, everyone who buys or sells a security has become an investor, regardless of what he buys, or for what purpose, or at what price, or whether for cash or on margin." Graham grimly observed, "The distinction between investment and speculation in common stocks has always been a useful one and its disappearance is cause for concern."[22]

As an antidote to the risky behavior that is speculation, Graham proposed an investment approach for selecting stocks that relied on what he called the *margin of safety*. He reasoned that a margin of safety existed for a common stock if its price was below its intrinsic value. And the obvious next question is, How does one determine intrinsic value? Again, Graham starts his answer with a no-nonsense definition: intrinsic value is "that value which is determined by the facts." These facts include a company's assets, its earnings and dividends—in other words, quantitative factors.

Graham decried the emphasis routinely placed on qualitative factors. His experience led him to believe that to the extent investors moved away from hard assets and toward intangibles, they invited a potentially risky way of thinking. Opinions about management and the nature of a business are not easily measured, and that which is difficult to measure can be badly measured. If, however, a greater amount of a company's intrinsic value is the sum of measurable, quantitative factors, Graham figured that the investor's downside was more limited. Fixed assets are measurable. Dividends are measurable. Current and historical earnings are measurable. Each of these factors can be demonstrated by figures and becomes a source of logic referenced by actual experience.

According to legend, Graham once said that having a good memory was a burden. The memory of being financially ruined twice in a lifetime led him to embrace an investment approach that stressed downside protection over upside potential. There are two rules to investing, he said. The first rule is, don't lose. The second rule is, don't forget the first rule. He solidified this "don't lose" philosophy for buying stocks into two specific, tangible guidelines cementing his margin-of-safety approach: (1) buy a company for less than two-thirds of its net asset value and (2) focus on low price-to-earnings ratios.

Although the margin of safety is considered the perfect hedge, it is not *always* the perfect hedge. Graham believed if glamorous projections for future growth went unfulfilled it was far better to focus on current assets, even if they were not generating much of an economic return, because someone, somewhere, somehow would squeeze out a decent return even from a poorly operating business. As a last resort, the assets could be liquidated. Of course, this presupposed that someone would always stand ready to buy the book value of bad companies.

In transitioning from the Buffett Partnership to Berkshire Hathaway, Warren Buffett learned firsthand why Graham's method of purchasing companies with low price-to-earnings ratios and high book values was not always foolproof. He soon discovered that the price he received for selling the book value of companies that generated little cash earnings was often less than desirable.

Using Graham's investment method of buying the common shares of companies, Buffett accumulated several businesses for the newly reconstructed Berkshire Hathaway. Although buying cheap stocks of bad businesses during the partnership years worked out well, largely because Buffett could quickly sell them and move on, he came to learn that buying and holding cheap assets of companies with poor economics for Berkshire was a failed strategy. "My punishment," Buffett said, "was an education in the economics of short-line farm implement manufacturers, third-place department stores, and New England textile manufacturers."[23] The farm implement manufacturer was Dempster Mill Manufacturing, the department store was Hochschild Kohn, and the textile manufacturer was Berkshire Hathaway. Although Buffett had the benefit of owning these companies outright, thereby being in charge of capital allocation, the economic returns of these subpar businesses were, in a word, miserable. These companies were not the penny weighing machines Buffett sought to own for his new Berkshire Hathaway.

As Buffett later explained, if you paid $8 million for a company whose assets are worth $10 million, you will profit handsomely if the assets are sold on a timely basis. However, if the underlying economics of the business are poor and it takes 10 years to sell the business, your total return is likely to be below average. "Time is the friend of a wonderful business," Buffett learned, "the enemy of mediocre."[24] Unless he could, in a timely basis, liquidate a poorly performing company and profit from the difference between the purchase price and the market value of the company's assets, his performance would replicate the poor economics of the underlying business.

One might think the failed investments in Dempster Mill, Hochschild Kohn, and Berkshire Hathaway would cause Buffett to turn away from Ben Graham's teachings. But this did not occur—far from it. Today, Buffett strongly urges investors to pay close attention to Graham's invaluable and timeless advice in two chapters of *The Intelligent Investor*: Chapter 8, "The Investor and Market Fluctuations," and Chapter 20, "Margin of Safety as the Central Concept of Investment." Both chapters contain philosophical pearls of wisdom.

Value Investing

In the final chapter of *The Intelligent Investor*, Graham wrote, "Confronted with a challenge to distill the secret of sound investment into three words, we venture the motto, Margin of Safety."[25] Writing in the 1990 Berkshire Hathaway Annual Report, Warren Buffett confessed "forty-two years after reading that, I still think those are the right three words."[26] The margin-of-safety concept, buying an investment at a price below intrinsic value, has been and will continue to be the cornerstone to value investing.

The conflict Warren Buffett had with Graham's teachings did not lie with the concept of buying only stocks with a margin of safety, but with how to think about long-term intrinsic value. If an investor bought a company with poor economics priced below the value of its hard assets and at a low price-to-earnings ratio, yes they were operating with Graham's concept of margin of safety, but once the stock repriced nearer to the fair value of its assets, the same investor was often left with the poor economic returns of a mediocre company. What Buffett learned in the early days of Berkshire was that the economics of better companies able to compound their earnings at high rates of return required him to think differently about intrinsic value. The game was no longer about buying hard assets on the cheap but learning to think intelligently about the fair value of cash-generating compounders, companies with better long-term economic returns.

Although Graham's method for picking stocks was not isolating the types of businesses Buffett wanted to own for his compounding conglomerate, it was Graham's temperament, more than anything else, that encouraged Buffett's philosophy about investing. Two things were particularly critical: how to think about the market's inherent volatility and understanding the difference between investment and speculation.

In Chapter 8 of *The Intelligent Investor*, "The Investor and the Market Fluctuations," Ben Graham introduced readers to "Mr. Market." Buffett, in turn, relayed the story of Mr. Market to the Berkshire shareholders in the 1987 Annual Report: "Ben Graham, my friend and teacher, long ago described the mental attitude toward market fluctuations that I believe are most conducive to investment success."

Buffett continues:

> You should imagine market quotations as coming from a remarkably accommodating fellow named Mr. Market who is your partner in a private business. Without fail, Mr. Market appears daily and names a price at which he will either buy your interest or sell you his.
>
> Even though the business that the two of you own may have economic characteristics that are stable, Mr. Market's quotations will be anything but. For sad to say, the poor fellow has incurable emotional problems. At times he feels euphoric and can see only the favorable factors affecting the business.

> When in that mood, he names a very high buy-sell price because he fears that you will snap up his interests and rob him of imminent gains. At other times, he is depressed and can see nothing but trouble ahead for both the business and the world. On these occasions he will name a very low price, since he is terrified that you will unload your interest on him.

Then Buffett gets to the heart of Graham's message of how to think about market fluctuations: "Mr. Market has another endearing characteristic, he doesn't mind being ignored. If his quotation is uninteresting to you today, he will be back with a new one tomorrow. Transactions are strictly at your option. Under these conditions, the more manic-depressive his behavior, the better for you."

Next Buffett frames the story of Mr. Market as it relates to the concept of self-reliance that had become deeply ingrained into his own thinking about investing and the markets:

> Mr. Market is there to serve you, not to guide you. It is his pocketbook, not his wisdom that you will find useful. If he shows up some day in a particularly foolish mood, you are free to either ignore him or take advantage of him, but it will disastrous if you fall under his influence. Indeed if you aren't certain that you understand and can value your business far better than Mr. Market, you don't belong in the game. As they say in poker, 'If you've been in the game 30 minutes and you don't know who the patsy is, *you're* the patsy.'[27]

Buffett concludes: "An investor will succeed by coupling good business judgment with an ability to insulate his thoughts and behavior from the super-contagious emotions that swirl about the marketplace. In my own efforts to stay insulated, I have found it highly useful to keep Ben's Mr. Market concept firmly in mind."[28]

In his inimitable fashion, Buffett has thus showed us that, other than the mathematical concept of the margin of safety, his deep connection to Ben Graham is more philosophical than the methodological approach of buying companies with low price-to-earnings and low price-to-book-value ratios.

The dedication that Warren Buffett has held for Ben Graham is well known, having lasted for 75 years. If we look closely at the set of beliefs and values they share from the perspective of underlying investment philosophy, we see a clear link. Warren Buffett's philosophical foundation had already been formed by his father, but now he had the natural connection that combined what he learned from his father to Graham's writings.

Roger Lowenstein explained, "Ben Graham opened the door, and in a way spoke to Buffett personally. He gave Buffett the tools to explore the market's manifold possibilities and also an approach that fit his student's temper." As a result, "Armed with Graham's techniques . . . and steeled by the example of Graham's character, Buffett would be able to work with his trademark self-reliance."[29] But his relationship with Ben Graham went deeper than this. Although he readily took in Graham's investment methods and philosophy he "saw Graham in idealized terms—as a 'hero' like his father." Indeed, Buffett once said that "Ben Graham was far more than an author or teacher. More than any other man, except my father, he influenced my life."[30]

Buffett reminds us, "To invest successfully over a lifetime does not require a stratospheric IQ. What is needed is a sound intellectual framework for making decisions and the ability to keep emotions from corroding that framework."[31] Ben Graham gave to Warren Buffett the philosophical architecture on how to think smartly about markets. What was left for Buffett to learn was how to polish his business judgment and to understand the attributes that make for a good business.

Philip Fisher: Discerning a Good Business

In 1958, Phil Fisher wrote the first investment book ever to make the *New York Times* bestseller list, *Common Stocks and Uncommon Profits*. Fisher advocated a buy-and-hold approach for growth stocks based on fundamental analysis. Going further, he recommended investors invest in a concentrated, low-turnover portfolio. "If the job has been correctly done when a common stock is purchased the time to sell is almost never."[32]

After Warren Buffett read Fisher's book, he sought out the writer. "When I met him, I was as impressed by the man as by his ideas. Much like Ben Graham, Fisher was unassuming, generous in spirit and an extraordinary teacher."[33]

While Ben Graham and David Dodd were writing *Security Analysis*, Philip Fisher was beginning his career as an investment counselor. After graduating from Stanford's Graduate School of Business Administration, he began work as an analyst at the Anglo London & Paris National Bank in San Francisco. In less than two years, he was made head of the bank's statistical department. From this perch, he witnessed the 1929 stock market crash. Then, after a brief and unproductive career with a local brokerage house, Fisher decided to start his own firm. On March 31, 1931, Fisher & Company began soliciting clients.

Starting an investment counseling firm in the early 1930s might have appeared foolhardy, but Fisher figured he had two advantages. First, any investor who had any money left after the stock market crash was probably very unhappy with their existing broker. Second, in the midst of the Depression, businesspeople had plenty of time to sit and talk with Fisher.

At Stanford, one of Fisher's business classes required him to accompany his professor on periodic visits to companies in the San Francisco area. The professor would get the business managers to talk about their operations and often helped them solve an immediate problem. Driving back to Stanford, Fisher and his professor would recap what they observed about the companies and managers they had visited. "That hour each week," Fisher later said, "was the most useful training I ever received."[34]

From these experiences, Fisher came to believe that superior profits could be made by investing in companies with both above-average potential and highly capable management. To isolate these companies, Fisher developed a "15 Point System" that qualified a company according to the characteristics of its business and management:[35]

> 1. Does the company have products or services with sufficient market potential to make possible a sizable increase in sales for at least several years?

2. Does management have a determination to continue to develop products or processes that will still further increase total sales potential when the growth potentials of currently attractive product lines have largely been exploited?
3. How effective are the company's research-and-development efforts in relation to its size?
4. Does the company have an above-average sales organization?
5. Does the company have a worthwhile profit margin?
6. What is the company doing to maintain or improve profit margins?
7. Does the company have outstanding labor and personnel relations?
8. Does the company have outstanding executive relations?
9. Does the company have depth to its management?
10. How good are the company's cost analysis and accounting controls?
11. Are there other aspects of the business, somewhat peculiar to the industry involved, which will give the investor important clues as to how outstanding the company may be in relation to its competition?
12. Does the company have a short-range or long-range outlook in regard to profits?
13. In the future will the growth of the company require sufficient equity financing so that the larger number of shares then outstanding largely cancel the existing stockholder's benefit from this anticipated growth?
14. Does management talk freely to investors about its affairs when things are going well but "clam up" when troubles and disappointments occur?
15. Does the company have management of unquestionable integrity?

The one characteristic of a company that most impressed Fisher was its ability to grow sales and profits over the years at rates greater than the industry average. To do that, Fisher believed that a company needed to possess "products or services with sufficient market potential to make possible a sizable increase in sales for several years."[36] He was not so much concerned with consistent annual increase in sales. Rather, he judged a company's success over a period of several years. He was aware that changes in the business cycle would have a material effect on sales and earnings. However, he believed that two types of companies would, decade by decade, show promise of above-average growth: (1) those that were "fortunate and able" and (2) those that were "fortunate because they were able."[37]

Aluminum Company of America (Alcoa) was an example, he said, of the first type. The company was "able" because the founders were great people of great ability. Alcoa's management foresaw the commercial uses of its products and worked aggressively to capitalize the aluminum market to increase sales. The company was also "fortunate," said Fisher, because events outside management's immediate control were having a positive impact on the company and the market. Specifically, the swift development of airborne transportation was rapidly increasing sales of aluminum. Because of this, Alcoa was benefitting far more than management had originally envisioned.

DuPont, Fisher said, was a good example of a company that was "fortunate because it was able." If DuPont had stayed with its original product, blasting powder, the company would have fared as well as most typical mining companies. But because management capitalized on the knowledge it had gained by manufacturing gunpowder, DuPont was able to launch new products—including nylon, cellophane, and Lucite—that created their own markets, ultimately producing billions of dollars in sales for DuPont.

A company's research and development efforts, Fisher noted, contributed mightily to the sustainability of its above-average growth in sales. Obviously, he explained, neither DuPont nor Alcoa would have succeeded over the long term without a significant commitment to research and development. Even nontechnical businesses need a dedicated research effort to produce better products and more efficient services.

Next, Fisher examined a company's sales organization. He believed a company could develop outstanding products and services but, unless they were "expertly merchandised," the research and development effort would never translate into revenues. It is the responsibility of the sales organization, he explained, to help customers understand the benefits of a company's products and services. A sales organization should also monitor its customers' buying habits and be able to spot changes in customers' needs. The sales organization, he concluded, becomes the invaluable link between the marketplace and the research and development unit.

The Significance of Profit

However, market share alone is insufficient. Fisher believed that a company, even one capable of producing above-average sales growth, was an inappropriate investment if it was unable to generate a profit for shareholders. "All the sales growth in the world wouldn't produce the right type of investment vehicle if, over the years, profits did not grow correspondingly."[38] Accordingly, Fisher sought companies that not only were the lowest-cost producers of products and services but were also dedicated to remaining so. A company with a low break-even point, or a correspondingly high profit margin, is better able to withstand depressed economic environments. Ultimately, it can drive out weaker competitors, thereby strengthening its own market position.

No company, he said, will be able to sustain its profitability unless it is able to break down the costs of doing business while simultaneously understanding the cost of each step in the manufacturing process. To do so, a company must install adequate accounting controls and cost analysis. This cost information, in turn, enables a company to direct its resources to those products or services with the highest economic potential. Furthermore, accounting controls will help identify snags in a company's operations. These snags, or inefficiencies, act as an early-warning device aimed at protecting the company's overall profitability.

Fisher's sensitivity about a company's profitability was linked to another important concern: a company's ability to grow in the future without requiring equity financing. If the only way a company can grow is to sell shares, he said, the larger number of shares outstanding will cancel out any benefit that stockholders might realize from the company's growth. A company with high profit margins, he explained, is better able to generate funds internally, and these funds can be used to sustain its growth without diluting shareholder's ownership. In addition, a company that is able to maintain adequate cost controls over its fixed assets and working capital needs is better able to manage its cash needs and avoid equity financing.

The Significance of Management

Fisher was aware that superior companies not only possess above-average business characteristics but also, equally important, are directed by people with above-average management capabilities. These managers are determined to develop new products and services long after the current products and services have reached the end of their natural market life. Many companies, Fisher said, have adequate growth prospects because their lines of products and services will sustain them for several years, but few companies have policies in place to ensure consistent gains for 10 or 20 years. "Management must have a viable policy for attaining these ends with all the willingness to subordinate immediate profits for the greater long-range gains that this concept requires."[39] But subordinating immediate profits, he cautioned, should not be confused with *sacrificing* immediate profits. An above-average manager has the ability to implement the company's long-range plans while simultaneously focusing on daily operations.

Fisher emphasized another critical manager trait: Does the business have a management of unquestionable integrity and honesty? Do the managers behave as if they are trustees for the stockholders, or does it appear they are only concerned with their own well-being?

One way to determine management's intentions, Fisher suggested, is to observe how managers communicate with shareholders. All businesses, good and bad, will experience a period of unexpected difficulties. Commonly, when the business is good, management talks freely, but when business declines, some managers clam up rather than talk openly about the company's difficulties. How management responds to business difficulties tells a lot about the people in charge of the company's future.

Fisher went deeper. For a business to be successful, he explained, management must also develop good working relations with all its employees. Employees should genuinely feel good about their place of work. Blue-collar employees should feel that they are treated with respect and decency. Executive employees should feel that promotion is based on ability, not favoritism.

Fisher also considered the depth of management at a company. Does the chief executive officer have a talented team, and is that person able to delegate authority to run parts of the business?

Finally, Fisher examined the specific characteristics of a company: its business and management aspects and how it compares to other businesses in the same industry. In this search, Fisher tried to uncover clues that might lead him to understand the superiority of a company in relation to its competitors. He argued that reading only a company's financial reports is not enough to justify an investment. The essential step in prudent investing, he believed, is to uncover as much about the company as possible from people who are familiar with the company. Fisher admitted that this was a catchall inquiry that would yield what he called *scuttlebutt*. Today, we might call it the business grapevine. If handled properly, Fisher claimed, scuttlebutt will provide substantial clues that will enable the investor to identify outstanding investments.

Fisher's scuttlebutt investigation led him to interview as many sources as possible. He talked with customers and vendors. He sought out former employees as well as consultants who had worked for the company. He contacted research scientists at universities, government employees, and trade association executives. He also interviewed competitors. Although executives may sometimes be hesitant to disclose too much about their own company, Fisher found that they never lacked an opinion about their competitors. "It is amazing what an accurate picture of the relative points of strength and weakness of each company in an industry can be obtained from one representative cross-section of the opinions of those who in one way or another are concerned with any particular company."[40]

Without question, the time and commitment Phil Fisher felt was necessary to understand a company is far more extensive than the mathematical exercise of calculating the accounting ratios of earnings and book value that formed the crux of Ben Graham's value approach. Graham studied balance sheets, Fisher studied companies and people. Fundamental analysis is more laborious than quantitative analysis—necessarily so, as the insights needed to judge a company's long-term intrinsic value are more challenging than taking a snapshot of company's current value.

Clearly, developing a scuttlebutt network and arranging interviews are time-consuming activities; for today's investors, the thought of replicating the scuttlebutt process for numerous companies under consideration can be overwhelming. Phil Fisher to the rescue. He found a simple way to reduce his workload; he reduced the number of companies he owned in his portfolio. Whereas Ben Graham recommended owning a large number of stocks broadly diversified across industries, Phil Fisher typically owned 10 companies or less with three or four companies representing 75 percent of his portfolio. "I don't want a lot of good investments; I want a few outstanding ones."[41]

The Circle of Competence

Fisher believed that, to be successful, investors needed to do only a few things well. One was investing in companies that were within their scope of understanding. Fisher said his earlier mistakes were "to project my skill beyond the limits of my experience. I began investing outside the industries which I believed I thoroughly understood, in completely different spheres of activities; situations where

I did not have comparable background knowledge."[42] Fisher's confession is identical to Warren Buffett's realization that successful investing occurs by staying within one's circle of competence. Not by straying into industries and companies one does not understand.

In an interview with *Forbes* magazine in 1969, Buffett noted "I'm 15% Philip Fisher and 85% Benjamin Graham."[43] At that time, it was not surprising that Graham's influence over Buffett was expansive. Buffett was first an interested reader, then student, then employee, then collaborator, and finally his peer. Graham had molded Buffett's untrained mind. However, those who consider Buffett to be the singular product of Graham have discounted the influence of Phil Fisher.

From his earliest investment mistakes running Berkshire Hathaway, Buffett began moving away from Graham's strict teachings. "I evolved, but I didn't go from ape to human or human to ape in a nice even manner."[44] The problem had been identified decades earlier by the British economist John Maynard Keynes: "The difficulty lies not in the new ideas but in escaping the old ones."[45] My escape, Buffett added, "was long delayed, in part because most of what I had been taught by the same teacher had been (and continues to be) so extraordinarily valuable." However, "Ultimately, business experience, direct and vicarious, produced my strong preference for businesses that possess large amounts of enduring goodwill (intrinsic value in excess of book value) and that utilize a minimum of tangible assets."[46]

In the 1983 Berkshire Hathaway Annual Report, Buffett told shareholders: "My own thinking on investing has changed drastically from 35 years ago when I was taught to favor tangible assets and to shun businesses whose value depended largely upon economic goodwill."[47] Buffett later updated his reasoning: "Phil's all about understanding what makes a company great. I am overwhelmingly in sync with Phil's ideas."[48]

However, for Buffett, the transition from Graham's quantitative method for buying cheap stocks to Fisher's qualitative approach for isolating great companies was not simply an academic exercise. It was the influence of his newfound friend, investing colleague, and soon-to-be vice chairman of Berkshire Hathaway, Charlie Munger. More than any other single individual, Charlie Munger enriched Buffett's thinking on investing.

"It took Charlie Munger to break my cigar-butt habits and set the course for building a business [Berkshire Hathaway] that could combine huge size with satisfactory profits. From my perspective, Charlie's most important architectural feat was the design of today's Berkshire. The blueprint he gave me was simple: Forget what you know about buying fair businesses at wonderful prices; instead, buy wonderful businesses at fair prices."[49]

Charlie Munger: An Intellectual Perspective

When Warren Buffett began his investment partnership in 1956, he had just over $100,000 in capital. One early task, therefore, was to persuade additional investors to sign on. One auspicious day, Buffett was making his usual and carefully detailed pitch to his neighbors, Dr. and Mrs. Edwin Davis, when suddenly Dr. Davis interrupted him and abruptly announced they'd give him $100,000. When Buffett asked why, Davis replied, "Because you remind me of Charlie Munger."[50]

In the category of "it's a small world," Charlie Munger was born in Omaha, Nebraska, on January 1, 1924. He grew up only 200 yards from where Buffett lives today. He even worked in Ernest Buffett's grocery store, although because of the age difference he and Buffett never met as kids. Munger left Omaha and attended the University of Michigan and the California Institute of Technology, but World War II interrupted his education; he served as a meteorological officer in the Army Air Forces. After the war, despite the lack of an undergraduate degree, Munger was admitted to Harvard Law School and graduated in 1948.

Even though both men grew up in Omaha and had many acquaintances in common, Buffett and Munger did not actually meet until 1959. By that time Munger had moved to southern California. When he returned to Omaha for a visit after his father's death, Dr. Davis decided it was time the two young men met, and brought them together for a dinner at a local restaurant. It was the beginning of an extraordinary partnership.

Charlie Munger, the son of a lawyer and grandson of a federal judge, had established a successful law practice in Los Angeles, but his interest in the stock market was already strong. At the first dinner, Buffett and Munger found much to talk about, including stocks. From then on they communicated often, with Buffett frequently urging Munger to quit law and concentrate on investing. "I told him law was a fine hobby, but he could do better."[51]

In 1962, Munger formed an investment partnership (Charles Munger Partnership), much like Buffett's, while maintaining his law practice. Three successful years later, he left law altogether, although to this day the firm still bears his name.

Munger's investment partnership in Los Angeles and Buffett's partnership in Omaha were similar in approach. Both sought to purchase stocks at some discount to underlying value and both achieved outstanding investment results. It is not surprising, then, that they bought some of the same stocks. Munger, like Buffett, began buying shares of Blue Chip Stamps in the late 1960s, and eventually became chairman of its board. When Berkshire Hathaway and Blue Chip Stamps merged in 1978, Charlie Munger became Berkshire's vice chairman.

To their working relationship, Charlie Munger brought not only financial acumen but also the foundation of business law. He also brought an intellectual perspective that was quite different from Buffett's. Munger was passionately interested in many areas of knowledge—science, history, psychology, philosophy, mathematics—and believed each of these fields hold important concepts that thoughtful people can, and should, apply to all their endeavors, including investment decisions.

Together, all these threads—financial knowledge, background in law, and appreciation of the lessons from other disciplines—produced in Munger an investment philosophy that enriched Buffett's. Whereas Buffett, unwaveringly dedicated to Ben Graham, continued to search for stocks selling at bargain prices, Munger was moving towards the principles outlined by Phil Fisher.

How exactly did Charlie Munger convince Buffett to cross over the Rubicon of cigar-butt investing and begin to consider higher-quality companies? We can find the answer in a box of chocolates. See's Candies to be exact.

In 1921, a 71-year-old grandmother named Mary See opened a small neighborhood candy shop in Los Angeles, selling chocolates made from her own recipes. With the help of her son and his partner, the business grew into a small chain in Southern and Northern California. It survived the Depression, overcame sugar rationing during World War II, and endured intense competition, through one unchanging strategy: Never compromise the quality of the product.

Some 50 years later, See's had become the premier chain of candy shops on the West Coast, and Mary See's heirs were ready to move to the next phase of their lives. Chuck Huggins, who had joined the company 30 years earlier, was given the job of finding the best buyer and coordinating the sale. Several suitors came calling, but no engagement was announced.

Late in 1971, an investment advisor to Blue Chip Stamps, of which Berkshire Hathaway was then the majority shareholder, proposed that Blue Chip should buy See's. The asking price was $40 million, but because See's had $10 million in cash, the net price was actually $30 million. Buffett was skeptical, See's was valued at three times book value, a very steep price according to Graham's value-based precepts.

Munger convinced Buffett that paying what he thought was a steep price was actually a good deal. Buffett offered $25 million and the sellers accepted. It was the beginning of a plate-tectonic shift in Buffett's thinking and he acknowledged it was Charlie Munger who pushed in a new direction. "It was," Munger later remarked, "the first time we paid for quality."[52] Ten years later, Buffett was offered $125 million to sell See's—five times the 1972 purchase price. He decided to pass.

Did See's Candies qualify as a penny weighing machine for Berkshire? In the 2014 Berkshire Hathaway Annual Report, Warren Buffett recapped the economic return to Berkshire shareholders.

Over the 22 years since being owned, he reported, this little penny weighing machine called See's Candies had distributed $1.9 billion in pretax earnings requiring only $40 million in added capital reinvestment. Said differently, for roughly $1.8 million per year in further investment, See's returned on average $86 million per year in pretax earnings.

Warren Buffett seized this opportunity to pound home the lesson of compounding. "See's has thus been able to distribute huge sums that have helped Berkshire buy other businesses that, in turn, have themselves produced large distributable profits (envision rabbits breeding). Additionally, through watching See's in action, I gained a business education about the powerful value of brands that opened my eyes to other profitable investments."[53] Buffett's experience owning See's Candies is thought to be a major motivating factor for his purchase, years later, of The Coca-Cola Company and Apple.

The Workings of a Polymath

It has been said that Warren Buffett's first attraction to Charlie Munger was largely based on how much Munger reminded him of Ben Graham. Both men fostered a belief in independent thought. Both were known for their "integrity and dedication to objectivity and realism."[54] And both were voracious readers with deep interests in history, literature, and science. Graham's preferences leaned more to the classical writings, whereas Munger devoured hundreds of biographies, one after another. Graham and Munger were also admirers of Benjamin Franklin and both absorbed Franklin's message of lifelong learning.

Charlie Munger was a polymath. The scope of his knowledge was staggering; there appeared to be little he didn't know. And, like Graham, his ability to reach conclusions with lightning speed was mesmerizing. "Charlie has the best 30-second mind in the world," Buffett once said. "He goes from A to Z in one move. He sees everything before you finish the sentence."[55] With all that Charlie Munger had accomplished, he deserved his own book. Thankfully we have several: *Poor Charlie's Almanack: The Wit and Wisdom of Charles T. Munger* and other fine books have captured the magnificence of Munger's mind.[56]

If we were to investigate the deep well that is Charlie Munger's knowledge, we would pull up three distinct buckets: the *pursuit of worldly wisdom*, the *study of failure*, and the *moral imperative to embrace rationality*.

In April 1994, Charlie Munger's wellspring of knowledge burst forth onto the scene in a remarkable lecture he gave to Dr. Guilford Babcock's "Student Investment Seminar" at the Marshall School of Business at the University of Southern California. The students were primed to hear Munger's thoughts about the stock market and perhaps pick up a few investment tips. Instead, Munger announced he was going to play a little joke on them. Rather than talking about investing directly, he was going to talk about "stock picking as a subdivision of the art of achieving worldly wisdom." For the next hour and a half, he challenged the students to think of the market, finance, and economics not as individual topics but as one composite element in a larger collection of studies that would also include physics, biology, social studies, mathematics, philosophy, and psychology.

It was straight out of the playbook of one of Charlie Munger's heroes. In 1749, Benjamin Franklin, who identified himself as B. Franklin Printer, published a pamphlet entitled *Proposals Relating to the Education of Youth in Pensilvania*. In it, he laid out his views on the fundamental purpose of higher education and proposed establishing an academy built on those ideas. It was astonishingly radical. At the time, institutions of higher education were meant to prepare young men for the ministry; Franklin's vision was much broader. He believed it was vital to educate young people for leadership in business and government, and to do so they should be exposed to many disciplines. He also firmly believed that such education should be available to students from the working class as well as the upper classes that then dominated most campuses. To make his vision a reality, he carefully nurtured the support of some of Philadelphia's leading citizens, and in 1751 the Academy and

Charitable School in the Province of Pennsylvania (which we know today as the University of Pennsylvania) opened its doors.

It's almost impossible to overstate how groundbreaking Franklin's ideas were. Dr. Richard Beeman, the former dean of Penn's College of Arts and Sciences, calls Benjamin Franklin the originator of the liberal arts education. Franklin believed that after students had mastered the basic skills of reading, writing, arithmetic, physical education, and public speaking, they should turn their attention to discovering the connections that exist among the wider bodies of knowledge. Dr. Beeman describes this as Franklin cultivating certain habits of mind.

We can see a straight line from Benjamin Franklin's *habits of mind* to Charlie Munger's focus on achieving *worldly wisdom*. According to Munger, we do not need to become an expert in every discipline in order to reach worldly wisdom; all we need is a basic understanding of the major mental models within each discipline. We would then have, in effect, a liberal arts education in investing, and we would be well on the way to enjoying what Munger called *the lollapalooza impact* of worldly wisdom.

But what exactly would a liberal arts education in investing look like?[57]

Foundations of Worldly Wisdom

In physics, we would certainly study Isaac Newton. In *Principia Mathematica* Newton outlines the three laws of motion, the third of which—for every action there is an equal and opposite reaction—connects directly to established principles of economics, primarily the principles of supply and demand. When they are in balance, we can say the economy is in equilibrium. But if this equilibrium becomes displaced by accidents in production or consumption, then the economy will react with countervailing forces of comparable strength that will restore equilibrium balance. Disequilibrium cannot long survive. Studying Isaac Newton helps us absorb this immutable truth.

However, there are many who do not see an economy and a stock market from a physics point of view. Perhaps they are more naturally drawn to biology, in which case Charlie Munger would recommend reading Charles Darwin, who taught us that living systems learn, evolve, adapt, and can change unexpectedly. There is no doubt markets are living, breathing systems. That makes them the exact opposite of atomic physical systems, which are highly predictable and can repeat the same actions thousands of times with near precision. They act most often in perfect equilibrium. Biological systems, by contrast, exhibit non-equilibrium traits whereby small effects can sometimes have large consequences, whereas large effects can have small consequences. In physics, negative feedback pushes the system predictably back to equilibrium. But in biology, we observe positive feedback loops that can push the system into new and unforeseen directions—just like the stock market.

Studying sociology gives us another mental model: The most optimal and efficient societal body is one that is most diverse. It is referred to as the wisdom of the crowd's effect. But once diversity collapses, when the agents become of one mindset, the system becomes unstable, leading to booms and busts—again, just like the stock market.

From mathematics we learn about probability theory, formulated by Blaise Pascal and Pierre de Fermat. We take additional note of the 18th-century Presbyterian minister Thomas Bayes, whose theorem gave us a mathematical procedure for updating our original beliefs and thus changing the relevant odds. Taken together, Pascal, Fermat, and Bayes give us an outline to properly estimate the future free cash flows of companies, which in turn makes it possible to determine the intrinsic value of our investments. To this we can add probability theory, which also helps to optimize the weightings of common stocks in a portfolio.

In philosophy we would study the modern philosophers René Descartes, Francis Bacon, Immanuel Kant, and David Hume; we will meet them again later in this chapter. Investors would also read Ludwig Wittgenstein, the Austrian-born philosopher whose field of study included logic, mathematics, and the philosophy of language. From Wittgenstein we learn that when we speak of "meaning," we are referring to the words we use to create a description that ultimately leads to our explanation of events. And that when we fail to explain outcomes it is often because we did not form the proper description.

Our studies of philosophy would be incomplete without studying Ralph Waldo Emerson and William James. We made the acquaintance of Emerson previously in this chapter, identifying his influence on Howard Buffett, who in turn relayed the writings of Emerson onto his son. Investors are right to study William James, considered one of the founders of the unique American philosophy called *pragmatism*. Being a pragmatist made possible Buffett's shift from Graham's asset-centric valuation techniques to the future free cash flow estimates of better businesses articulated by Charlie Munger.

But no liberal arts study of investing is complete without a deep dive into psychology. And doing so takes us immediately into the study of failure, Munger's second bucket of knowledge. In Charlie Munger's mind, although it is important to study what works, it is absolutely imperative to study what doesn't work. And getting to the root of failure starts with psychology, for almost without exception our failures, our mistakes, start with errors in thinking that are embedded in psychological missteps.

For his part, Charlie Munger said he had always been interested in standard thinking errors. Even as a young college student he wanted to understand the psychology of decision-making, but he found little help from his formal curriculum. So, soon after receiving his law degree in 1948, Munger began what he called "a long struggle to get rid of the most dysfunctional part of my idea of x."[58]

Note the year 1948. It is important to appreciate that Charlie Munger's quest to understanding the psychology of decision-making occurred during a period when little was published about the link between psychology and investing. What today is popularly known as behavioral finance did not exist as a field of study in the 1950s, 1960s, or 1970s. The first serious work, *Judgment Under Uncertainty: Heuristics and Biases,* by Daniel Kahneman and Amos Tversky, did not appear until 1982, and even then it was buried deep in academia. Two years later, Robert Cialdini wrote one of Munger's favorite books, *Influence: The Psychology of Persuasion*.

Today, 40 years later, investors still struggle with understanding mental errors, a journey Charlie Munger began 75 years earlier. In short, he drew his own road map for how to avoid cognitive failures long before the rest of the world had named the problem.

It should come as no surprise that Charlie Munger took control of his "struggle to get rid of psychological ignorance" by building his own road map for improving decision-making. Soon after the lecture at the Marshall School of Business in 1994, Munger gave two back-to-back talks at the Cambridge Center for Behavioral Studies, one in fall 1994, the other in spring 1995. Under the title "The Psychology of Human Misjudgment," Munger offered a list of what he called "psychology-based tendencies that often mislead along with the antidotes to errors."[59] That list comprised 25 tendencies, from "reward and punishment/super-response tendency" to "lollapalooza tendency—the tendency to get extreme consequences from confluences of psychological tendencies acting in favor of a particular outcome." With each one, Munger provided a detailed description of thinking errors, followed by antidotes on how to avoid future missteps. All 25 tendencies and their antidotes can be found in *Poor Charlie's Almanack*.

Here's an example: number 15 is called "social-proof tendency." It describes the very common and very human tendency to adopt the beliefs and behaviors of people around us, without considering their worth. Essentially it is about self-confidence. A person's behavior becomes oversimplified, Munger warned, when he "automatically thinks and does what he observes to be thought and done around him." So, by the actions of others, investors risk being pulled into misguided action. Or equally dangerous, they are lulled into inaction at times when action is precisely what is needed. Munger's antidote is simple: "Learn how to ignore the examples of others when they are wrong. Few skills are more worth having."[60]

Note that when Charlie Munger defined the tendencies in "The Psychology of Human Misjudgment" he didn't just name one or two, he described 25. And in writing 25 antidotes he challenged investors to continually reassess their positioning. "In the practical world," he asked "what good is the thought system laid out in this list of tendencies?" He answered his own question: "The psychological thought system described, when properly used, enables the spread of wisdom and good conduct and facilitates the avoidance of disaster."[61] Here, in one tidy sentence, Charlie Munger summed up his main themes—developing worldly wisdom, learning to avoid failure, and conducting oneself intelligently. He called that last one *good conduct* and it gives us a natural lead-in to investigating his third bucket: the *embrace of rationality*.

Rational Thinking Roger Lowenstein, Warren Buffett's biographer, said that Buffett's "genius was largely a genius of character—of patience, discipline, and rationality."[62] Without question the same can be said about Charlie Munger. It was he who said, "Berkshire is sort of a temple to rationality."[63] But for Charlie Munger rationality was not just a passing definition; it was the moral compass that guides everything. For him, being rational was the highest calling one can answer. That makes it the most important mental bucket in the formation of Munger's thinking, and it compels us to parse its full meaning.

Rationalism is one of those words that have developed a slippery coating over the years. In its purest sense, the philosophical construct named rationalism refers to a theory of how we gain knowledge. In this theory (simplified here), rationalists learn by thinking and analyzing—that is, through deductive reasoning and the power of the mind. This is referred to as *a priori* knowledge. The antithesis is known as empiricism, which holds that the only way we gain knowledge is through direct observation of our sense experiences *(a posteriori)*. To empiricists, nothing is true unless they can see it, hear it, taste it, and so on. Of course, in real life people can, and generally do, use both approaches according to the circumstances at hand. It's not an either/or game.

However, in casual conversations we often use the word *rational* much more loosely. When we hear someone say, "You're not being rational," they usually mean not being logical or sensible, or not thinking straight.

Both Warren Buffett and Charlie Munger refer to this concept of rationality. As we will soon see, they tend to value it over all other mental models. So when they talk about the importance of being rational, it behooves us to listen. But do we know for sure what they mean? Are they using the term in its more casual sense of being logical, sensible? Or are they thinking of the classic arguments between two academic schools of thought?

I believe it is an amalgam of the two. Warren Buffett and Charlie Munger spent decades reading and thinking about important concepts and sculpting their own sense of truth from many sources. It is worthwhile to explore the various philosophical threads that have led to this uniquely Berkshirist approach to rationality.

Two important figures in modern philosophy—Francis Bacon and René Descartes—illustrate the two opposite views. The two men were contemporaries, from the late 16th to mid-17th centuries, and both rejected the teachings of medieval universities they inherited but disagreed on what should come next. Francis Bacon, an empiricist, argued all knowledge must either originate with or be testable by actual experience. He believed in the value of practical knowledge, like that acquired by carpenters, farmers, sailors, and scientists with their telescopes and microscopes. They were, in his view, united in their philosophical inquiry by how things actually are, not by how they imagine things may be. Descartes, a rationalist, epitomizes the opposite camp, wherein true knowledge can be achieved only by reason, by inference of first principles of self-evident truths. The tension between the empiricists and rationalists was quite real, and offered little guidance for those attempting to define a personal philosophy to help navigate life's challenges.

A century later, during the Age of Enlightenment, a new voice emerged. Immanuel Kant, one of history's great philosophical minds, is credited with bridging the impasse between rationalists and the empiricists by synthesizing their concepts. Starting in 1755 and continuing for the next four decades, Kant taught at the University of Königsberg, in what was then known as Prussia, where he himself had been a student years earlier. His lectures reflected an astonishingly wide range of interests, including physics, astronomy, mathematics, geography, anthropology, and psychology—a perfect example of worldly wisdom.

In his struggles to resolve the dispute between rationalists and empiricists, Kant turned to David Hume, the Scottish philosopher, economist, and historian. Hume eschewed the debate; he was much more interested in understanding how the mind works. Hume's major philosophical work was *A Treatise of Human Nature* written in 1739. Years later he rewrote his masterpiece, dividing the *Treatise* into two books, *An Enquiry Concerning Human Understanding* (1748) and *An Enquiry Concerning the Principles of Morals* (1751). In *Human Understanding* Hume argues that we form "mental habits of connecting ideas together" such that whenever we think of x our mind automatically and immediately goes to y with such inevitability that we assume both ideas must be connected.

Hume's idea of how the mind works was the insight Kant needed to develop a metatheory that would combine both the rationalists' and empiricists' approaches to knowledge. In Kant's new perspective, later referred to as Kantianism, both are right and both are wrong. A. C. Grayling, the British philosopher and philosophy historian, summarizes it this way: "The empiricists are right to insist there cannot be knowledge without sensory experience but they are wrong to say the mind is a blank slate. The rationalists are right to insist that there are *a priori* concepts supplied by our mind, but they are wrong to say *a priori* concepts are sufficient by themselves for knowledge of the world."[64]

Rational Investing Now let's consider these two theories as it relates to investing. We can look at Ben Graham as a rationalist, firmly in René Descartes' camp. Graham's knowledge was built through a series of mental steps, each connected and then carefully reviewed until the chain is complete. His approach is mathematical, relying on self-evident truths. His estimation of value, for example, is built on *a priori* reasoning, not the actual experience of running the companies he bought. Thus, Graham tended toward cheap stocks with low price-to-earnings and low book-value ratios—data that can be collected through research rather than through hands-on sensory experience.

Charlie Munger resides in the Francis Bacon camp. For Charlie, truth was based on observable facts and personal experiences that provide evidence toward knowledge. When Munger began his investment partnership in 1962, he was aware of Graham's teachings but not fully convinced. For his own investment approach, Munger favored identifying good businesses through the process of observing and analyzing the full scope of the company's operations, not simply a bargain price.

Examining Warren Buffett's investment philosophy, we can see Immanuel Kant at work. On the one hand, Buffett is a rationalist. He pledges allegiance to Graham's method of buying a stock only when its low price, lower than the company's intrinsic value, provides a margin of safety. On the other hand, he also appreciates the lessons learned from the experiences of owning companies, and from that we can say he is an empiricist. Hands-on experiences that come from actually owning a business added mightily to Buffett's understanding of investing. We appreciate the philosophical bridge that Charlie Munger built for Warren Buffett when Buffett says, "I am a better investor because I am a businessman and a better businessman because I am an investor."[65] David Hume would explain that when Buffett sees a stock (x), he automatically thinks about the business (y) and that when he analyzes a business (y) he is thinking about a stock (x).

At dinner one night, Charlie Munger was asked what one quality accounts for his success. "I'm rational," he replied. "That's the answer. I am rational."[66] He added, "People who say they are rational should know how things work, what works, and what doesn't, and why."[67] It wasn't a passing idea; it was fundamental to him. As he often said, "It's a moral duty to be as rational as you can make yourself."[68]

The good news is rationality can be learned. "An increase in rationality is not just something you choose or don't choose," Munger said.[69] "Becoming more rational is a long process. It's something you get slowly, with a variable result. But there's hardly anything more important."[70]

Charlie Munger sat by Warren Buffett's side for longer than the time Buffett shared with his father, Howard Buffett, or his teacher,

Ben Graham. Buffett and Munger met in 1959 and became instant friends. When Charlie Munger started his own investment partnership in 1962, they became investment buddies. And in 1978, when Munger became vice chairman of Berkshire Hathaway, they cemented a business partnership that lasted nearly five decades. Through the years, the two men shared a 65-year friendship, a 62-year passion for investing, and a 45-year pilot-copilot relationship that steered Berkshire Hathaway into becoming one of the largest and most respected companies in the world. In all, over half of their lives were spent in the company of each other.

The working relationship between Munger and Buffett was not formalized in an official partnership agreement, but it evolved over the years into something perhaps closer and more symbiotic. Even before Munger joined the Berkshire board, the two made many investment decisions together, often conferring daily; gradually their business affairs became more interlinked.

In every way, Charlie Munger functioned as Buffett's acknowledged co-managing partner and alter ego. To get a sense of how closely the two were aligned, you only have to count the number of times Buffett reported "Charlie and I" did this, or decided that, or believe this, or looked into that, or think this—almost as if "Charlie and I" were the name of one person.

CHAPTER 3

Business-Driven Investing

"Investment is most intelligent when it is most *businesslike*."[1]

This is the summation of Ben Graham's landmark book, *The Intelligent Investor*.

"These are the nine most important words ever written about investing."[2]

That's Warren Buffett, Graham's most famous pupil.

When the world's greatest investor tells us Graham's words are the nine most important ever written about investing, we are well advised to focus and pay acute attention to exactly what is being said. Although we have moved past Graham's methods for valuing businesses, his counsel for how to think about stocks as businesses, explains Buffett, is both enduring and invaluable.

As far back as 1917, when Graham wrote his first article for *The Magazine of Wall Street,* he held a steadfast belief that there was a better way to think about investing, and it was *not* speculating about what the next fellow was going to do with his shares. At the heart of Graham's advice was an appreciation that, in the world of investing, the temperament of a businessperson was far superior to that of a speculator. Having said this, he was dismayed to "see how many capable businessmen try to operate in Wall Street with complete disregard of all sound principles through which they have gained success in their own undertaking."[3]

Graham believed that someone who purchased common shares in a company had earned "double status" and that it was their choice to decide what action to take. They could view themselves as a "minority stockholder in a business" whose fortune was "dependent on the profits of the enterprise or on a change in the underlying value of its assets." Or they could see themselves holding "a piece of paper, an engraved stock certificate, which could be sold in a matter of minutes at a price which varies from moment to moment—when the market is open, that is—and often far removed from the balance-sheet value."[4] That is, one has to choose between being a business owner or a stock speculator.

According to Warren Buffett, there is no fundamental difference between buying a business outright and buying the common shares of that business. Of the two options, Buffett has always preferred to directly own a company because it permits him to influence the business's most critical issue: capital allocation. Buying its common stocks instead has one big disadvantage: You can't control the business. But this is offset, explains Buffett, by two distinct advantages: First, the arena for selecting noncontrolled businesses—the stock market—is significantly larger. Second, said Buffett, "occasionally the stock market offers us the chance to buy non-controlling pieces of extraordinary businesses at truly ridiculous prices—dramatically below those commanded in negotiated transactions that transfer control."[5] In either case, Buffett invariably follows the same strategy. He looks for companies he understands, with favorable long-term prospects, that are operated by honest and competent people, and, importantly, are available at attractive prices.

Most investors spend too much time analyzing the stock market and forecasting the economy; then they assemble a broadly diversified, non-correlative portfolio only to constantly buy and sell stocks in a futile attempt to outperform the market. Buffett disregards the lot. "When investing," he said, "we view ourselves as business analysts, not as market analysts, not as macroeconomic analysts, and not even as security analysts."[6] This means that Buffett works first and foremost from the perspective of a businessperson. He looks at the business holistically, examining all quantitative and qualitative aspects of the business, its management, its financial position, and its purchase price.

Reading the Berkshire Hathaway Annual Report dating back to 1966, looking for commonalities, it is possible to discern a set of basic principles, or tenets, that have guided Warren Buffett's decisions. If we extract these tenets and spread them out for a closer look, we see that they naturally group themselves into four categories:

- Business tenets—three basic characteristics of the business itself
- Management tenets—three important qualities that senior executives must display
- Financial tenets—four critical financial markers that a company must maintain
- Value tenets—two interrelated purchase guidelines

These 12 tenets are timeless principles that Buffett thinks about when buying wholly owned companies as well as shares of common stocks in the market.

Tenets of *The Warren Buffett Way*

Business Tenets
Is the business simple and understandable?
Does the business have a consistent operating history?
Does the business have favorable long-term prospects?

Management Tenets
Is management rational?
Is management candid with shareholders?
Does management resist the institutional imperative?

Financial Tenets
Focus on return on equity, not earnings per share.
Calculate "owner earnings."
Look for companies with high profit margins.
For every dollar retained, make sure the company has created at least one dollar of market value.

Value Tenets
What is the value of the business?
Can the business be purchased with a margin of safety?

Business Tenets

For Warren Buffett, stocks are an abstraction.[7] He doesn't think in terms of market theories, macroeconomic concepts, or sector trends. He makes decisions based only on how a business operates. Buffett believes when people are drawn to an investment because of superficial notions rather than business fundamentals, they are more likely to get scared away at the first sign of trouble, and, in all likelihood, will lose money in the process. Instead, Buffett concentrates on learning all he can about the business under consideration. He focuses on three main areas:

- ☐ A business must be simple and understandable.
- ☐ A business must have a consistent operating history.
- ☐ A business must have favorable long-term prospects.

Simple and Understandable

In Buffett's view, investors' financial success is correlated to how well they understand their investment. This is a distinguishing trait that separates investors with a business orientation from those hit-and-run type investors who are constantly buying and selling stocks.

Over the years, Buffett has owned a vast array of businesses in many different industries. Some of these companies he controlled; in others, he was or is a minority shareholder. But he is acutely aware of how all these businesses operate. He understands the revenues, expenses, cash flows, pricing flexibility, and capital allocation needs of every single one of Berkshire's holdings. Buffett is able to maintain this high level of knowledge about Berkshire's businesses, and common stock holdings, because he purposely limits his selection to companies that are within his area of financial and intellectual understanding. His logic is compelling. If you own a company (either outright or as a shareholder) in an industry you do not fully understand, you cannot possibly interpret developments accurately or make wise decisions.

Investment success is not a matter of how much you know but how realistically you define what you don't know. "Invest in your circle of competence," Buffett counsels. "It's not how big the circle is that counts; it's how well you define the parameters."[8]

Consistent Operating History

Warren Buffett not only avoids the complex but also avoids companies that are either solving difficult business problems or fundamentally changing direction because their previous plans were unsuccessful. It has been his experience that the best returns are achieved by companies that have been producing the same products and services for several years. Undergoing major business changes increases the likelihood of committing major business errors.

Buffett observed, "Severe change and exceptional returns usually don't mix."[9] Most people, unfortunately, invest as if the opposite were true. Investors tend to be attracted to fast-changing industries or companies that are in the midst of a corporate reorganization. For some unexplained reason, says Buffett, investors are so infatuated with what tomorrow may bring that they ignore today's business reality.

Buffett cares very little for stocks that are popular at any given moment. He is far more interested in buying into companies that he believes will be successful and profitable for the long term. And although predicting the future success is certainly not foolproof, a steady track record is a relatively reliable performance indicator. When a company has demonstrated consistent results with the same type of products or services year after year, it is not unreasonable to assume that those results will continue.

Buffett also tends to avoid businesses that are solving difficult problems. Experience has taught him that turnarounds seldom turn. It can be more profitable to look for good businesses at reasonable prices than difficult businesses at cheaper prices. "Charlie and I have not learned how to solve difficult business problems," he once said. "What we have learned to do is to avoid them. To the extent that we have been successful, it is because we have concentrated on identifying one-foot hurdles that we can step over rather than because we acquired any ability to clear seven-footers."[10]

Favorable Long-Term Prospects

Buffett divides the economic world into two unequal parts: a small group of great businesses, which he terms *franchises,* and a much larger group of mediocre businesses, of which most are not worth purchasing. He defines a franchise as a company providing a product or service that is (1) needed or desired, (2) has no close substitute, and (3) is not regulated. These traits enable the company to hold its prices, and occasionally raise them, without fear of losing market share or unit volume. This pricing flexibility is one of the defining characteristics of a great business; it enables the company to earn above-average returns on capital.

"We like stocks that generate high returns on invested capital," says Buffett, "where there is a strong likelihood that [they] will continue to do so."[11] He added, "I look at the long-term competitive advantage, and [whether] that's something that is enduring."[12]

Individually and collectively, these great businesses create what Buffett calls a *moat*—something that gives the company a clear advantage over others and protects it against incursion from competition. The bigger the moat, and the more sustainable, the better he likes it. "The key to investing is determining the competitive advantage of any given company and above all, the durability of the advantage. The products and services that have wide, sustainable moats around them are ones that deliver rewards to investors. The most important thing for me is figuring out how big a moat there is around the business. What I love, of course, is a big castle and a big moat with piranhas and crocodiles."[13]

Conversely, a mediocre business offers a product that is virtually indistinguishable from the products of its competitors—a commodity. Despite mammoth advertising budgets, they are unable to achieve meaningful product differentiation. Commodity businesses, generally, are low-returning businesses and prime candidates for profit trouble. Their product is basically no different from anyone else's, so they can compete only on the basis of price, which of course cuts into profit margins. The most dependable way to make a commodity business profitable is to become the low-cost provider. The only other time commodity businesses turn a healthy profit is during periods of tight supply, a factor that can be extremely difficult to predict. A key to determining the long-term profit of a commodity business, notes Buffett, is the ratio of "supply-tight to supply-ample years." However, this ratio is often fractional. "What I like," he confides, "is economic strength in an area where I understand it and where I think it will last."[14]

Last, Buffett tells us, in one of his many succinct bits of wisdom, "The definition of a great company is one that will be great for 25 to 30 years."[15]

Management Tenets

When considering new investment or a business acquisition, Buffett looks very hard at the quality of management. He tells us that the companies or stocks Berkshire purchases must be operated by honest and competent managers whom he admires and trusts. "We do not wish to join with managers who lack admirable qualities," he says, "no matter how attractive the prospects for their business. We've never succeeded with making good deals with a bad person."[16]

When he finds managers he admires, Buffett is generous with his praise. Year after year, readers of the chairman's letter in Berkshire's annual reports find Buffett's warm words about those who manage the various Berkshire companies. He is just as thorough when it comes to the management of companies whose stock he owns. In particular, he looks for three traits:

☐ Is management rational?
☐ Is management candid with shareholders?
☐ Does management resist the institutional imperative?

The highest compliment Buffett can pay a manager is that he or she unfailingly behaves and thinks like an owner of the company. Managers who behave like owners tend not to lose sight of the company's prime objective—increasing shareholder value—and they tend to make rational decisions that further that goal. Buffett also greatly admires managers who take seriously their responsibility to report candidly and fully to shareholders. And those who have the courage to resist what he has termed the *institutional imperative*, that is, blindly following industry peers.

Rational Management

The most important management act is the allocation of capital. It is the most important because allocation of capital, over time, determines shareholder value. Deciding what to do with the company's earnings—reinvest in the business or return money to shareholders—is, in Buffett's mind, an exercise in logic and rationality. "Rationality is the quality that Buffett thinks distinguishes the style with which he runs Berkshire—and the quality he often finds lacking in other corporations," wrote Carol Loomis of *Fortune* magazine.[17]

The question of where to allocate earnings is linked to where the company is in its life cycle. As a company moves through its economic life cycle, its growth rates, sales, earnings, cash flows, and returns on capital change dramatically. In the developmental stage, a company loses money as it develops products and establishes markets. During the next stage, rapid growth, the company is profitable but growing so fast that it must retain all of its earnings. In the last stage, decline, the company experiences declining sales and earnings but continues to generate excess cash. It is in phase three that the question arises: How should those earnings be allocated?

If the extra cash, reinvested internally, can produce above-average return on equity, a return higher than the cost of capital, then the company should retain all of its earnings and reinvest them. That is the only logical course. Retaining earnings in order to reinvest in the company at *less* than the average cost of capital is completely irrational. It is also quite common.

A company that provides average or below-average investment returns but generates cash in excess of its needs has three options: (1) It can ignore the problem and continue to reinvest at below-average rates, (2) it can buy growth, or (3) it can return money to shareholders. It is at this crossroads that Buffett keenly focuses on management's decisions, for it is here that management will behave rationally or irrationally.

Generally, managers who continue to reinvest despite below-average returns do so in the belief that the situation is temporary. They are convinced that with managerial prowess, they can improve their company's profitability. Shareholders become mesmerized with management's forecast of improvements. If a company continually ignores this problem, cash will become an increasingly idle resource and the stock price will decline.

A company with poor economic returns, excess cash, and a low stock price will attract corporate raiders, which is the beginning of the end of current management tenure. To protect themselves, executives frequently choose the second option instead: purchasing growth by acquiring another company.

Announcing acquisition plans has the effect of exciting shareholders and dissuading corporate raiders. However, Buffett is skeptical of companies that need to buy growth. For one thing, growth often comes at an overvalued price. For another, a company that must integrate and manage a new business is apt to make mistakes that could be costly for shareholders.

In Buffett's mind, the only reasonable and responsible course of action for companies that have a growing pile of cash that cannot be reinvested at above-average rates is to return that money to shareholders. For that, two methods are available: (1) initiating or raising a dividend and (2) buying back shares.

With cash in hand from their dividends, shareholders have the opportunity to look elsewhere for higher returns. On the surface, this seems like a good deal, and therefore many people view increased dividends as a sign of companies that are doing well. Buffett believes this is true only if investors can get more from their cash than the company could generate if it retained the earnings and reinvested in the company.

If the real value of dividends is misunderstood, the second mechanism for returning earnings to the shareholders—stock repurchases—is even more so. That's because the benefit to the owners is, in many respects, less direct, less tangible, and less immediate.

When management repurchases stock, Buffett feels that the reward is twofold. If the stock is selling below its intrinsic value, then purchasing shares makes good business sense. If a company's stock price is $50 and its intrinsic value is $100, then each time management buys its stock, it is acquiring $2 intrinsic value for every $1 spent. Transactions of this nature can be very profitable for remaining shareholders.

Furthermore, Buffett says, when executives actively buy the company's stock in the market selling at prices below intrinsic value, they are demonstrating that they have the best interests of their owners at heart, rather than the careless need to expand the corporate structure. That kind of stance sends signals to the market, attracting other investors looking for a well-managed company that increases shareholder wealth. Frequently, shareholders are rewarded twice—once from the initial open market purchase and then subsequently as increased investor interest has a positive effect on the stock price.

Candid Management

Buffett holds in high regard managers who report their company's financial performance fully and genuinely, who admit mistakes as well as share successes, and in all aspects are candid with shareholders. In particular, he respects managers who are able to communicate the performance of their company without hiding behind generally accepted accounting principles (GAAP). Buffett explains: "What needs to be reported is data—whether GAAP, non-GAAP, or extra GAAP—that helps the financially literate readers answer three key questions: (1) Approximately how much is the company worth? (2) What is the likelihood that it can meet its future obligations? (3) How good a job are its managers doing, given the hand they have been dealt?"[18]

Buffett also admires managers who have the courage to discuss failure openly. Over time, every company makes mistakes, both large and inconsequential. Too many managers, he believes, report with excess optimism rather than honest explanations, serving perhaps their own interests in the short term but no one's interest in the long run.

Most annual reports, he says bluntly, are a sham. That's why in his own annual reports to Berkshire Hathaway shareholders, Buffett is very open about Berkshire's economics and management performance, both good and bad. Throughout the years, he has admitted the difficulties that Berkshire encountered in both the textile and insurance businesses, and his own management failures in regard to these businesses. In the 1989 Berkshire Hathaway Annual Report, he started a practice of listing his mistakes formally, called "Mistakes of the First Twenty-Five Years (A Condensed Version)." Two years later, the title was changed to "Mistakes Du Jour." Here, Buffett confessed not only mistakes made but also opportunities lost because he failed to act appropriately—what he calls "failures of omission."

Critics have noted that it's a bit disingenuous for Buffett to publicly admit his mistakes; because of his large personal ownership of Berkshire's common stock, he never has to worry about being fired. This is true. But by modeling candor, Buffett is quietly creating a new approach to management reporting. It is Buffett's belief that candor benefits the manager at least as much as the shareholder. "The CEO who misleads others in public," he says, "may eventually mislead himself in private."[19] Buffett credits Charlie Munger with helping him understand the value of studying one's mistakes, rather than concentrating only on successes.

The Institutional Imperative

If management stands to gain wisdom and credibility by facing mistakes, why do so many annual reports trumpet only success? If allocation of capital is so simple and logical, why is capital so poorly allocated? The answer, Buffett has learned, is an unseen force he calls the *institutional imperative*—the lemming-like tendency of corporate managers to imitate the behavior of others, no matter how silly or irrational.

It was the most surprising discovery of his business career. At school he was taught that experienced managers were honest and intelligent, and automatically made rational business decisions. Once in the business world, he learned instead that "rationality frequently wilts when the institutional imperative comes into play."[20]

Buffett believes that the institutional imperative is responsible for several serious and distressingly common conditions: "(1) [The organization] resists any change in its current condition; (2) just as work expands to fill available time, corporate projects or acquisitions will materialize to soak up available funds; (3) any business craving of the leader, however foolish, will quickly be supported by detailed rate-of-return and strategic studies prepared by his troops; (4) the behavior of peer companies, whether they are expanding, acquiring, setting executive compensation or whatever, will be mindlessly imitated."[21]

Buffett learned his lesson early. Jack Ringwalt, head of National Indemnity, which Berkshire acquired in 1967, made what seemed like a stubborn move. While most insurance companies were writing policies on terms guaranteed to produce inadequate returns—or worse, a loss—Ringwalt stepped away from the market and refused to write new policies. Buffett recognized the wisdom of Ringwalt's decision and followed suit. Today, all of Berkshire's insurance companies still operate on this principle: Just because everyone else is doing something, that doesn't make it right.

What is behind the institutional imperative that drives so many businesses? Human nature. Most managers are unwilling to look foolish with, for example, an embarrassing quarterly loss when others in the industry are still producing quarterly gains, even though they assuredly are heading like lemmings into the sea.

It's never easy to make unconventional decisions or shift direction. Still, a manager with strong communication skills should be able to persuade shareholders to accept a short-term loss in earnings and a change in the company's direction if that strategy will yield superior results over time. Inability to resist the institutional imperative, Buffett has learned, often has less to do with the owners of the company than the willingness of its managers to accept fundamental change. And even when managers accept the need for radical change, carrying out this plan is often too difficult for most managers to accomplish. Instead, many succumb to the temptation to buy a new company rather than face the financial facts of the current problem.

Why would they do this? Buffett isolates three factors as being most influential in management's behavior:

- ☐ Most managers cannot control their lust for activity. Such hyperactivity often finds its outlet in business takeovers.
- ☐ Most managers are constantly comparing their business's sales, earnings, and executive compensation to other companies within and beyond their industry. These comparisons invariably invite corporate hyperactivity.
- ☐ Most managers have an exaggerated sense of their own capabilities.

Another common problem, we have learned, is poor allocation skills. CEOs often rise to their position by excelling in other areas of the company including administration, engineering, marketing, or production. With little experience in allocating capital, they turn instead to staff members, consultants, or investment bankers, and inevitably the institutional imperative enters the decision-making process. If the CEO craves a potential acquisition that requires a 15 percent return on investment to justify a purchase, it's amazing, Buffett points out, how smoothly the troops report back that the business can actually achieve 15.1 percent.

The final justification for the institutional imperative is mindless imitation. The CEO of Company D says to himself, "If Companies A, B, and C are all doing the same thing, it must be all right for us to behave in the same way."

They are positioned to fail—not, Buffett believes, because of venality or stupidity, but because the institutional dynamics of the imperative make it difficult to resist doomed behavior. Speaking before a group of University of Notre Dame students, Buffett displayed a list of 37 investment banking firms. Every single one, he explained, had failed, even though the odds for success were in their favor. He ticked off the positives: The volume of the New York Stock Exchange had multiplied 15fold, and the firms were headed by hardworking people with very high IQs, all of whom had an intense desire to succeed. Yet all failed. Buffett paused. "You think about that," he said sternly, his eyes scanning the room. "How could they get a result like that? I'll tell you—mindless imitation of their peers."[22]

The Measure of Management

Buffett would be the first to admit that evaluating managers along these dimensions—rationality, candor, and independent thinking—is more difficult than measuring the financial performance for the simple reason that human beings are more complex than numbers.

Indeed, many analysts believe that because measuring human activity is vague and imprecise, we simply cannot value management with Excel spreadsheet precision, and therefore the exercise is futile. Without a decimal point, they seem to suggest, there is nothing to measure. Others hold the view that the value of management is fully reflected in the company's performance statistics—including sales, profit margins, and return on equity—hence when you are placing a value on management it is a form of double accounting.

Both of these opinions have some validity, but neither is, in my view, strong enough to outweigh the original premise. The reason for taking the time to evaluate management is that it yields early warning signs of eventual financial performance. Financial facts tell you what has transpired. Evaluating management can give us insight as to what might yet occur. If you look closely at the words and actions of the management team, you will find clues that will help you measure the value of the team's work long before it shows up on the company's financial reports or in the stock pages of a daily newspaper.

For gathering the necessary information, Buffett offers a few tips. Review annual reports from a few years back, paying special attention to what management said then about the strategies for the future. Then compare those plans to today's results; how fully were the plans realized? Also compare the strategies of a few years ago to this year's strategies and ideas; how has the thinking changed? Buffett also suggests it can be very valuable to compare annual reports of the companies in which you are interested with the reports of similar companies in the same industry. It is not always easy to find exact duplicates, but even relative performance comparisons can yield insights.

It's worth pointing out that quality of management is by itself not sufficient to attract Buffett's interest. No matter how impressive management is, he will not invest in people alone, because he knows there is a point where even the brightest and most capable managers cannot rescue a difficult business. Buffett has been fortunate to work with some of the most talented managers in corporate America, including Tom Murphy and Dan Burke at Capital Cities/ABC, Roberto Goizueta and Donald Keough at Coca-Cola. However, he's quick to point out, "if you put these same guys to work in a buggy whip company it wouldn't have made much difference."[23] He adds, "When a management with a reputation for brilliance tackles a business with a reputation for poor fundamental economics, it is the reputation of the business that stays intact."[24] This being said, the best combination is to own great companies run by talented managers who will help keep the great business alive.

Financial Tenets

The financial tenets by which Buffett evaluates both managerial excellence and economic performance are all grounded in some typical Buffett-like principles. For one thing, he does not take yearly results too seriously. Instead, he focuses on five-year averages. Profitable returns, he wryly notes, don't always coincide with the time it takes the planet to circle the sun. He also has little patience with accounting sleight-of-hand that produces impressive year-end numbers but little value. Instead, he is guided by these four financial principles.

- Focus on return on equity, not earnings per share.
- Calculate "owner earnings" to get a true reflection of value.
- Look for companies with high profit margins.
- For every dollar retained, make sure the company has created at least one dollar of market value.

Return on Equity

Customarily, analysts measure annual company performance by examining earnings per share (EPS). Did EPS increase over the prior year? Did the company beat expectations? Are earnings high enough to brag about?

Buffett considers earnings per share a smoke screen. Because most companies retain a portion of their previous year's earnings as a way to increase their equity base, he sees no reason to get excited about EPS. There is nothing spectacular about a company that increases EPS at 10 percent if, at the same time, it is growing its earnings base by 10 percent. "Earnings per share will rise constantly on a dormant saving account or on a U.S. Savings Bond bearing a fixed rate of return simply because 'earnings' (the stated interest rate) are continually plowed back and added to the capital base," explains Buffett. "Thus, even a 'stopped clock' can look like a growth stock if the dividend payout ratio is low."[25]

To measure a company's annual performance, Buffett prefers return on equity: the ratio of operating earnings to shareholder's equity. "The primary test of managerial economic performance," says Buffett, "is the achievement of a high earnings rate on equity employed (without undue leverage, accounting gimmickry, etc.) and not the achievement of consistent earnings per share." He goes on to explain, "In our view, many businesses would be better understood by their shareholder owners, as well as the general public, if management and financial analysts modified the primary emphasis they place on earnings per share, and upon yearly changes in that figure."[26]

To use this ratio, we need to make several adjustments. First, all marketable securities should be valued at cost and not market value, because values in the stock market as a whole can greatly influence the returns on shareholder's equity in a particular company. For example, if the stock market rose dramatically in one year, thereby increasing the net worth of a company, a truly outstanding operating performance would be diminished when compared to a larger denominator. Conversely, falling prices reduce shareholders' equity, which means that mediocre operating results appear much better than they really are.

Second, we must also control the effects that unusual items may have on the numerator of this ratio. Buffett excludes all capital gains and losses, as well as any extraordinary items that may increase or decrease operating earnings. He is seeking to isolate the specific annual performance of a business. He wants to know how well management accomplishes its task of generating a return on operations of the business given the capital employed. That, he says, is the single-best judge of management's economic performance.

Furthermore, Buffett believes that a business should achieve good returns on equity while employing little debt or no debt. Buffett knows that companies can increase their return on equity by increasing the debt-to-equity ratio, but he is not impressed. "Good business or investment decisions," he says, "will produce quite satisfactory results with no aid from leverage."[27] Furthermore, highly leveraged companies are vulnerable during economic downturns. Buffett would rather err on the side of the financial quality than risk the welfare of Berkshire's owners by increasing the risk associated with high debt levels.

Buffett does not give any suggestions as to what debt levels are the most appropriate or inappropriate for a business. This is wholly understandable: Different companies, depending on their cash flows, can manage different levels of debt. What Buffett does say is that a good business should be able to earn a good return on equity without the aid of leverage. Companies that depend on debt for good returns on equity should be viewed suspiciously.

Owner Earnings

"The first point to understand," Buffett says, "is that not all earnings are created equal."[28] Companies with high assets compared to profits, he points out, tend to report ersatz earnings. Because inflation exacts a toll on asset-heavy businesses, the earnings of these companies take on a mirage-like quality. Hence, accounting earnings are useful to the analyst only if they approximate the company's expected cash flow.

But even cash flow, Buffett warns, is not a perfect tool for measuring value; in fact, it often misleads investors. Cash flow is an appropriate way to measure businesses that have large investments in the beginning and smaller outlays later on, such as real estate development, gas fields, and cable companies. Manufacturing companies, however, which require ongoing capital expenditures, are not accurately valued using only cash flow.

A company's cash flow is customarily defined as net income after taxes plus depreciation, depletion, amortization, and other noncash charges. The problem with this definition, explains Buffett, is that it leaves out a critical economic fact: capital expenditures. How much of this year's earnings must the company use for new equipment, plant upgrades, and other improvements needed to maintain an economic position and unit volume? According to Buffett, an overwhelming majority of US businesses require capital expenditures that are roughly equal to their depreciation rates. You can defer capital expenditures for a year or so, he says, but if over a long period you don't make the necessary capital expenditures, your business will surely decline. These capital expenditures are as much an expense as labor and utility costs.

Popularity of cash flow numbers heightened during the leverage buyout period because the exorbitant prices paid for businesses was justified by a company's cash flow. Buffett believes that cash flow numbers "are frequently used by marketers of businesses and securities in attempts to justify the unjustifiable and thereby sell what should be unsalable. When earnings look inadequate to service debt of a junk bond or justify a foolish stock price, how convenient it becomes to focus on cash flow."[29] But you cannot focus on cash flow, Buffett warns, unless you are willing to subtract the necessary capital expenditures.

Instead of cash flow, Buffett prefers what he calls *owner earnings*—a company's net income plus the noncash charges of depreciation, depletion, and amortization, less the amount of capital expenditures and any additional working capital that might be needed. Buffett admits that owner earnings do not provide the precise calculation that many analysts demand. Calculating future expenditures often requires estimates. Even so, it is far better to adjust reported GAAP income numbers adjusted for noncash charges and estimated capital expenditures than rely on net income alone.

Profit Margins

Similar to Philip Fisher, Buffett is aware that great businesses make lousy investments if management cannot convert sales into profits. There's no big secret to profitability: It all comes down to controlling costs. In Buffett's experience, managers of high-cost operations tend to find ways to continually add to overhead, whereas managers of low-cost operations are always finding ways to cut expenses.

Buffett has little patience with managers who allow costs to escalate. Frequently, these same managers have to initiate a restructuring program to bring costs in line with sales. Each time a company announces a cost-cutting program, he knows its management has not figured out what expenses can do to a company's owners. "The really good manager," Buffett says, "does not wake up in the morning and say, 'This is the day I'm going to cut costs,' any more than he wakes up and decides to practice breathing."[30]

Buffett singles out the accomplishments of some of the best management teams he has worked with, including Tom Murphy and Dan Burke at CapCities/ABC, for their relentless attacks on unnecessary expenses. These managers, he says, "abhor having a bigger head count than is needed," and both "attack costs as vigorously when profits are at record levels as when they are under pressure."[31]

Buffett himself can be tough when it comes to costs and unnecessary expenses. He understands the right size staff for any business operation and believes that for every dollar of sales, there is an appropriate level of expenses. Buffett is very sensitive about Berkshire's profit margins.

Berkshire Hathaway is a unique corporation. It does not have a legal department, or a public relations or investor relations department. There are no strategic planning departments staffed with MBA-trained workers plotting mergers and acquisitions. Berkshire's after-tax corporate expenses run less than 1 percent of operating earnings. Most companies of Berkshire's size have corporate expenses 10 times higher.

The One-Dollar Premise

Speaking broadly, the stock market eventually answers the fundamental question, What is this particular company worth? Buffett proceeds in the belief that if he has selected a company with favorable long-term economic prospects, run by able and shareholder-oriented managers, the proof will be reflected in the increased market value of the company. The same, Buffett explains, holds for retained earnings. If a company employs retained earnings unproductively (generating a return below the cost of capital) over an extended period of time, the market, justifiably, will price the shares lower. Conversely, if a company has been able achieve above-average returns on augmented capital, over time that success will be reflected in an increased stock price.

However, we also know that although the stock market will track business values reasonably well over long periods, in any one year prices can gyrate widely up and down for reasons other than long-term intrinsic value. So Buffett has created a quick test to judge not only the economic attractiveness of a business but also how well management has accomplished its goal of creating shareholder value: the one-dollar rule. The increase in value should, at the very least, match the amount of retained earnings dollar for dollar. If the value goes up more than retained earnings, so much the better. All in all, Buffett explains, within the stock market it is our job to select a business with economic characteristics that allow for the retention of one dollar of retained earnings to be translated into at least one dollar of market value.

Value Tenets

All the principles embodied in the tenets described thus far lead to one decision point: buying or not buying shares in a company. Anyone at this point must weigh two factors: Is this company a good value, and is this a good time to buy it—that is, is the price favorable?

Price is established by the stock market. Value is determined by the analyst, after weighing all the known information about a company's business, management, and financial traits. Price and value are not always equal. If the stock market was always efficient, prices would instantaneously adjust to all available information. Of course, we know this does not occur—at least not all the time. The prices of securities move above and below a company's value for numerous reasons, not all of them logical.

Theoretically, the actions of an investor are determined by the differences between price and value. If the price of the business is below its per-share value, a rational investor will purchase shares of the business. Conversely, if the price is higher than value, the investor will pass. As the company moves through its economic life cycle, the analyst will periodically reassess the company's value in relation to market price, and buy, sell, or hold shares accordingly.

In sum, rational investing has two components:

- ☐ What is the value of the business?
- ☐ Can the business be purchased at a significant discount to its value?

Determine the Value

In the 1992 Berkshire Hathaway Annual Report, 20 years after he purchased See's Candies, Warren Buffett articulated, for the first time, his revised thoughts on value investing. He began, "The very term 'value investing' is redundant. What is 'investing' if it is not the act of seeking value at least sufficient to justify the amount paid?" Buffett explained, "Consciously paying more for a stock than its calculated value—in the hope that it can be sold for still-higher price—should be labeled speculation (which is neither illegal, immoral nor—in our view—fattening)."[32]

Next he weighed in on the never-ending debate between value and growth investing. Buffett asked, "How does one decide what's attractive?" He responded, "Most analysts feel they must choose between two approaches customarily thought to be in opposition: 'value' and 'growth.'" He then admitted, "Many investment professionals see any mixing of the two terms as a form of intellectual cross-dressing. We view that as fuzzy thinking (in which, it must be confessed, I myself engaged some years ago)." Now, said Buffett, "our opinion [is] the two approaches are joined at the hip: Growth is always a component in the calculation of value, constituting a variable whose importance can range from negligible to enormous and whose impact can be negative as well as positive."[33]

Then Buffett drilled down into the specifics of the argument: "Whether appropriate or not, the term 'value investing' is widely used. Typically, it connotes the purchase of stocks having attributes such as a low ratio of price-to-book value, a low price-earnings ratio, or a high dividend yield. Unfortunately, such characteristics, even if they appear in combination, are far from determinative as to whether an investor is indeed buying something for what it is worth and therefore truly operating on the principle of obtaining value in his investments."[34]

His point was profound, but what Buffett wrote next turned the value investing community upside down: "Correspondingly, opposite characteristics—a high ratio of price-to-book value, a high price-to-earnings ratio, and a low dividend yield—are in no way inconsistent with a 'value' approach."[35]

To settle the matter, Buffett next introduced John Burr Williams to the Berkshire shareholders. Williams had written *The Theory of Investment Value* in 1938, four years after Graham and Dodd had written *Security Analysis*. Williams' definition of value, now embraced by Buffett, is "the value of any stock, bond, or business today is determined by the cash inflows and outflows—discounted at an appropriate interest rate—that can be expected to occur during the remaining life of the asset."[36] Whether a stock is undervalued or overvalued, explained Buffett, is not determined by its price-to-book value or price-to-earnings ratio.

Williams' discounted present value of the future free cash flow is popularly referred to as the dividend discount model and sometimes as the discounted cash flow model. The mathematical exercise, Buffett tells us, is very similar to valuing a bond. A bond has both a coupon and a maturity date that determines its future cash flows. If you add up all the bond's coupons and divide the sum by the appropriate discount rate (the interest rate of the bond), the price of the bond will be revealed.

To determine the value of a business, an analyst estimates the coupons (owner earnings) that the business will generate for a period of time in the future, and then discounts all of these coupons back to the present. For Buffett, determining a company's value is relatively easy so long as you plug in the right variables: the stream of cash flow and the proper discount rate. In his mind, the predictability of a company's future cash flow should take on a "coupon-like" certainty that can be found in bonds. If the business is simple and understandable, and if it has operated with consistent earnings power, Buffett is able to determine the future cash flows with a high degree of certainty. If he cannot, he will not attempt to value a company. This is the distinction of his approach.

The next question then becomes, what is the appropriate discount rate? Abbreviated answer: cost of capital. In the standard cash flow model, a company's cost of capital is used as the discount rate for determining the value of future cash flows. And so, how do we determine a company's cost of capital? The cost of debt is straightforward: the weighted-average interest rate of its debt outstanding. But determining a company's equity cost of capital requires some additional thinking.

Academicians argue the appropriate discount rate applied to the discounted cash flow model is the risk-free rate (10-year US Treasury Note) plus an equity risk premium, added to reflect the uncertainty of the company's future cash flows. But as we will learn later, Buffett dismisses the concept of the equity risk premium because it is an artifact of the capital asset pricing model that, in turn, uses price volatility as a measure of risk. In simple terms, the higher the price volatility, the higher equity risk premium.

Buffett thinks the whole idea that price volatility is a measure of risk is nonsense. In his mind, business risk is reduced, if not eliminated, by focusing on companies with consistent and predictable earnings. "I put a heavy weight on certainty," he says. "If you do that, the whole idea of a risk factor doesn't make sense to me. Risk comes from not knowing what you're doing."[37] In Buffett's mind, the predictability of a company's future cash flow should take on a coupon-like certainty found in the bonds.

When *The Warren Buffett Way* was first published in 1994, Warren Buffett explained that he used the risk-free rate, the 10-year US Treasury, to discount stocks. During the decade of the 1990s, the average yield of the 10-year Treasury was 8.55 percent. We wrote that Buffett used this risk-free rate and adjusted the purchase price, the margin of safety, relative to the riskiness of the business. However, over the last 10 years with the yield of the 10-year Treasury well below 5.00 percent, Buffett has had to think of a different discount rate.

It appears both Buffett and Munger had a solution. "We just look to do the most intelligent thing we can with the capital we have," said Buffett. Munger was more precise: "We measure everything against our alternatives." For emphasis, he added, "It's your alternatives that matter."[38]

Munger, by speaking of alternatives, framed the question as opportunity cost. People who invest in the stock market have an expectation of earning at least a 10 percent return, which is the average historical return of the stocks since 1900.[39] That is their investment opportunity. Thus, we can say an investor's cost of capital for "lending" their money to the stock market is 10 percent. Conversely, someone who decides not to invest in the stock market has made a decision to forgo a 10 percent annual return. Said differently, capital has an opportunity cost.[40] All this said, with the risk-free rate below 10 percent, I believe a 10 percent discount rate is appropriate for calculating the intrinsic value of a stock.

Intrinsic business value, Buffett explains, is an economic calculation based on the future cash flows of a business discounted back to present value: Anyone calculating intrinsic value necessarily comes up with a highly subjective figure that will change both as estimates of future cash flows are revised and interest rates move. Despite the fuzziness, however, intrinsic value is all-important and is the only logical way to evaluate the relative attractiveness of investments and businesses.[41]

Buffett is not the only one to recognize intrinsic value as an elusive concept. Although Ben Graham did not apply the discounted net present value model, he also cautioned that intrinsic value was not a precise estimate. "The essential point," said Graham, "is that security analysis does not seek to determine exactly what is the intrinsic value of a given security. It only needs to establish either the value is adequate to protect a bond or justify a stock purchase. For such purposes an indefinite and approximate measure of the intrinsic value may be sufficient."[42] Seth Klarman thinks along the same lines. In his book, *Margin of Safety*, he writes, "Many investors insist on affixing exact values to their investment, seeking precision in an imprecise world, but business value cannot be precisely determined."[43] Buffett echoes both Graham and Klarman: "Intrinsic value is an estimate rather than a precise figure."[44]

With Wall Street's obsession over target prices and single-point estimates, Buffett's admission that the calculation of intrinsic value lacks precision sounds anomalous, but it is perfectly logical. Although Buffett likes to buy certainties at a discount, in reality business returns can and do fluctuate. So business analysts must think in a range of possibilities, knowing full well there are various scenarios that can occur. How does Warren Buffett think about the different outcomes? "We take the probability of loss times the amount of possible loss from the probability of gain times the amount of possible gains," explains Buffett. "It is imperfect, but that's what it is all about."[45] Thus, expected intrinsic value is the weighted average value for a distribution of possible outcomes. Warren Buffett, channeling John Maynard Keynes, has often said, "I would rather be approximately right than precisely wrong."[46]

Buy at Attractive Prices

Focusing on good businesses—those that are understandable, with enduring and attractive economics, run by shareholder-oriented managers—by itself is not enough to guarantee success, says Buffett. First, an investor has to buy at sensible prices and then the company has to perform to the investor's expectations. If we make mistakes, Buffett points out, it is either because of (1) the price we paid, (2) the management we joined, or (3) the future economics of the business. Miscalculations in the third instance are, he notes, the most common.

It is Buffett's intention to not only identify businesses that earn above-average economic returns but also to purchase them at prices below their indicated value. Graham's fundamental principle was the importance of buying a stock only when the difference between its price and its value represented a margin of safety.

The margin-of-safety principle assists Buffett in two ways. First, it protects him from downside price risk. If he calculates the value of a business to be only slightly higher than its per-share price, he will not buy the stock; he reasons that if the company's intrinsic value were to dip even slightly because of misappraised future cash flows, eventually the stock price would drop, too, perhaps below what he paid for it. But if the margin between purchase price and intrinsic value is large enough, the risk of declining intrinsic value is less. If Buffett purchases a company at a 25 percent discount to intrinsic value and the value subsequently declines by 10 percent, his original purchase price will still yield an adequate return.

The margin of safety also provides for extraordinary stock returns. If Buffett correctly identifies a company with above-average economic returns, the value of the stock over the long term will steadily march upward as the share price mimics the returns of the business. If a company consistently earns 15 percent on equity, its share price will advance more each year than that of a company that earns 10 percent on equity. Additionally, if Buffett, by using the margin of safety, is able to buy this outstanding business at a significant discount to intrinsic value, Berkshire will earn an extra bonus when the market corrects the price of the business. He said, "The market, like the Lord, helps those who help themselves, but unlike the Lord, the market does not forgive those who know not what they do."[47]

An Intelligent Investor

The most distinguishing trait of Warren Buffett's investment approach and philosophy is the clear understanding that, by owning shares of stock, he owns businesses, not pieces of paper. The idea of buying a stock without an understanding of the company's prospects, managers, and economics is unconscionable, says Buffett.

Investors have a choice: They can decide to conduct themselves like the owner of a business, with all that implies, or spend their time trading stocks just for the sake of being in the game—or indeed for any reason other than business fundamentals.

Owners of common stocks who perceive they merely own a piece of paper are far removed from the company's financial statements. They behave as if the market's ever-changing price is a more accurate reflection of their stock's value than the business's balance sheet and income statement. They draw and discard stocks like playing cards. Buffett considers this the height of foolishness. In his view there is no difference between owning a company and owning a share of a company—the same mentality should apply to both.

When Buffett launched the Buffett Partnership Limited in 1956, he began buy buying common stocks and then later bought entire companies. When he took full control of Berkshire Hathaway in 1969, he started with wholly owned businesses but soon added common stocks. In his mind the investment decisions of owning companies or shares of companies are interchangeable. There is no difference. And that insight became for Warren Buffett, the investor, his competitive advantage. Most don't appreciate how powerfully the force and experience of owning both companies and common stocks has led to Warren Buffett's extraordinary success.

Although only a few investors will have the benefit of owning, outright, a company or companies while also investing in the stock market, there is nothing that prevents an investor who doesn't fully own a company from thinking and behaving like a business owner when investing in stocks.

Buffett is often asked what types of stocks he will purchase in the future. First, he says, he will avoid businesses and managers in whom he has little confidence. What he will purchase is the type of company he understands, one that possesses good economics and is run by trustworthy managers. Buffett believes, "A good business is not always a good purchase, although it is a good place to start."[48]

CHAPTER 4

Common Stock Purchases
FIVE CASE STUDIES

When the Buffett Partnership took control of Berkshire Hathaway in 1965, stockholder's equity had dropped by half and loss from operations exceeded $10 million. Buffett and Ken Chace, who managed the textile group, labored intensely to turn the textile mills around. Results were disappointing; return on equity struggled to reach double digits.

Amid the gloom, there was one bright spot, a sign of things to come: Buffett's deft handling of the company's common stock portfolio. When Buffett took over, the company had $2.9 million in marketable securities. By the end of the first year, Buffett had enlarged the securities account to $5.4 million. In 1967, the dollar return from investing was three times the return of the entire textile division, which had 10 times the equity base.

Over the next decade Buffett had come to grips with certain realities. First, the very nature of the textile business made high returns on equity improbable. Textiles are commodities and commodities, by definition, have a difficult time differentiating their products from those of competitors. Foreign competitors, which employed a cheap labor force, were squeezing profit margins. Second, to stay competitive, the textile mills would require significant capital improvements—a prospect that is frightening in an inflationary environment and disastrous if the business returns are anemic.

Buffett made no attempt to hide the difficulties, and on several occasions he explained his thinking. The textile mills were the largest employer in the area; the work force was an older age group with relatively nontransferable skills; management had shown a high degree of enthusiasm; the unions were being reasonable; and, lastly, he believed that the textile business could attain some profits.

However, Buffett made it clear that he expected the textile group to earn positive returns on modest capital expenditures: "I won't close down a business of subnormal profitability merely to add a fraction of a point to our corporate returns. I also feel it inappropriate for even an exceptionally profitable company to fund an operation once it appears to have unending losses in prospect. Adam Smith would disagree with my first proposition and Karl Marx would disagree with my second; the middle ground is the only position that leaves me comfortable."[1]

In 1980, the annual report revealed ominous clues for the future of the textile group. That year, the group lost its prestigious lead-off position in the chairman's letter. By the next year, textiles were not discussed in the letter at all. Then, the inevitable: In July 1985, Buffett closed the books on the textile group, thus ending a business that had started some 100 years earlier.

The experience was not a complete failure. First, Buffett learned a valuable lesson about corporate turnarounds: They seldom succeed. Second, the textile group generated enough capital in the earlier years to buy an insurance company, and that is a much brighter story.

In March 1967, Berkshire Hathaway purchased, for $8.6 million, the outstanding stock of two insurance companies headquartered in Omaha: National Indemnity Company and National Fire & Marine Insurance Company. It was the beginning of a phenomenal success story. Berkshire Hathaway the textile company would not long survive, but Berkshire Hathaway the investment company that encompassed it was about to take off.

For a seasoned stock picker like Buffett, it was perfect. In two years, he increased the combined stock and bond portfolios of his two new insurance companies from $32 million to nearly $42 million. At the same time, the insurance businesses themselves were doing quite well. In just one year, the net income of National Indemnity rose from $1.6 million to $2.2 million.

To appreciate the phenomenon, we must recognize the true value of owning an insurance company. Sometimes insurance companies are good investments, sometimes not. They are, however, terrific investment *vehicles*. Policyholders, by paying premiums, provide a constant stream of cash, known as float. As Buffett explains:

> One reason we are attracted to the property-casualty [P/C] business was its financial characteristics. P/C insurers receive premiums upfront and pay claims later. This collect-now, pay later model leaves P/C companies holding large sums—money we call "float"—that will eventually go to others. Meanwhile, insurers get to invest this float for their benefit.
>
> If our premiums exceed the total of our expenses and eventual losses, we register an underwriting profit that adds to the investment income our float produces. When such a profit is earned, we enjoy the use of free money—and, better yet, get *paid* for holding it.[2]

Insurance companies set aside cash and short-term Treasury Bills to pay claims each year, based on their best estimates, and invest the rest. To give themselves a high degree of liquidity, because it is seldom possible to know exactly when claim payments will need to be paid, most opt to invest in marketable securities, primarily stocks and bonds. Thus Warren Buffett acquired not only two healthy insurance companies but also a cast-iron vehicle for managing investments. Over the next decade, Buffett purchased three additional insurance companies and organized five more. And he didn't slow down. As of 2023, Berkshire Hathaway owns 13 different insurance companies including Alleghany Corporation, General Re, and GEICO Insurance.

Over the years, Buffett's common stock purchases have become part of Berkshire folklore. There have been successes and failures, but Buffett, not surprisingly, has had many more hits than strikeouts along with some monster home runs. Behind each investment is a unique story. The purchase of the Washington Post Company in 1973 was far different from the 1980 purchase of GEICO. And the $517 million investment in Cap Cities in 1985, which in turn helped Tom Murphy buy the American Broadcasting Company, was unlike his billion-dollar investment in The Coca-Cola Company.

What unites these four companies is each achieved permanent holding status, a "till-death-do-us-part" attitude, which placed these investments on the same commitment level as Berkshire's controlled businesses. And to this distinguished group of common stock holdings we will also examine what history will likely recount as Warren Buffett's greatest investment: a $36 billion purchase in the world's largest market capitalization stock, a 5.9 percent stake in Apple, now worth $162 billion. It accounts for roughly 20 percent of the total market value of Berkshire Hathaway.

For those hoping to better understand fully Warren Buffett's thinking, all of these five common stock purchases share one very important trait. They enable us to observe his business, management, financial, and value tenets. At the time, each of these companies possessed attributes that qualified them for purchase. It is these attributes that are worth studying.

The Washington Post Company

In 1931, the *Washington Post* was one of the five dailies competing for readers in the nation's capital. Two years later, the *Post*, unable to pay for its newsprint, was placed in receivership. That summer, the company was sold at auction to satisfy creditors. Eugene Meyer, a millionaire financier, bought the *Washington Post* for $825,000. For the next two decades, he supported the paper until it turned a profit. Management of the paper passed to Philip Graham, a brilliant Harvard-educated lawyer, who had married Meyer's daughter Katharine. In 1954, Philip Graham convinced Eugene Meyer to purchase a rival newspaper, the *Times-Herald*. Later, Graham purchased *Newsweek* magazine and two television stations before his tragic suicide in 1963. It is Phil Graham who is credited with transforming the *Washington Post* into a media and communications company.

After Graham's death, the control of the *Washington Post* passed to Katharine Graham. Although she had no experience in managing a major corporation, she quickly distinguished herself by confronting difficult business issues. Much of Katharine Graham's success can be attributed to her genuine affection for the *Post*.[3] She had observed how her father and husband struggled to keep the company viable, and she realized that to be successful, the company would need a decision-maker, not a caretaker. "I quickly learned that things don't stand still," she said. "You have to make decisions."[4] And she made two doozies, decisions that had a profound impact on the newspaper: hiring Ben Bradlee as managing editor and then inviting Warren Buffett to become a director of the company. Bradlee encouraged Katharine Graham to publish the Pentagon Papers and to pursue the Watergate investigation, which earned the *Washington Post* a reputation for prize-winning journalism. For his part, Buffett taught Katharine Graham how to run a successful business.

Warren Buffett first met Katharine Graham in 1971. At the time, he owned stock in the *New Yorker*. Hearing the magazine might be for sale, he asked Katharine Graham whether the *Washington Post* would be interested in purchasing it. Although the sale never materialized, Buffett came away very much impressed with the publisher of the *Post*.

About that time, the *Washington Post*'s financial structure was headed for profound changes. Under the terms of the trust established by Eugene and Agnes Meyer, Katharine and Philip Graham owned all of the *Post*'s voting stock. After Phil Graham's death, Katharine Graham inherited control of the company. Over the years, Eugene Meyer had gifted thousands of shares of private *Post* stock to several hundred employees in gratitude for their loyalty and service. He also funded the company's profit-sharing plan with private stock. As the company prospered, the value of the *Washington Post* skyrocketed from $50 per share in the 1950s to $1,154 in 1971.

The profit-sharing plan and the personal holdings of employees required the company to maintain a market for the stock, an arrangement that proved to be an unproductive use of the company's cash. In addition, the Graham and Meyer family was facing stiff inheritance taxes. Having a publicly traded stock would aid both the company, its employees, and its founding family owners.

In 1971, Katharine Graham decided to take the *Washington Post* public, thus erasing the burden of maintaining a market in its own stock, and enabling the family heirs to more profitably plan for their estates. The Washington Post Company was divided into two classes of stock. Class A common stock elected a majority of the board of directors, and class B elected a minority. Katharine Graham held 50 percent of the Class A stock, thus effectively controlling the company. In June 1971, the Washington Post Company issued 1,354,000 shares of Class B stock. Remarkably, two days later, despite government threats, Katharine Graham gave Ben Bradlee permission to publish the Pentagon Papers. In 1972, the price of both Class A and B shares climbed steadily, from $24.75 in January to $38.00 by December.

But the mood on Wall Street was turning gloomy. In early 1973, the Dow Jones Industrial Average began to slide. By spring, the Dow was down more than 100 points to 921. The Washington Post Company share price was slipping as well. By May, the stock was down to $23. Wall Street brokers were buzzing about IBM—the stock had declined more than 69 points, breaking through its 200 day moving average. They warned that the technical breakdown was a bad omen for the rest of the market. That same month, gold bounced through $100 per ounce, the Federal Reserve boosted the discount rate to 6 percent, and the Dow fell another 18 points, its biggest loss in three years. By June, the discount rate was raised again and the Dow plunged further, passing through the 900 level. And all the while, Warren Buffett was quietly buying shares in the *Washington Post*. By June, he had purchased 467,150 shares at an average price of $22.75, a purchase worth $10,628,000.

At first, Katharine Graham was unnerved. The idea of a non-family member owning so much *Post* stock, even though it was noncontrolling, was unsettling. Buffett assured Graham that Berkshire's purchase was for investment purposes only. To reassure her, he suggested that Don Graham, Katharine's son, be given a proxy to vote Berkshire's shares. Don Graham had graduated magna cum laude from Harvard in 1966, having majored in English history and literature. He was the editor of the *Crimson*, the university's newspaper. In 1971, Don Graham joined the *Post* as a metro reporter. Later, he worked 10 months as a reporter for *Newsweek* before returning to the *Post* in 1974 when he became the assistant managing sports editor. Buffett's willingness to allow Don Graham to control his *Washington Post* stock was all that Katharine Graham needed to hear. She responded by inviting Buffett to join the board of directors, and soon made him chairman of the finance committee.

Warren Buffett's role at the *Washington Post* is widely known. He helped Katharine Graham persevere during the pressman strikes of the 1970s, and he also tutored Don Graham in business, helping him understand the role of management and its responsibility to its owners. Don, in turn, was an eager student who listened to everything Buffett preached. Writing years later as the CEO of the Washington Post Company, Don Graham promised to "continue to manage the company for the benefit of shareholders, especially long-term shareholders whose perspective extends well beyond the quarterly or even yearly results." He vowed always to "manage costs rigorously" and "to be disciplined about the uses we make of our cash."[5] Buffett's business lessons had made an impact.

Tenet: Simple and Understandable

Buffett's grandfather once owned and edited the *Cuming County Democrat*, a weekly newspaper in West Point, Nebraska. His grandmother helped out at the paper and also set the type at the family's printing shop. His father, while attending the University of Nebraska, edited the *Daily Nebraskan*. Buffett himself was once the circulation manager for the *Lincoln Journal*. Some thought that had Buffett not embarked on a business investing career he would have likely pursued a career in journalism.

In 1969, Buffett bought his first newspaper, the *Omaha Sun*, along with a group of weekly papers. Although he respected high-quality journalism, Buffett thought of newspapers first and always as a business. He expected profits, not influence, to be the rewards for a paper's owners. Owning the *Omaha Sun* taught him the dynamics of a newspaper company. He had four years of hands-on experience owning a newspaper before he bought his first share of the Washington Post Company.

Tenet: Consistent Operating History

Warren Buffett told Berkshire Hathaway shareholders that his first financial connection to the Washington Post Company was at age 13. He delivered both the *Washington Post* and the *Times-Herald* on his paper route while his father served in Congress. Buffett liked to remind others that with his dual delivery route, he merged the two papers long before Phil Graham bought the *Times-Herald*.

Obviously Buffett was aware of the newspaper's rich history and he considered *Newsweek* magazine a predictable business. The Washington Post Company had for years been reporting stellar performance of its broadcast division, and Buffett quickly learned the value of the company's television stations. Buffett's personal experience with the company and his own successful history of owning newspapers led him to believe that the company was a consistent and dependable business performer.

Tenet: Favorable Long-Term Prospects

"The economics of a dominant newspaper," Buffett wrote in 1984, "are excellent, among the very best in the world."[6] Take note: what Buffett said was a full decade before the internet's potential and its eventual impact on the media industry, including newspapers, was fully realized.

In the early 1980s, there were 1,700 newspapers in the United States and approximately 1,600 operated without any direct competition. The owners of newspapers, Buffett noted, like to believe that the exceptional profits they earn each year are a result of their paper's journalistic quality. The truth, explained Buffett, is that even a third-rate newspaper can generate adequate profits if it is the only paper in town. Now it's true that a high-quality paper will achieve a higher penetration rate, but even a mediocre paper, he said, is essential to a community for its bulletin-board appeal. Every business in town, every home seller and every individual who wants to get a message out to the community needs the circulation of a newspaper to do so. Similar to Canadian media entrepreneur Lord Thomson, Buffett believed that owning a newspaper was like receiving a royalty on every business in town that wanted to advertise.

In addition to their franchise quality, newspapers possess valuable economic goodwill; the value of a newspaper is greater than the company's book value, its hard assets.

Newspapers have low capital needs, so they can easily translate sales into profits. Even when a newspaper has installed expensive computer-assisted printing presses and electronic newsroom systems, they were quickly paid for by lower fixed-wage costs. During the 1970s and early 1980s, a period of hyperinflation, newspapers were able to increase prices easily, thereby generating above-average returns on invested capital.

Tenet: Determine the Value

In 1973, the total market value for the Washington Post Company (WPC) was $80 million. Yet Buffett claimed that "most security analysts, media brokers, and media executives would have estimated WPC's intrinsic value at $400 million to $500 million."[7] How did Buffett arrive at the estimate? Let's walk through the numbers, using Buffett's reasoning.

We'll start by calculating owner earnings for the year: net income ($13.3 million) plus depreciation and amortization ($3.7 million) minus capital expenditures ($6.6 million) yields 1973 owner earnings of $10.4 million. If we divide these earnings by the long-term US government yield (6.81 percent), the value of the Washington Post Company reaches $150 million, almost twice the market value of the company but well short of Buffett's estimate.

Buffett tells us that, over time, the capital expenditures of a newspaper will equal depreciation and amortization charges, and therefore net income should approximate owner earnings. Knowing this, we can simply divide net income by the risk-free rate (defined as the 10-year US bond yield) and now reach a valuation of $196 million.

If we stop here, the assumption is that the increase in owner earnings will equal the rise in inflation. But we know that newspapers have unusual pricing power; because most are monopolies in their community, they can raise prices at rates higher than inflation. If we make one last assumption—the *Washington Post* has the ability to raise real prices by 3 percent—the value of the company is closer to $350 million. Buffett also knew that the company's 10 percent pretax margins were well below its 15 percent historical average margins, and he knew Katharine Graham was determined that the *Post* would once again achieve these margins. If pretax margins improved to 15 percent, the present value of the company would increase by $135 million, bringing the total intrinsic value to $485 million.

Tenet: Buy at Attractive Prices

Even the most conservative calculation of the company's value indicates that Buffett bought the Washington Post Company for at least half its intrinsic value. He maintains that he bought the company at less than one-quarter of its value. Either way, he clearly bought the company at a significant discount to its then market value. Therefore, Buffett satisfied Ben Graham's premise that buying at a discount creates a margin of safety.

Tenet: Return on Equity

When Buffett purchased the stock of the *Washington Post*, its return on equity was 15.7 percent. That was the average return for most newspapers and only slightly better than that of the Standard & Poor's (S&P) 500 Index. But within five years, the *Post*'s return doubled. By then it was twice as high as the S&P 500 Index and 50 percent higher than the average newspaper. Over the next

10 years, the *Post* maintained its supremacy, reaching a high of 36 percent return on equity in 1988.

These above-average returns are more impressive when we observe that the company had, over time, reduced its debt. In 1973, the ratio of long-term debt to shareholder's equity stood at 37 percent, the second-highest ratio in the newspaper group. Astonishingly, by 1978 Katharine Graham had reduced the company's debt by 70 percent. In 1983, long-term debt to equity was 2.7 percent—one-tenth the newspaper group average—yet the Washington Post Company generated a return on equity 10 percent higher than these companies. In 1986, after investing in the cellular telephone systems and purchasing Capital Cities' 53 cable systems, debt in the company was an uncharacteristically high $336 million. Within a year it was reduced to $155 million. By 1992, long-term debt was $51 million and the company's long-term debt to equity was 5.5 percent compared to the industry average of 42.7 percent.

Tenet: Profit Margins

Six months after the Washington Post Company went public, Katharine Graham met with Wall Street security analysts. The first order of business, she told them, was to maximize profits for the company's operations. Profits continued to rise at the television stations and *Newsweek*, but profitability at the newspaper was leveling off. Much of the reason, said Mrs. Graham, was high production costs, namely, wages. After the *Post* purchased the *Times-Herald*, sales surged. However, each time the unions struck the paper (1949, 1958, 1966, 1968, 1969), management opted to pay their demands rather than risk a shutdown of the paper. During this time, Washington, DC, was still a three-newspaper town. Throughout the 1950s and 1960s, increasing wage costs dampened profits. This problem, Mrs. Graham told the analysts, was going to be solved.

As union contracts began to expire in the 1970s, Katharine Graham enlisted labor negotiators who took a hard line with the unions. In 1974, the company defeated a strike by the Newspaper

Guild and, after lengthy negotiations, the printers settled on a new contract. Katharine Graham's firm stance came to a head during the pressmen's strike in 1975. The strike turned bitter and violent. The pressmen lost sympathy when they vandalized the pressroom before striking. Management worked the presses; members of the Guild and the printer's union crossed the picket lines. After four months, Mrs. Graham announced that the paper was hiring nonunion pressmen. The company had won.

In the early 1970s, the financial press wrote that "the best that could be said about the Washington Post Company's performance was it rated a gentleman's C in profitability."[8] Pretax margins in 1973 were 10.8 percent—well below the company's historical average 15 percent margins earned in the 1960s. After successfully renegotiating the union contracts, the *Post*'s fortunes improved. By 1988, pretax margins reached a high of 31.8 percent, which compared favorably to its newspaper group average of 16.9 percent and the S&P Industrial average of 8.6 percent.

Tenet: Rational Management

The Washington Post Company generated substantial cash flow for its owners. Because it generated more cash than it could reinvest at high rates in its primary businesses, management was confronted with two choices: return the money to shareholders and/or invest the cash into new opportunities. It was Buffett's preference to have companies return excess cash earnings to shareholders. The Washington Post Company, while Katharine Graham was chief executive officer, was the first newspaper in its industry to repurchase shares in large quantities. Between 1975 and 1991, the company bought an astonishing 43 percent of its shares outstanding at an average price of $60.

A company can also choose to return money to shareholders by increasing the dividend. In 1990, confronted with substantial cash reserves, the Washington Post Company voted to increase the annual dividend to shareholders from $1.84 per share to $4.00, a 117 percent increase.

Tenet: The One-Dollar Premise

Buffett's goal is to select companies in which each dollar of retained earnings is translated into at least one dollar of market value, preferably more than one dollar of market value. This test can quickly identify companies whose managers, over time, have been able to optimally invest in their company's capital. If retained earnings are invested in the company and produce above-average returns, returns above the cost of capital, the proof will be a proportionally greater rise in the company's market value.

From 1973 to 1992, the Washington Post Company earned $1.755 billion for its owners. From these earnings, the company returned $299 million to shareholders and retained $1.456 billion to reinvest in the company. In 1973, the total market value of the Washington Post Company was $80 million. By 1992, the market value of the company had grown to $2.630 billion. Over those 20 years, for every $1.00 the company retained, it created $1.75 in market value for shareholders.

Still, there is one more way to judge the success of the Washington Post Company under Katharine Graham's leadership. In his insightful book, *The Outsiders: Eight Unconventional CEOs, and Their Radically Rational Blueprint for Success*, William Thorndike helps us best appreciate how well both the company and its CEO actually performed:

"From the time of the company's IPO in 1971, until Katharine Graham stepped down as chairman in 1993, the compounded annual return for shareholders was a remarkable 22.3 percent, dwarfing both the S&P (7.4 percent) and her peers (12.4 percent). A dollar invested at the IPO was worth $89 when she retired versus $5 for the S&P and $14 for her peer group. Katharine Graham outperformed the S&P by *eighteenfold* and her peers by over *sixfold*. She was simply the best newspaper executive in the country during her 22-year period by a wide margin."[9]

In the early 1990s, Buffett concluded that media businesses, newspapers included, were destined to become less valuable than anyone had predicted. Advertisers had found cheaper ways to reach their customers: cable television, direct mail, newspaper inserts, and—most of all—the internet.

"The fact is," said Buffett, "that newspapers, television, and magazine properties have begun to resemble *businesses* more than *franchises* in their economic behavior." Franchises include companies that have a product or service that is desired and in high demand and, most important, has no close substitute. But this had now changed particularly with the advent of cable television and the internet. "Consumers looking for information and entertainment enjoy greatly broadened choices as to where to find them," said Buffett. "Unfortunately, demand can't expand in response to this new supply: 500 million American eyeballs and a 24-hour day are all that's available. The result is that competition has intensified, markets have fragmented and the media has lost some of its franchise strength."[10]

The secular changes in the media industry reduced the earnings of newspapers, which, in turn, reduced the intrinsic value of the properties. Many local newspapers folded. A good number merged to form efficiencies to help offset the decline in profitability. However, the *Washington Post* fared better than most. First, explained Buffett, the *Post*'s modest level of long-term debt ($50 million) was more than offset by its $400 million in cash. The *Post* was the only public newspaper that operated essentially free of debt. Thus the decline in intrinsic value was moderate compared to others as its assets were not hobbled by the burden of debt.

Twenty years later, in 2013, Jeff Bezos, the founder of Amazon, purchased the *Washington Post* for $250 million, a price that was once unthinkable. What remained of the Washington Post Company included seven television stations, cable properties, and Kaplan, a higher education business. The remnants were renamed Graham Holdings Company.

In 2014, Buffett swapped his remaining $1.1 billion investment in Graham Holdings for a Miami, Florida, television station (folded into BH Media Group) along with cash and Berkshire Hathaway shares held by Graham Holdings including 2,107 shares of Class A and 1,278 Class B shares, thus ending a 41-year relationship with the *Washington Post*.

Although the intrinsic value of The Washington Post Company had steadily declined for nearly 20 years, principally because of the declining value of the *Washington Post*, Berkshire's investment proved to be value-added.

What was the total return for Berkshire's investment in the *Washington Post* starting with $11 million and cashing out with $1.1 billion? The answer is 9,900 percent—an 11.89 percent compounded average growth rate. What was the total return of the S&P 500 Index over the same time period? The answer is 7,228 percent (dividends reinvested)—an 11.03 percent compounded average return. Put differently, an $11 million investment in the S&P 500 Index, over the same time period that Berkshire owned the Washington Post Company, would have returned $803 million. Buffett bested the S&P 500 by nearly $300 million with his Washington Post Company stock.

GEICO Corporation

The Government Employees Insurance Company (GEICO) was founded in 1936 by Leo Goodwin, an insurance accountant.[11] He envisioned a company that insured only preferred-risk drivers and sold this insurance directly by mail. He had discovered that government employees, as a group, had fewer accidents than the general public. He also knew that by selling directly to the driver, the company would eliminate the overhead expenses associated with paying agents to sell the policies, typically 10 to 25 percent of every premium dollar. Goodwin figured that if he isolated careful drivers and passed along the savings from issuing insurance policies directly, he would have a recipe for success.

Goodwin invited a Fort Worth, Texas, banker named Cleaves Rhea to be his partner. Goodwin invested $25,000 and owned 25 percent of the company; Rhea invested $75,000 for 75 percent. In 1948, the company moved from Texas to Washington, DC. That year the Rhea family decided to sell its interest in the company and Rhea enlisted Lorimer Davidson, a Baltimore bond salesperson, to help with the sale. In turn, Davidson asked David Kreeger, a Washington, DC, lawyer, to help him find buyers, and Kreeger approached the Graham-Newman Corporation. Ben Graham decided to buy half of Rhea's stock for $720,000; Kreeger and Davidson's Baltimore associates bought the other half. The Securities and Exchange Commission forced Graham-Newman, because it was an investment fund, to limit its holding in GEICO to 10 percent of the company, so Graham distributed GEICO's stock to the fund's partners. Years later, when GEICO became a billion-dollar company, Graham's personal shares were worth millions.

It has been a mystery as to why Ben Graham personally owned GEICO shares that didn't pass the "don't lose" litmus test he was preaching in *Security Analysis*. Not much is written about the subject. The most logical explanation offered is that Graham certainly understood and appreciated the potential return from owning GEICO. However, analyzing the complexity of an insurance company was difficult—management decision-making is critical for success—and, Graham knew, a stock that sold above book value at a higher price-to-earnings ratio could result in a loss. His tenet to buy only low price-to-earnings ratio stocks selling below book value was a simple method that didn't require analyzing management nor forecasting the long-term prospects of a company. Also, his mathematical approach to selecting stocks, outlined in *Security Analysis*, was so sensible and easy that it had become very popular with investors.

Lorimer Davidson, at Goodwin's invitation, joined GEICO's management team. In 1958, he became chairman and led the company until 1970. During this period, the board extended the eligibility for GEICO's car insurance to include professional, managerial, technical, and administrative workers. GEICO's insurance market now included 50 percent of all car owners, up from 15 percent. The new strategy was a success. Underwriting profits soared.

These were the company's golden years. In the 1960s, insurance regulators were mesmerized by GEICO's success, and shareholders saw their share price climb. The company's premium-to-surplus ratio rose above 5:1. This ratio measures the risk that a company takes (premiums written) compared to its policyholder surplus (capital that is used to pay the claims). Because regulators were so impressed with GEICO, the company was allowed to exceed the industry average.

However, by the late 1960s, GEICO's fortunes were beginning to dim. At first, few took notice. Then, the shocking news. In 1969, the company reported that it had underestimated its reserves for that year by $10 million. Instead of earning $2.5 million, the company actually posted a loss. The adjustment to income was made the next year, but again the company underestimated reserves—this time by $25 million—and the underwriting profit in 1970 showed a disastrous loss.

In 1970, Davidson retired and was replaced by David Kreeger, the Washington lawyer. Running the company fell to Norman Gidden, who had served as president and chief executive officer. What happened next suggests that GEICO was attempting to grow out of its reserve mess created in 1969 and 1970. Between 1970 and 1974, the number of new auto policies grew at an 11 percent annual rate compared to a 7 percent average from 1965 to 1970. In addition, the company embarked on an expensive and ambitious decentralized program that required significant investments in real estate, computer equipment, and personnel.

By 1973, the company, facing fierce competition, lowered its eligibility standards to expand its market share. Now GEICO's automobile drivers, for the first time, included blue-collar workers and drivers under age 21, two groups with checkered accident histories. Both of these strategic changes, the corporate expansion plan and the plan to insure a greater number of motorists, occurred simultaneously with the lifting of the country's price controls. Soon, auto repair and medical costs exploded. In 1974, underwriting losses soared.

In 1972, GEICO's share price reached an all-time high of $61. By 1973, the share price was cut in half, and in 1974 it fell further to $10. In 1975, when the company announced further projected losses and eliminated the $0.80 dividend, the stock dropped to $7.

At the March 1976 GEICO annual meeting, Gidden confessed another executive might have handled the company's problems better. He announced that the company's board of directors had appointed a committee to seek new management. GEICO's share price was still weakening—it was now $5 and heading lower.[12]

After the 1976 annual meeting, GEICO announced that John J. Byrne, a 43-year-old marketing executive from Travelers Corporation, would become the new president. Soon after Byrne's appointment, the company announced a $76 million convertible preferred stock offering to shore up its capital. But shareholders had lost hope, and the stock drifted down to $2 per share.

During this period, while GEICO's stock price was collapsing, Warren Buffett was quietly and doggedly buying stock. As the company teetered on the edge of bankruptcy, he invested $4.1 million, gathering 1,294,308 shares at an average price of $3.18.

Tenet: Simple and Understandable

When Buffett attended Columbia University in 1950, his teacher Ben Graham was a director of GEICO. His curiosity stimulated, one weekend Buffett took the train to Washington, DC, to visit the company. On a Saturday morning, he knocked on the company's front door and was let in by a janitor, who led him to the only executive in the office that day, Lorimer Davidson. Buffett peppered him with questions, and Davidson spent the next five hours schooling his young visitor on GEICO's distinctions. Philip Fisher would have been impressed.

Later, when Buffett returned to Omaha and his father's brokerage firm, he recommended that the firm's clients buy GEICO. He himself invested $10,000, approximately two-thirds of his net worth, in the stock. Many investors resisted his recommendation. Even Omaha's insurance agents complained to Howard Buffett that his son was promoting an "agentless" insurance company. Frustrated, Warren Buffett sold his GEICO shares a year later, at a 50 percent profit, and did not again purchase shares in the company until 1976 when he bought the stock for Berkshire Hathaway.

Undaunted, Buffett continued to recommend insurance stocks to his clients. He bought Kansas City Life at three times earnings. Later he added Massachusetts Indemnity & Life Insurance Company to Berkshire Hathaway's security portfolio. And after Berkshire purchased National Indemnity in 1967, Jack Ringwalt, the CEO of National Indemnity, schooled Buffett on the mechanics of profitably running an insurance company. The experience, more than any other, helped Buffett understand how an insurance company makes money. It also, despite GEICO's shaky financial situation, gave him confidence to purchase the company.

In addition to Berkshire's $4.1 million investment in GEICO's common stock in 1976, Buffett also invested $19.4 million in its convertible preferred issue, which raised additional capital for the company. Two years later, Berkshire converted these preferred shares into common, and in 1980 Buffett invested another $19 million of Berkshire's money in the company. Between 1976 and 1980, Berkshire invested a total of $47 million, purchasing 7.2 million shares of GEICO at an average price of $6.67 per share. By 1980, that investment had appreciated 123 percent. It was now worth $105 million and had become Berkshire Hathaway's largest common stock holding.

Tenet: Consistent Operating History

On first reaction, we might assume that Buffett violated his consistency tenet. Clearly, GEICO's operations in 1975 and 1976 were anything but consistent. When Byrne became president of GEICO his job was to turn around the company, and turnarounds, Buffett knew, seldom turn. So how do we explain Berkshire's purchase of GEICO?

In the 1980 Berkshire Hathaway Annual Report, Buffett explains his reasoning: "We have written in past reports about the disappointments that usually result from purchases and operation of 'turnaround' businesses. Literally hundreds of turnaround possibilities in dozens of industries have been described to us over the years and, either as participants or observers, we have tracked performance against expectations. Our conclusion is that, with few exceptions, when a management with a reputation for brilliance tackles a business with poor fundamental economics, it is the reputation of the business that remains intact."[13]

Buffett continued: "GEICO may appear to be an exception, having turned around from the very edge of bankruptcy in 1976. It certainly is true that managerial brilliance was needed for its resuscitation, and that Jack Byrne, upon arrival that year, supplied the ingredient in abundance. But it is also true that the fundamental advantage that GEICO had enjoyed—an advantage that previously produced staggering success—was still intact within the company, although submerged in a sea of financial and operating troubles."[14]

Buffett reminded Berkshire shareholders: "GEICO was designed to be the low-cost operation in an enormous marketplace (auto insurance) populated largely by companies whose marketing structures restricted adaptation. Run as designed, it could offer unusual value to its customers while earning unusual returns for itself. For decades, it had been run in just this manner. Its troubles in the mid-70s were not produced by any diminution or disappearance of this essential economic advantage."[15]

Then Buffett referenced an interesting analogy. "GEICO's problems," said Buffett, "at the time put it in position analogous to that of American Express in 1964 following the salad oil scandal." Readers will recall Buffett made a bold bet on American Express at the time, investing 25 percent of the assets of the Buffett Limited Partnership. Buffett believed the salad oil scandal, which almost bankrupted the company, had no impact on the franchise qualities of the American Express Credit Card or the sale of American Express Travelers Cheques. And once the ramifications of the financial punishment related to the salad oil scandal passed, the company would resume its superior investment performance. It did, tripling its share price in two years and netting the partnership a $20 million profit. Buffett explains further: "Both [American Express and GEICO] were one-of-a-kind companies temporarily reeling from the effects of the fiscal blow that did not destroy their exceptional underlying economics. The GEICO and American

Express situations, extraordinary business franchises with a localized excisable cancer (needing, to be sure, a skilled surgeon), should be distinguished from the true 'turnaround' situation in which the managers expect—and need—to pull off a corporate Pygmalion."[16]

Importantly for Buffett, GEICO was not terminal, only wounded. Its franchise of providing low-cost agentless insurance was still intact. Furthermore, in the marketplace, there still existed safe drivers who could be insured at rates that would provide a profit for the company. On a price basis, GEICO would always beat competitors. For decades, GEICO generated substantial profits for its owners by capitalizing on its competitive strengths.

Tenet: Favorable Long-Term Prospects

As long as there are automobiles, motorcycles, boats, and homes individuals will need insurance policies. Although insurance is a commodity product, undifferentiated from other insurance products, Buffett reminds us that a commodity business can make money if it has a cost advantage, being the low-cost provider, that is sustainable and wide. This description aptly fits GEICO. We also know that management in a commodity business is a crucial variable. GEICO's leadership, since Berkshire's purchase, has demonstrated that it, too, had a competitive advantage.

Tenet: Candid Management

When Jack Byrne took over GEICO in 1976, he convinced insurance regulators and competitors that if GEICO went bankrupt, it would be bad for the entire industry. His plan for rescuing the company included raising capital, obtaining a reinsurance treaty with other companies to reinsure a portion of GEICO's business, and cutting costs aggressively. "Operation Bootstrap," as Byrne called it, was the battle plan aimed at returning the company to profitability.

In his first year, Byrne closed 100 offices, reduced employment from 7,000 to 4,000 and returned GEICO's license to sell insurance in both New Jersey and Massachusetts. Byrne told New Jersey regulators he would not renew the 250,000 policies that were costing the company $30 million per year. Next, he did away with the computerized systems that enabled policyholders to renew their insurance without providing updated information. When Byrne required the new information, he found the company was underpricing 9 percent of its renewal policies. When GEICO repriced them, 400,000 policyholders decided to discontinue their insurance. Altogether, Byrne's actions reduced the number of policyholders from 2.7 million to 1.5 million, and the company went from being the nation's 18th largest insurer in 1975 to 31st a year later. Despite this reduction, after losing $126 million in 1976, GEICO earned an impressive $58.6 million on $463 million in revenues in 1977, Byrne's first full year of responsibility.

Clearly, GEICO's dramatic recovery was Byrne's doing, and his steadfast discipline on corporate expenses sustained GEICO's economic performance for many years. Byrne told shareholders that the company must return to its first principle of being the low-cost provider of insurance. His reports detailed how the company continually reduced costs. Even in 1981, when GEICIO was the seventh-largest writer of automobile insurance, Byrne shared his secretary with two other executives. He boasted how the company serviced 378 policies per GEICO employee, up from 250 policies years earlier. During the turnaround years, he was always a great motivator. "Byrne," said Buffett, "is like the chicken farmer who rolls an ostrich egg into the henhouse and says, 'Ladies, this is what the competition is doing.'"[17]

Over the years, Byrne happily reported the successful progress of GEICO. He was equally candid when the news turned bad. In 1985, the company temporarily stumbled when it had underwriting losses. Writing in the company's first-quarter report to shareholders, Byrne "likened the company's plight to that of the pilot who told his passengers, 'the bad news is that we are lost, but the good news is that we are making great time.'"[18] The company quickly regained its footing and the following year posted profitable underwriting results. But, just as important, the company gained a reputation for being candid with its shareholders.

Tenet: Rational Management

Over the years, Jack Byrne demonstrated rational behavior managing GEICO's assets. After he took charge, he positioned the company for controlled growth. It was more profitable, Byrne figured, to grow at a slower rate that enabled the company to carefully monitor its losses and expenses than to grow twice as fast if it meant losing financial control. Even so, this controlled growth continued to generate excess returns for GEICO, and the mark of rationality is what the company did with the cash.

Starting in 1983, the company was unable to invest its excess cash at profitable high returns so it decided to return the money to its shareholders. Between 1983 and 1992, GEICO purchased 30 million shares, reducing the company's total common shares outstanding by 30 percent. In addition to buying back stock, GEICO also began to increase the dividend it paid to its shareholders. In 1980, the company's dividend was $.09 per share. In 1992, it was $0.60 per share, a 21 percent annual increase.

Tenet: The Institutional Imperative

One could argue that managing an agentless insurance company is evidence of an ability to resist the institutional imperative when the overwhelming majority of insurance companies rely on agents to sell policies. But there is also another litmus test.

Recall insurance companies can profit in two ways: (1) earning an underwriting profit on the insurance policies they issue and (2) investing smartly the premium dollars that policyholders pay. As a general rule, profits from underwriting are small compared to the profits generated by investments—so much that when the financial markets offer high returns, insurance companies are willing to sell policies at lower prices, sacrificing profitability to gather more premium dollars to invest. It is the company's chief investment officer who manages the investment portfolio, and their skill set can make a significant difference in whether or not the investment returns on float are additive.

Between 1980 and 2004, the chief investment officer was Lou Simpson. He graduated with a master's degree in economics from

Princeton. After a brief stint as a teacher at his alma mater, he accepted a position with the investment firm of Stein Roe & Farnham. In 1969, Simpson joined Wester Asset Management, where he became president and chief executive officer before joining GEICO in 1979. When Buffett, along with Jack Byrne, interviewed Simpson, he impressed them with his independent attitude. "He was the ideal temperament for investing," Buffett said. "He derives no particular pleasure from operating with or against the crowd. He is comfortable in his own reason."[19]

The willingness to act and think independently is found in the investment guidelines that Simpson developed for GEICO's investment portfolio.[20] The first guideline was "think independently." Simpson was skeptical of Wall Street's conventional wisdom. Instead, he searched for his own. Like Buffett, he was a voracious reader of daily newspapers, magazines, journals, and annual reports. Simpson believed that after receiving the basic financial training, the most important job of an investment manager is to keep reading until an idea materializes. Simpson was constantly on the prowl for good ideas while resisting the overt suggestions of most brokerage analysts. "Lou is a quiet guy. In the modern world, everybody would rather talk on the phone than do the basic work. Lou does the basic work," said one former GEICO director.[21]

GEICO's second guideline was "invest in high-return businesses run for shareholders." Simpson sought companies with sustainable above-average profitability. Then he interviewed the company management to ascertain whether their priorities were maximizing shareholder value or expanding the corporate empire. Simpson looked for managers who had a significant investment stake in their own company and were straightforward in their dealing with the company's owners, treating them like partners. Last, he quizzed management on their willingness to divest unprofitable divisions and use the excess cash to repurchase shares for the owners.

GEICO's third guideline was "pay only a reasonable price, even for an excellent business." Simpson was a very patient investor. He was willing to wait until the price of a business became attractive. The greatest business in the world, Simpson confessed, was a bad investment if the price was too high. The fourth guideline was "invest for the long-term." Simpson paid no attention to the stock market and never tried to predict short-term market movements. "In many ways," he wrote, "the stock market is like the weather in that if you don't like the current conditions all you have to do is wait awhile."[22]

GEICO's last guideline was "do not diversify excessively." Simpson figured that a widely diversified portfolio would only provide mediocre results. He admitted that his talks with Buffett helped crystallize his thinking on the subject. Simpson's tendency was to concentrate his equity holdings. In 1991, GEICO's $800 million equity portfolio contained eight stocks.

From 1980, when Simpson assumed control, to 2004, the equity portfolio generated an average annual compounded rate of return of 20.3 percent compared to the 13.5 percent return for the Standard & Poor's 500 Index.

Over the years, Simpson steered GEICO's investment portfolio away from junk bonds and risky real estate holdings. While other insurance investment officers surrendered to the institutional imperative and risked the net worth of their company, Simpson, investing conservatively, produced above-average returns for GEICO's shareholders. In a nutshell, the value of Lou Simpson to the economic gains for GEICO, independent of the policies written by GEICO, was enormous.

Buffett instinctively knew that Simpson had the characteristics necessary to resist the institutional imperative and avoid mindless imitation. They were exactly like his own. "Lou Simpson," trumpeted Buffett, "is the best investment manager in the property-casualty business."[23] Buffett went further in the 1995 Berkshire Hathaway Annual Report: "Lou takes the same conservative, concentrated approach to investments that we do at Berkshire, and it is an enormous plus to have him on the board. One point that goes beyond Lou's GEICO work: His presence on the scene assures us that Berkshire would have an extraordinary professional immediately available to handle its investments if something were to happen to Charlie and me."[24]

Tenet: Return on Equity

In 1980, with its financial troubles largely behind it, GEICO's return on equity was 30.8 percent—almost twice as high as the peer group average. By the late 1980s, the company's return on equity began to decline, not because the business was floundering, but because its equity grew faster than its earnings. Hence, part of the logic of paying out increasing dividends and buying back stock worked to reduce equity capital and maintain an acceptable return on equity.

Tenet: Profit Margins

Investors can compare profitability of insurance companies in several ways. Pretax margins are one of the best measures. Over the 10-year period from 1983 to 1992, GEICO's average pretax margins were the most consistent, with the lowest standard deviation, of any peer group company.

GEICO paid meticulous attention to all its expenses and closely tracked the expenses associated with settling insurance claims. During this period, corporate expenses as a percentage of premiums written averaged 15 percent—half the industry average. This low ratio partly reflects the cost of insurance agents that GEICO does not have to pay.

GEICO's combined ratio of corporate expenses and underwriting losses was demonstrably superior to the industry average. From 1977 through 1992, the industry average beat GEICO's combined ratio only once, in 1977. From then, GEICO's combined ratio averaged 97.1 percent, more than 10 percentage points better than the industry average. GEICO posted an underwriting loss only twice—once in 1985 and again in 1992. The underwriting loss in 1992 was accentuated by the unusual number of natural disasters that struck the country that year. Without Hurricane Andrew and other major storms, GEICO's combined ratio would have been a low 93.8 percent.

Tenet: Determine the Value

When Buffett first started to buy shares of GEICO for Berkshire Hathaway, GEICO was close to bankruptcy. But he said GEICO was worth a substantial sum, even with a negative net worth, because of the company's insurance franchise. Still, in 1976, because the company had no earnings, it defied the discounted present value determination of value put forth by John Burr Williams. Even so, despite the uncertainty over GEICO's future cash flows, Buffett was sure that the company would survive and earn money in the future. How much and when was open to debate.

In 1980, Berkshire owned one-third of GEICO, invested at a cost of $47 million. That year, GEICO's total market value was $296 million. Even then, Buffett estimated that the company possessed a significant margin of safety. In 1980, the company earned $60 million on $705 million in revenues. Berkshire's share of GEICO's earnings (unreported in Berkshire's net income) was $20 million. According to Buffett, "to buy a similar $20 million of earnings in a business with first-class economic characteristics and bright prospects would cost a minimum of $200 million"—more if the purchase was for a controlling interest in the company.[25]

Even so, Buffett's $200 million assumption is realistic, given Williams' valuation theory. Assuming that GEICO could sustain this $60 million in earnings without the aid of any additional paid-in capital, the present value of GEICO, discounted by the then-current 12 percent rate of the 30-year US government bond, would have been $500 million—almost twice GEICO's 1980 market value. If the company could grow this earnings power at 2 percent real, the present value would increase to $600 million, and Berkshire's share would equal $200 million. In other words, in 1980, the market value of GEICO's stock price was less than half the discounted present value of its earnings power.

At year-end 1995, Berkshire Hathaway completed the purchase of GEICO, then the seventh-largest auto insurer in the US, with about 3.7 million cars insured. Buffett agreed to pay $2.3 billion for the half of the company Berkshire Hathaway didn't own. That price, Buffett pointed out, valued GEICO at $4.6 billion for 100 percent of a business that then had tangible net worth of $1.9 billion.

"The excess over tangible net worth of the implied value of $2.7 billion," said Buffett, "was what we estimated GEICO's 'goodwill' to be worth at the time. That goodwill represented the economic value of the policyholders who were then doing business with GEICO." Buffett confessed, "By industry standards, that was a very high price. But GEICO was no ordinary insurer: Because of the company's low costs, its policyholders were consistently profitable and unusually loyal."[26]

Buffett goes on to explain. Premium volume in 2010 was $14.3 billion and growing. "Yet," he said, "we carry the goodwill of GEICO on our books at only $1.4 billion, an amount that will remain unchanged no matter how much the value of GEICO increases." Based on the same metrics he used to value a GEICO customer in 1995, the real value of GEICO's economic goodwill in 2010, said Buffett, was $14 billion. "And this value," Buffett believed, "is likely to be much higher ten and twenty years from now. GEICO is the gift that keeps giving."[27]

Capital Cities/ABC

Cap Cities had its beginning in the news business. In 1954, Lowell Thomas, the famous journalist, and his business manager, Frank Smith, along with a group of associates bought Hudson Valley Broadcasting Company, which included an Albany, New York, television and radio station. At the time, Tom Murphy was a product specialist at Lever Brothers. Frank Smith, who was a golfing partner of Murphy's father, hired the younger Murphy to manage the company's television station. In 1957, Hudson Valley purchased a Raleigh–Durham television station, and the company's name was changed to Capital Cities Broadcasting, reflecting that both Albany and Raleigh were capitals of their respective states.

In 1960, Tom Murphy hired Dan Burke to manage the Albany station. Burke was the brother of one of Murphy's Harvard classmates, Jim Burke, who later became chairman of Johnson & Johnson. Dan Burke, an Albany native, was left in charge of the television station while Murphy returned to New York, where he was named president of Capital Cities in 1964. Thus began one of the most successful corporate partnerships in US business. During the next three decades, Murphy and Burke ran Capital Cities and together they made more than 30 broadcasting and publishing acquisitions, the most notable being the purchase of American Broadcasting Company (ABC) in 1985.

Buffett first met Tom Murphy in the late 1960s at a New York luncheon arranged by one of Murphy's classmates. The story goes that Murphy was so impressed with Buffett that he invited him to join the board of directors at Capital Cities.[28] Buffett declined, but he and Murphy became close friends, keeping in touch over the years.

In December 1984, Murphy approached Leonard Goldenson, chairman of American Broadcasting Company, with the idea of merging the two companies. Although initially rebuffed, Murphy contacted Goldenson again in January 1985. The Federal Communications Commission (FCC) had increased the number of television and radio stations that a single company could own from 7 to 12, effective in April that year. This time Goldenson agreed. Goldenson, then 79 years old, was concerned about his successor. Although ABC had several potential candidates, none was, in his opinion, ready for leadership. Murphy and Burke had gained a reputation as the best managers in the media and communications industry. By agreeing to merge with Capital Cities, Goldenson was ensuring that ABC would remain in strong management hands. American Broadcasting Company entered the negotiating room with high-priced investment bankers. Murphy, who always negotiated his own deals, brought his trusted friend Warren Buffett. Together they worked out the first-ever sale of a television network and the largest media merger in history up to that point.

Capital Cities offered American Broadcasting Company a total package worth $121 per ABC share ($118 in cash per share and one-tenth warrant to purchase Capital Cities worth $3 per share). The offer was twice the value at which ABC's stock traded at the day before the announcement. To finance the $3.5 billion deal, Capital Cities would borrow $2.1 billion from a banking consortium, sell overlapping television and radio stations worth approximately $900 million, and also sell restricted properties that a network was not allowed to own, including cable properties, subsequently sold to the Washington Post Company. The last $517.5 million came from Berkshire Hathaway.

Warren Buffett agreed that Berkshire would purchase three million newly issued shares of Cap Cities at a price of $172.50 per share. Buffett also provided Tom Murphy and Dan Burke with a highly unusual agreement that spoke to his confidence in both men. As long as Murphy or Burke remained the chief executive officer of this newly merged company, they could vote Berkshire's shares. Buffett's reasoning was that such an arrangement would leave Murphy and Burke to run Capital Cities/ABC as if it were a private company, thereby thinking and acting like long-term owners of the company without worrying about the distractions that come from short-term traders of the stock. Tom Murphy again asked his friend to join the board and this time Buffett agreed.

Tenet: Simple and Understandable

After serving on the board of the Washington Post Company for more than 10 years, Buffett understood the business of television broadcasting, adding to his long history of understanding newspapers and magazines. He was acutely aware of the economics of the media businesses. Buffett's business understanding of television networks also grew with Berkshire's own purchase of American Broadcasting Company common stock in 1978.

Tenet: Consistent Operating History

Both Capital Cities and American Broadcasting Company had profitable business histories dating back more than 50 years, the records of which were available for review and analysis. ABC averaged 17 percent return on equity with 21 percent debt to equity from 1975 through 1984. Cap Cities, during the 10 years before its offer to purchase ABC, averaged 19 percent return on equity with 20 percent debt to equity.

Tenet: Favorable Long-Term Prospects

Prior to the advent of the internet, broadcasting companies and networks were blessed with above-average economics. Similar to newspapers, and for much the same reason, they generated a great deal of economic goodwill, which is economic value beyond the value of brick and mortar. Once a broadcasting tower was built, capital reinvestment and working capital needs are minor and inventory investment is nonexistent. Much the same can be said about cable properties after they have strung cable lines to reach customers. Movies and programs could be bought on credit and settled later when advertising dollars rolled in. Thus, as a general rule, broadcasting companies produced above-average returns on capital and generated substantial cash in excess of operating needs.

At the time, the risk to networks and broadcasters included government regulations, technology disruption, and shifting advertising dollars. Governments can deny the renewal of a company's broadcasting license, but it is rare. Cable programs, in 1985, were a minor threat to networks. Although some viewers tuned in cable shows, the overwhelming majority of television viewers still preferred network programming. Also during the 1980s, advertising dollars targeting free-spending consumers were growing substantially faster than the country's gross domestic product. To reach a mass audience, advertising companies still counted on network broadcasting. The basic economics of networks and broadcasting companies were, in Buffett's mind, above average, and in 1985, the long-term prospects for these businesses was highly favorable.

Tenet: Determine the Value

Berkshire's $517 million investment in Capital Cities at that time was the single-largest investment Buffett ever made. How Buffett determined the value of Capital Cities and American Broadcasting Company is open for debate. Murphy agreed to sell Buffett three million shares of Capital Cities/ABC for $172.50 per share. But we know price and value are often two different figures. Buffett's practice, we have learned, is to acquire a company only when there is a significant margin of safety between the company's intrinsic value and its purchase price. However, with the purchase of Capital Cities/ABC, he admittedly compromised this principle. But, as we will learn, that unconventional decision was ultimately justified.

If we discount Buffett's offer of $172.50 per share by 10 percent (the approximate yield of the 30-year US government bond in 1985) and multiply this value by 16 million shares (Cap Cities had 13 million shares outstanding plus three million issued to Berkshire Hathaway), the present value of this business would need to have earning power of $276 million. Capital Cities' 1984 earnings net after depreciation and capital expenditures was $122 million, and ABC's net income after depreciation and capital expenditures was $320 million, making the combined earnings power $442 million. But the combined company would also have substantial debt: the $2.1 billion that Murphy had borrowed would cost $220 million a year in interest. So, the net earnings of the combined company was approximately $200 million.

There were additional considerations. Murphy's reputation for improving the cash flow of purchased businesses simply by reducing expenses was legendary. Capital Cities' operating margins were 28 percent, whereas ABC's were 11 percent. If Murphy could improve operating margins of the ABC properties by one-third to 15 percent, the company would throw off an additional $125 million each year, and the combined earnings power would equal $325 million annually. The per-share present value of a company earning $325 million with 16 million shares outstanding discounted at 10 percent was $203 per share—a 15 percent margin of safety over Buffett's $172.50 purchase price. "I doubt if Ben's up there applauding me on this one," Buffett quipped, in fond reference to Ben Graham.[29]

The margin of safety that Buffett accepted could be expanded if we make certain assumptions. Buffett says the conventional wisdom during this period argued that newspapers, magazines, or television stations would be able to increase earnings forever at 6 percent annually—without the need for additional capital.[30] The reasoning, he explained, was that capital expenditures would equal depreciation rates and the need for working capital would be minimal; hence, income could be thought of as freely distributed earnings. This means that an owner of a media company possessed a perpetual annuity that would grow at 6 percent for the foreseeable future without the need for any additional capital.

Compare that, Buffett suggested, to a company that is able to grow only if capital is reinvested. If you owned a media company that earned $1 million and expected to grow at 6 percent, it would be appropriate, says Buffett, to pay $25 million for this business ($1 million divided by a risk-free rate of 10 percent less the 6 percent growth rate). Another business that earned $1 million but could not grow earnings without reinvested capital might be worth $10 million ($1 million divided by 10 percent).

If we take Buffett's finance lesson and apply to it Cap Cities, the value of Cap Cities increased from $203 per share to $507, or a 66 percent margin of safety over the $172.50 price that Buffett agreed to pay. But there are a lot of ifs in these assumptions. Would Murphy be able to sell a portion of Capital Cities/ABC combined properties for $900 million? (He actually got $1.2 billion.) Would he be able to improve operating margins at American Broadcasting Companies? Would he be able to continually count on the growth of advertising dollars?

Buffett's ability to obtain a significant margin of safety in Capital Cities was complicated by several factors. The stock price of Cap Cities had been rising over the years. Murphy and Burke were doing an excellent job managing the company and the company's share price reflected this. So, unlike GEICO, Buffett did not have the opportunity to purchase Cap Cities cheaply because of a temporary business decline. The stock market, which had been steadily rising, didn't help either. And, because this was a secondary stock offering, Buffett had to take a price for Cap Cities' shares that was close to its then value.

If there was any disappointment over the issue of price, Buffett was comforted by the quick appreciation of those same shares. On Friday, March 15, 1985, Capital Cities' share price was $176. On Monday afternoon, March 18, Capital Cities announced it would purchase American Broadcasting Companies. The next day, by market close, Capital Cities' share price was $202.75. In four days, the price had risen 26 points, a 15 percent appreciation. Buffett's profit was $90 million and the deal was not due to close until January 1986.

The margin of safety that Buffett received investing in Capital Cities was significantly less than for other purchases. So why did Buffett proceed? The answer was Tom Murphy. Had it not been for Murphy Buffett admitted he would not have invested in the company. Murphy was Buffett's margin of safety. Capital Cities/ABC was an exceptional business, the kind of business that attracts Buffett. But there is also something special about Murphy. "Warren adores Tom Murphy," said John Byrne, "Just to be partners with him is attractive to [Buffett]."[31]

Cap Cities' management philosophy is decentralization, the exact management approach applied by Buffett and Munger at Berkshire Hathaway. Murphy and Burke hire the best people possible and then leave them alone to do their job. All decisions are made at the local level. Burke found this out early in his relationship with Murphy. Burke, while managing the Albany TV station, mailed updated reports to Murphy, who never responded. Burke finally got the message. Murphy promised Burke, "I won't come to Albany unless you invite me—or I have to fire you."[32] Murphy and Burke set yearly budgets for their companies and reviewed operating performance quarterly. With these two exceptions, managers were expected to operate their businesses as if they owned them. "We expect a great deal from our managers," wrote Tom Murphy.[33]

And the one thing Capital Cities' managers were expected to do was control costs. When they failed, Murphy was not shy about getting involved. When Capital Cities purchased ABC, Murphy's managerial talent for cutting costs was badly needed. Television networks tend to think in terms of ratings, not profits. Whatever was needed to increase ratings, the networks thought, superseded cost evaluation. This mentality abruptly stopped when Murphy took over. With the help of carefully selected committees at ABC, Murphy pruned payrolls, perks, and expenses. Some 1,500 people, given generous severance packages, were let go. The executive dining rooms and private elevator at ABC were closed. The limousine at ABC Entertainment in Los Angeles that was used to drive Murphy during his first tour of the company's operation was discharged. On his next trip, he took a cab.

Such cost-consciousness was a way of life at Capital Cities. The company's Philadelphia television station, WPVI, the number one station in the city, had a news staff of 100 compared to 150 at the CBS affiliate across town. Before Murphy arrived at ABC, the company employed 60 people to manage ABC's five television stations. Soon after the Cap Cities' acquisition, six people managed eight stations. WABC-TV in New York employed 600 people and generated 30 percent pretax margins. Once Murphy reconfigured the business, the station employed 400 people with pretax margins north of 50 percent. Once a cost crisis was resolved, Murphy depended on Burke to manage the operating decisions. He concentrated on acquisitions and shareholder assets.

Tenet: The One-Dollar Premise

From 1985 through 1992, the market value of Capital Cities/ABC grew from $2.9 billion to $8.3 billion. During this period, the company retained $2.7 billion in earnings, thereby creating $2.01 in value for every $1 reinvested. This accomplishment was especially noteworthy considering that the company endured both a cyclical downturn in earnings in the 1990–1991 economic recession and a decline in its intrinsic value in the network broadcasting business.

Tenet: Rational Management

In 1988, Capital Cities/ABC announced it had authorized the repurchase of up to two million shares, 11 percent of the company's outstanding stock. In 1989, the company spent $233 million purchasing 523,000 shares of stock at an average price of $445 per share—7.3 times cash flow, compared to the asking price of other media companies that were selling for 10 to 12 times cash flow. The following year, the company purchased 926,000 shares of stock at an average price of $477 per share, or 7.6 times operating cash flow. In 1992, the company continued to buy back its stock. That year it purchased 270,000 shares at an average price of $434 per share, or 8.3 times operating cash flow. Murphy explained, the price it paid for itself buying back shares was still less than the price of other advertiser-supported media companies that he and Burke considered attractive. From 1988 through 1992, Capital Cities/ABC purchased a total of 1,953,000 shares of stock, investing $866 million to reduce shares outstanding.

In November 1993, the company announced an auction to purchase up to two million shares of stock at prices between $590 and $630 per share. Berkshire participated in the auction, submitting one million of its three-million-share investment in Cap Cities. This act alone caused widespread speculation. Was the company unable to find an appropriate acquisition, putting itself up for sale? Was Buffett, by selling a third of his position, giving up on the company? Cap Cities denied the rumors. Opinions surfaced that Buffett would have not tendered stock that surely would have fetched a higher price if indeed the company was for sale. Capital Cities/ABC eventually purchased 1.1 million shares of stock, one million from Berkshire at an average price of $630 per share. Buffett was able to redeploy $630 million into other investments.

Tenet: The Institutional Imperative

The basic economics of the broadcasting and network business ensured Cap Cities would generate ample cash flow. However, the industry's basic economics, coupled with Murphy's penchant for controlling costs, meant Cap Cities would have overwhelming cash flow. From 1988 through 1992, Cap Cities generated $2.3 billion in unencumbered cash. Given such resources, some managers might be unable to resist the temptation to spend money, buying businesses and expanding the corporate domain. Murphy, too, bought a few businesses. In 1990, he spent $61 million acquiring small properties but barely putting a dent in the $2.3 billion he had accumulated over the previous five years. At the time, the general market for most media properties was priced too high, said Murphy.

Acquisitions had always been very important to Cap Cities in the development of its growth. Murphy was always on the lookout for media properties, but he was steadfast in his discipline not to overpay for a company. Cap Cities, with its enormous cash flow, could easily gobble up other media properties, but as *BusinessWeek* reported, "Murphy would sometimes wait for years until he found the right property. He never made a deal just because he had resources available to do it."[34] Murphy and Burke also realized that the media business was cyclical, and if a purchase was built on too much leverage, the risk to shareholders would be unacceptable. "Murphy never did a deal that either of us thought was capable of mortally wounding us," said Burke.[35]

There is another example of how Tom Murphy resisted the institutional imperative. In *The Outsiders*, William Thorndike contrasted the differences between the management styles of Tom Murphy with the legendary Bill Paley, who ran CBS.[36] When Tom Murphy became CEO of Capital Cities in 1966, CBS was the country's dominant media business with TV and radio stations in some of the largest markets, coupled with publishing and music properties. Under Murphy, Cap Cities began with a few smaller-market TV and radio stations. The market value of CBS's stock was 16 times the size of the smaller Cap Cities. Thorndike points out when Capital Cities/ABC sold the company to the Walt Disney Company 30 years later Capital Cities' market capitalization was three times more valuable than CBS. How did this occur?

Thorndike points out that Paley and Murphy took two different pathways to growing the intrinsic value of their businesses. Paley, flush with the cash that media companies generate, latched on to the popular and often imitated idea of buying unrelated businesses in a quest to diversify the economic streams of the businesses so as to negate the risk of being tied solely to just one industry. It was the conventional road map that many large businesses took at the time, transforming single-line businesses into conglomerates. CBS bought a toy business, the New York Yankees, and a very expensive landmark building in midtown Manhattan. Paley's management strategy was focused on making CBS not only larger but more economically diversified.

Murphy was the exact opposite. He was not interested in how big Capital Cities became but how more valuable he could make the company. Murphy stuck to his knitting, staying within the confines of the media industry, which he knew well. "We just kept opportunistically buying assets, intelligently leveraging the company, improving the operations, and then we'd . . . take a bite of something else."[37]

Along the way, Murphy would pay down debt and then look for another media property. Because Murphy was unwilling to pay high asking prices for media properties, and because he resisted the institutional imperative to buy unrelated businesses, he instead returned the money to shareholders. We took note of Murphy's stock repurchase program that enriched remaining shareholders. He also worked aggressively to reduce debt. In 1986, after the acquisition of ABC, long-term debt at Cap Cities was $1.8 billion, and the debt-to-equity capital ratio was 48.6 percent. Cash and cash equivalents at 1986 year-end amounted to $16 million. By 1992, long-term debt was $964 million and the debt-to-capital ratio had dropped to 20 percent. Furthermore, cash and cash equivalents increased to $1.2 billion, making the company essentially debt free. Murphy's strengthening of the Cap Cities balance sheet substantially reduced the company's risk while simultaneously increasing intrinsic value.

Warren Buffett has observed the operations and management of countless businesses over the years. But according to him, Cap Cities was the best-managed publicly owned company in the country. As mentioned, when Buffett invested in Cap Cities he assigned all voting rights to Murphy and Burke. He helped the company finance its acquisition of American Broadcasting Company, and in 1996 Buffett helped to orchestrate the sale of Capital Cities/ABC to the Walt Disney Company. Buffett's decades-long relationship with the management of Cap Cities is telling. And if that is not enough to convince you of the high regard he held for Murphy and Burke, consider this: "Tom Murphy and Dan Burke are not only great managers," said Buffett. "They are precisely the sort of fellows you would want your daughter to marry."[38]

The Coca-Cola Company

In 1998, Coca-Cola was the world's largest manufacturer, marketer, and distributor of carbonated soft drink concentrates and syrups. It still is. The company's soft drink product was first sold in the

United States in 1886. Today, it is sold in more than 200 countries worldwide.

Warren Buffett's relationship with Coca-Cola, as you recall, dates back to his childhood. He drank his first Coca-Cola when he was five years old. Soon afterwards, he started buying six Cokes for 25 cents from his grandfather's grocery store and reselling them in his neighborhood for five cents each. For the next 50 years, Buffett admitted, he observed the phenomenal growth of Coca-Cola but instead invested in textile mills, department stores, and farming equipment manufacturers. Even in 1986, when he formally announced that Coca-Cola was the official drink of Berkshire Hathaway's annual meetings, Buffett still had not purchased his first share of its stock. It was not until two years later, in summer 1988, that he began to buy shares of Coco-Cola.

Tenet: Simple and Understandable

The business of Coca-Cola is relatively simple. The company purchases commodity inputs and combines them to manufacture a concentrate that is sold to bottlers, who combine the concentrate with other ingredients to make the soft drink. The bottlers then sell the finished product to retail outlets, including supermarkets, minimarts, and vending machines. The company also provides soft drink syrups to restaurants and fast food companies who sell soft drinks to their customers in cups and glasses. At the time, the company's name brand products included Coca-Cola, Diet Coke, Sprite, Mr. PiBB, Mello Yellow, Ramblin' Root Beer, Fanta soft drinks, Tab, and Fresca. Other drinks included Hi-C brand fruit drinks, Minute Maid orange juice, Powerade, Nestea, and Nordic Mist. In the 1980s, the company also owned bottlers including a 44 percent interest in Coca-Cola Enterprises, the largest bottler in the United States, and 53 percent of Coca-Cola Amatil, an Australian bottler that had interests not only in Australia but also in New Zealand and Eastern Europe. The strength of Coca-Cola was not only its name-brand products but also its unmatched worldwide distribution system.

Tenet: Favorable Long-Term Prospects

Shortly after Berkshire Hathaway's 1989 public announcement that it owned 6.3 percent of The Coca-Cola Company, Buffett was interviewed by Mellisa Turner, a business writer for the *Atlanta Journal-Constitution*. She asked him the question that he has been often asked: Why didn't he purchase shares in the company sooner? By way of an answer, Buffett related his thinking at the time he finally made the decision: "Let's say you were going away for ten years and you wanted to make one investment and you know everything that you know now, and you couldn't change it while you were gone. What would you think about?"[39]

Of course the business would have to be simple and understandable. Of course the company would have had to demonstrate a great deal of business consistency over the years. And of course the long-term prospects would have to be favorable. Buffett goes on: "If I came up with anything in terms of certainty, where I knew the market was going to continue to grow, where I knew the leader was going to continue to be the leader—I mean worldwide—and where I knew there could be big unit growth, I just don't know anything like Coke. I would be relatively sure that when I came back they would be doing a hell of a lot more business than they do now."[40]

But why purchase at that particular time? Coca-Cola's business attributes, as described by Buffett, have existed for several decades. What caught his eye, he said, were the changes occurring at Coca-Cola during the 1980s under the leadership of Roberto Goizueta.

The 1970s was a dismal period for Coca-Cola. The decade was marred by disputes with bottlers, accusations of mistreatment of migrant workers at the company's Minute Maid groves, environmentalists' claims that Coke's "one way" containers contributed to the country's growing pollution problem, and the Federal Trade Commission's charges that the company's exclusive franchise system violated the Sherman Anti-Trust Act. Coca-Cola's international business was reeling as well. The Arab boycott of Coke, caused by the company's issuing an Israeli franchise, dismantled years of investment. Japan, where the company's earnings were growing the fastest, was a battlefield of mistakes. Coke's 26-ounce take-home bottles were exploding—literally—on store shelves. In addition, Japanese consumers angrily objected to the company's use of artificial coal tar coloring in Fanta Grape. When the company developed a new version using real grape skins, the bottles fermented, and the grape soda was tossed in Tokyo Bay.

During the 1970s, Coca-Cola was a fragmented and reactive company rather than an innovator setting the pace within the beverage industry. Paul Austin was appointed chairman of the company in 1971, after serving as president since 1962. Despite its problems, the company continued to generate millions of dollars in earnings. But instead of reinvesting it its own beverage market, Austin diversified the company, investing in water projects and shrimp farms, despite slim profit margins. Austin also purchased a winery. Shareholders bitterly opposed the acquisition, arguing Coca-Cola should not be associated with alcohol. To deflect criticism, Austin directed unprecedented amounts of money into advertising campaigns.

Meanwhile, Coca-Cola earned 20 percent on equity. However, pretax margins were slipping. The market value of the company at the end of the 1973–1974 bear market was $3.1 billion. Six years later, the value of the company was $4.1 billion. From 1974 to 1980, the company's market value rose an average annual rate of 5.6 percent, vastly underperforming the Standard & Poor's 500 Index. For every dollar the company reinvested in those six years, it only created $1.02 of market value.

Coca-Cola's corporate woes were exacerbated by Austin's behavior.[41] He was intimidating and unapproachable. Furthermore, his wife, Jeanne, was a disruptive influence within the company. She redecorated corporate headquarters with modern art, shunning the company's classic Norman Rockwell paintings. She even ordered a corporate jet to help her facilitate the search for works of art. But it was her last order that contributed to her husband's downfall.

In May 1980, Mrs. Austin ordered the company's park closed to employee luncheons. Their food droppings, she complained, attracted pigeons on the well-manicured lawns. Employee morale hit an all-time low. Robert Woodruff, the company's 91-year-old patriarch, who led Coca-Cola from 1923 to 1955 and was still chairman of the board's finance committee, had heard enough. He demanded Austin's resignation and replaced him with Robert Goizueta.

Goizueta, raised in Cuba, was Coca-Cola's first foreign chief executive officer. Goizueta was as outgoing as Austin was reticent. One of Goizueta's first acts was to bring together Coca-Cola's top 50 managers for a meeting in Palm Springs, California. "Tell me what we're doing wrong," he said. "I want to know it all and once it's settled, I want 100 percent loyalty. If anyone is not happy, we will make you a good settlement and say goodbye."[42] From this meeting evolved the company's "Strategy for the 1980s," a 900-word pamphlet outlining the corporate goals for Coca-Cola.

Goizueta encouraged his managers to take intelligent risks. He wanted Coca-Cola to initiate action rather than be reactive. Goizueta, similar to many new chief executives, began cutting costs. Furthermore, he demanded that any company Coca-Cola owned must optimize its return on assets. These actions translated, immediately, into increasing profit margins.

Tenet: Profit Margins

Coca-Cola's pretax profit margins, in 1980, were a low 12.9 percent. Margins had been falling for five straight years and were substantially below the company's 1973 margins of 18 percent. In Goizueta's first year, pretax margins rose to 13.7 percent. By 1988, when Buffett bought his first Coca-Cola shares, margins had climbed to a record 19 percent.

Tenet: Return on Equity

In the company's "Strategy for the 1980s," Goizueta demanded that the company divest any business that no longer generated acceptable returns on equity. Any new business venture must have sufficient real growth potential to justify an investment. Coca-Cola was no longer interested in battling for shares in a stagnant market. "Increasing earnings per share and effecting increased return on equity are still the name of the game," argued Goizueta.[43] His words were followed by actions. Coca-Cola's wine business was sold to Seagram in 1983. Although the wine business earned a respectable 20 percent on equity during the 1970s, Goizueta was not impressed. He demanded better returns and the company obliged. By 1988, Coca-Cola's return on equity had increased to 31.8 percent.

By any measurement, Goizueta's Coca-Cola was doubling and tripling the financial accomplishments of Austin's Coca-Cola. The results could be seen in the market value of the company. In 1980, Coca-Cola had a market value of $4.1 billion. By the end of 1987, even after the stock market crash in October that year, the market value of Coca-Cola had risen to $14.1 billion. In seven years, Coca-Cola's market value rose an average annual rate of 19.3 percent. For every dollar Coca-Cola retained during the period, it gained $4.66 in market value.

Tenet: Candid Management

Goizueta's strategy for the 1980s pointedly included shareholders. In addressing them he wrote, "We shall, during the next decade, remain totally committed to our shareholders and to the protection and enhancement of their investment. In order to give our shareholders an above average total annual return on their investment, we must choose businesses that generate returns in excess of inflation."[44]

Goizueta not only had to grow the business, which required capital reinvestment, but also he was obliged to increase shareholder value. To do so, Coca-Cola, by increasing profit margins and return on equity, was able to pay higher dividends while simultaneously reducing the dividend payout ratio. In the 1980s, dividends to shareholders were increasing 10 percent per year while the payout ratio was declining from 65 percent to 40 percent. This enabled Coca-Cola to reinvest a greater percentage of the company's earnings to help sustain the growth rate of the company while not shortcutting the dividend return to shareholders.

Each year in its annual report, Coca-Cola begins the financial review and management's discussion by stating its primary goal: "Management's primary objective is to maximize shareholder value over time." The company's business strategy emphasizes the intent to maximize long-term cash flows. In order to do so, the company will continue to focus on investing in the high-return soft drink business, increasing returns on existing businesses, and optimizing the costs of capital. If successful, the evidence will be growth in cash flow, increased return on equity, and an increased total return to shareholders.

Tenet: Rational Management

The growth in net cash flow enabled Coca-Cola to increase its dividend to shareholders and also repurchase its shares in the open market. In 1984, the company authorized its first ever buyback, announcing it would repurchase six million shares of stock. The company continued to repurchase shares every year through 1992, 414 million shares for a total investment of $5.3 billion. This represented more than 25 percent of the company's outstanding shares at the beginning of 1984. It was a good investment. The value of the shares repurchased, based on the closing price on December 31, 1993, was $18.5 billion.

In July 1992, Coca-Cola advanced its share repurchase program by announcing that through the year 2000 it would buy back 100 million shares of stock, representing 7.6 percent of the company's outstanding shares. Remarkably, the company would be able to accomplish this while it continued its aggressive investment in overseas markets. The buyback, claimed Goizueta, could be accomplished because of the company's strong cash-generating ability.

Tenet: Owner Earnings

In 1973, owner earnings (net income plus depreciation/amortization minus capital expenditures) were $152 million. By 1980, owner earnings were $262 million, an 8 percent annual compounded growth rate. From 1981 through 1988, owner earnings grew from

$262 million to $828 million, a 17.8 percent average annual compounded growth rate. The growth in owner earnings is reflected in the share price of Coca-Cola. In analyzing 10-year periods, total return of Coca-Cola's share price, from 1973 to 1982, grew at 6.3 percent average annual rate. From 1983 to 1992, the total return of Coca-Cola's share price grew at a 31.1 percent average annual rate.

Tenet: Determine the Value

When Buffett first purchased Coca-Cola in 1988, people asked, "Where is the value of Coke?" The company's price was 15 times earnings and 12 times cash flow, a 30 percent and 50 percent premium to the market average. Value investors devoted to Ben Graham's teachings howled in protest, claiming Buffett had turned his back on the master. It was four years later, in the 1992 Berkshire Hathaway Annual Report, that Buffett clarified: Value is not determined by multiples but by the discounted present value of the future cash flow stream.

Buffett paid five times book value for Coca-Cola. He was willing to do that because of Coca-Cola's extraordinary level of economic goodwill. The company was earning 31 percent on equity while employing relatively little in capital reinvestment. Of course, Buffett tells us, the value of Coca-Cola, similar to any other company, is determined by the net cash flows expected to occur over the life of the business, discounted by an appropriate interest rate.

In 1988, owner earnings of Coca-Cola equaled $828 million. The 30-year US Treasury Bond (the risk-free rate) at the time traded near a 9 percent yield. If Coca-Cola's 1988 owner earnings were discounted by 9 percent (remember, Buffett does not add an equity risk premium to the discount rate), the value of Coca-Cola would have been $9.2 billion. When Buffett purchased Coca-Cola, the market value of the company was $14.8 billion, indicating Buffett might have overpaid for the company. But the $9.2 billion represented the discounted value of Coca-Cola's current owner earnings. Because the market was willing to pay a price for Coca-Cola that was 60 percent higher than the $9.2 billion, it signaled that buyers perceived part of the value of Coca-Cola to be its future growth opportunities.

When a company is able to grow owner earnings without the need for additional capital, it is appropriate to discount owner earnings by the difference between the risk-free rate of return and the expected growth of owner earnings. Analyzing Coca-Cola, we found that owner earnings from 1981 through 1988 grew at a 17.8 percent annual rate—faster than the risk-free rate of return. When this occurs, analysts use a two-stage discount model known as the Gordon growth model. It is a way of calculating future earnings when a company has extraordinary growth for a limited number of years, followed by a period of constant, slower growth thereafter.

We used this two-stage model to calculate the 1988 discounted present value of Coca-Cola's future cash flows. In 1988 Coca-Cola's owner earnings were $828 million. If we assume that Coca-Cola would be able to grow owner earnings at a 15 percent rate per year for the next 10 years (a reasonable assumption because that growth rate was lower than the company's previous seven-year average), by year 10 owner earnings would equal $3.45 billion. We further assumed that starting in year 11, the growth rate of the company would slow to 5 percent per year. Using a discount rate of 9 percent (the long-term bond rate at the time), we calculated that the intrinsic value of Coca-Cola in 1988 was $48.38 billion.

We can repeat this exercise using different growth-rate assumptions. If we assume that Coca-Cola could grow owner earnings at 12 percent for 10 years followed by 5 percent growth, the present value of the company discounted at 9 percent would be $38.16 billion. At 10 percent growth for 10 years and 5 percent thereafter, the value of Coca-Cola would be $32.45 billion. And if we assumed only a steady 5 percent growth rate for the company, Coca-Cola would be worth at least $20.7 billion.

Tenets: Buy at Attractive Prices; The $1 Premise

In fall 1988, Donald Keough, the president of Coca-Cola, could not help but notice that someone was buying shares of the company's stock in a big way. Just a year after the 1987 stock market crash, Coca-Cola's shares were still trading 25 percent below their pre-crash high. But Coca-Cola's share price had finally found a floor because "some mysterious investor was gulping down shares by the caseload." When Keough discovered the broker who was doing the buying hailed from the Midwest, he immediately thought of his friend Warren Buffett and decided to give him a call.

"Well, Warren, what's going on?" Keough asked. "You don't happen to be buying any shares of Coca-Cola?" Buffett paused, then said, "It so happens that I am, but I would appreciate if you would stay quiet until I disclose my ownership."[45] If word had ever gotten out that Buffett was buying Coca-Cola, it would have created a rush of buying, ultimately driving the share price higher, and he was not done adding to Berkshire's position.

By spring 1989, Berkshire Hathaway shareholders learned that Buffett has spent $1.02 billion buying Coca-Cola shares. He had bet one-third of the Berkshire portfolio, and now owned 7 percent of the company. It was the single largest Berkshire investment to date, and already Wall Street was scratching its head.

From the time that Goizueta took control of Coca-Cola in 1980, the company's stock price had increased every year. In the five years before Buffett purchased his first shares of Coca-Cola, the average annual gain in the share price was 18 percent. The company's fortunes were so good that Buffett was unable to purchase any shares at distressed prices. During this period, the Standard & Poor's Index was gaining as well. Neither Coca-Cola nor the stock market presented Buffett with an opportunity to buy shares at low prices. Still, Buffett charged ahead.

The stock market's value of Coca-Cola in 1988 and 1989, during Buffett's purchase period, averaged $15.1 billion. But our estimation of the intrinsic value of Coca-Cola was anywhere from $20.7 billion (assuming 5 percent growth in owner earnings), $32.4 billion (assuming 10 percent growth for 10 years followed by 5 percent growth), $38.1 billion (assuming 12 percent growth for 10 years followed by 5 percent growth), to $48.3 billion (assuming 15 percent growth for 10 years followed by 5 percent growth).

So Buffett's margin of safety—the discount to intrinsic value—could have been as low as a conservative 27 percent or as high as 70 percent.

Ten years after Berkshire began investing in Coca-Cola, the market value of the company had grown from $25.8 billion to $143 billion. Over that time period, the company produced $26.9 billion in profits, paid out $10.5 billion in dividends to shareholders, and retained $16.4 billion for investment. For every dollar the company retained, it created $7.20 in market value. At year-end 1999, Berkshire's original $1.023 billion investment in Coca-Cola was worth $11.6 billion. The same amount invested in the S&P 500 Index was worth $3 billion.

The best business to own, says Buffett, is one that, over a long period of time, can employ ever larger amounts of capital at sustainable high rates of return. In Buffett's mind this was the perfect description of Coca-Cola. The company is one of the most widely recognized and esteemed name brands in the world. It is easy to understand why Buffett considered Coca-Cola to be the most valuable franchise in the world. That was until, 36 years later, he took a look at Apple.

Apple, Inc.

In 1971, Marcian "Ted" Hough, the architect of the first microprocessor, unveiled Intel's 4004 chip and in doing so launched the fifth technology revolution—what became known as the age of information and technology.[46] The microprocessor, a computer chip, is a component that performs the instructions and tasks involved in computer processing. The new technologies of the fifth revolution include microprocessors, computers, software applications, smartphones, and control systems. The new infrastructure includes global digital telecommunications with cable, fiber optics, radio frequencies, and satellites providing internet, electronic mail, and other e-services.

As Wall Street raced to monetize the inventions of the fifth technology revolution, Warren Buffett sat on the sidelines. New technology companies were quickly coming to the market, the likes of which included Dell Computer, Microsoft, Cisco Systems, and America OnLine. Investors, along with the financial media, were constantly pestering Buffett to take a look at those outperforming stocks. His response was always the same: technology companies were not within his circle of competence, so he had no competitive advantage when it came to analyzing them. "I could spend all my time thinking about technology for the next year," Buffett said, "and still not be the 100th, 1,000th, or even the 10,000th smartest guy in the country in analyzing those businesses."[47]

Actually, what prevented Buffett from buying technology companies was not that he didn't understand these companies; he understood them all too well. What had troubled him was the difficulty of predicting the future cash flows. The constant disruption and innovation inherent in the technology industry made those calculations difficult. Buffett was much more comfortable predicting the future economics of Coca-Cola, American Express, Procter & Gamble, and Walmart.

Then in fall 2011, 40 years after the unveiling of Intel's new microprocessor, Warren Buffett announced he had been purchasing shares of IBM. International Business Machines, founded in 1911, was considered the cornerstone of the US technology industry. But in the early 1990s IBM almost went bankrupt, losing $5 billion in 1992, the most money any US company had ever lost in a single year. Had it not been for the managerial talents of Lou Gerstner and then Sam Palmisano, today there might not be an IBM.

By year-end 2011, Berkshire Hathaway had purchased 63.9 million shares of IBM, about 5.4 percent of the company. It was a bold $10.8 billion purchase, the single biggest purchase of an individual stock Buffett had ever made. Berkshire Hathaway shareholders might have thought they would be getting a crash course on the competitive advantages of IBM's advanced information processing technology, but what they got instead was a tutorial on the talents of management and how to think about IBM's corporate strategy.

When Lou Gerstner joined IBM as CEO in 1993, he had a mandate to turn the struggling company around. So he sold low-margin technology assets and moved aggressively into software. Palmisano, who became CEO in 2002, sold the personal computer business and kept IBM focused not only on software but also consulting services and the internet. A testimonial that IBM had regained its cash-generating capabilities was evidenced by the repurchase of over half of IBM's shares outstanding during Gerstner's and Palmisano's respective tenures. To boot, Palmisano, in the decade he managed the company, raised the common stock dividend from $0.59 to $3.30, a 460 percent increase.

What attracted Buffett to IBM was not only the rational capital-allocation skills of Gerstner and Palmisano, but also the idea the information technology (IT) services industry was defensive in nature and provided relatively stable and predictable growth prospects. The IT industry is resilient because its revenues are recurring and tied to nondiscretionary budgets of larger corporations and governments. In Buffett's mind, IBM's IT services business had moat-like qualities because corporations and governments rarely switched providers.

Despite its new strategic plan, IBM struggled to grow revenues. One of the reasons for the drop in sales was the stiff competition from other companies that were providing the same level of data storage and software services at cheaper costs. The rise of cloud computing services offered by Amazon Web Services (AWS), Microsoft Azure, and Google Cloud Platform (GCP) were siphoning IBM's lucrative accounts. After nearly six years of declining revenues the share price of IBM sank to $140, below Berkshire's purchase price of $170.

In the 2016 Annual Report, Berkshire's common stock portfolio took note of a new addition—61 million shares of Apple, Inc. Buffett still owned IBM stock with a cost basis of $13.8 billion and a market value of $13.5 billion. There was no explanation of the Apple purchase. Below the portfolio holdings, Buffett simply wrote, "Some of the stocks in the table are the responsibility of either Todd Combs or Ted Weschler, who work with me in managing Berkshire's investments." Todd Combs joined Berkshire in 2010. Two years later, Ted Weschler was added to the team. Each was responsible for about $10 billion of Berkshire's portfolio, or about

20 percent of the total. At the time, people assumed that either Todd or Ted had made the Apple purchase.

Then in 2017, the shoe dropped. The Apple investment was enlarged to 166 million shares at a cost basis of $20 billion. The IBM investment was no longer listed. The following year, Berkshire added another 89 million shares of Apple, bringing the total investment to 255 million shares with a cost basis of $36 billion and a market value of $40 billion. Apple was now Warren Buffett's stock. The transition out of IBM and into Apple marked the changing of the guard in the technology industry. Once close competitors, these two industry giants now diverged onto different pathways. IBM focused on enterprise software solutions for the largest customers. Apple emerged and soon thrived as the dominant provider of consumer electronics.

Tenet: Simple and Understandable

Apple was founded on April 1, 1976, by Steve Wozniak, Steve Jobs, and Ronald Wayne to sell Wozniak's new Apple I personal computer. The company was incorporated in 1977 as Apple Computer, Inc., and went public on December 12, 1980, under the ticker symbol "AAPL" with a market capitalization of $1.778 billion.

A seminal moment in the history of Apple occurred on January 22, 1984, during the third quarter of the Super Bowl XVIII. A television commercial, directed by Ridley Scott, announced the launch of Apple's Macintosh computer. Called "1984," the commercial was hailed as one of the greatest advertisements in television history, and it proved to be a watershed event for Apple's success. The Apple Macintosh personal computer played a pivotal role in establishing desktop publishing as an easy-to-use general office function.

Years later, in 2001, the company opened its first two Apple stores (in Virginia and California) to showcase its products. Today, Apple has more than 500 stores worldwide. That same year Apple launched the iPod, a portable digital audio player that displaced the popular Sony Walkman that played tape cassettes. The iPod sold over 100 million units within six years. Two years later, Apple launched the iTunes store, a music service that offered, for 99 cents, downloads of songs that could integrate with the iPod. In five years, iTunes notched over 5 billion downloads, becoming the world's largest music retailer.

Then, in 2007, at the Macworld Expo, Steve Jobs introduced what was called a "game-changer" for Apple: a dramatically new cellphone with an unremarkable name.[48] The iPhone sold 270,000 units in the first 30 hours of sales and signaled that Apple had transitioned from its emphasis on computers to now becoming a consumer electronics giant. Next, in 2010, Apple unveiled a large-screen media device tablet called the iPad. It ran the same touch-based operating system as the iPhone, and all the apps on the iPhone were compatible on the iPad. Apple sold 300,000 iPads on the first day, and more than 500,000 by the end of the first week. In 2014, the company introduced a smartwatch, called the Apple Watch. At first a fashion statement, the watch became immensely popular because it could make and receive phone calls and also track health and fitness information. Late in 2016, AirPods, wireless headphones that could be used with the iPhone, iPad, and the Apple Watch, were launched just in time for the holidays.

Throughout this period, Apple and Microsoft were seen as chief technology competitors. Initially, Apple's computers and its proprietary operating system, iOS, were the principal economic driver for the company. Likewise, Microsoft was singularly focused and continued to gain market share selling its software, Microsoft Windows, a proprietary graphical operating system. But Apple broke away, expanding past computers and computer software into richly engineered and richly priced consumer electronics for the masses. And it was working. When Apple launched the iPad in 2010, its market capitalization surpassed that of Microsoft for the first time since 1989.

It is staggering to realize that a display of a full selection of all the consumer electronics of this $3 trillion market cap company can easily fit on top of a small breakfast table. But this is only half the story. The other half, and by some estimates half of the total value of the company, resides in Apple Services, a subscription-based service including Apple One, Apple TV+, Apple Music, Apple Arcade, Apple Fitness+, Apple News+, Apple Podcasts, Apple Books, Apple Care, iCloud, and the Apple Credit Card. And in this lineup, the Apple App Store is the most significant. The App Store is a digital distribution platform where individuals can buy and download digital software and applications for their iPhone and iPad. In return for access to Apple's customers, the company charges a 30 percent fee for apps designed by outside developers. For subscription-based apps, Apple charges 30 percent in the first year, which then drops to 15 percent for the subsequent years. In short, the App Store gushes money.

In 2023, Apple Services, the App Store included, generated more than $80 billion in revenues, representing nearly 20 percent of Apple's total $400 billion in sales with a much higher percentage contribution to net income. The company, alone, has over one billion paying subscribers for its array of digital services, up from 860 million subscribers the year before. Apple's active installed base, including iPhone, Mac, and iPad, crossed two billion by year-end 2022, up 11 percent year-over-year. Approximately 26 percent of the world's population of eight billion people own an Apple product.

Tenet: Return on Equity

When Warren Buffett first bought Apple, many were scratching their heads wondering why Berkshire wanted to buy a company similar to Nokia or Motorola, two cellphone manufacturers that had seen better days. But in another case of "failure to explain is caused by failure to describe," Apple wasn't Motorola or Nokia, it is Louis Vuitton. There is a reason why the Apple Store on Fifth Avenue in New York and on the Avenue des Champs-Elysees in Paris is next to the Louis Vuitton store. Apple is the luxury goods manufacturer of cellphones, and consumers have a strong affinity for its products. In short, the Apple iPhone became a status symbol.

Buffett was coming around to the idea that Apple was a very valuable product and that people were building their lives around the iPhone. "That's true of 8-year-olds and 80-year-olds. People want the product," said Buffett, "And they don't want the cheapest product."[49] On average, Apple has sold about 15 percent of the world's smartphones but captures 85 percent of the world's profits for smartphones.

The second value-added component of Apple is its rapidly growing services business, including the App Store. Apple's services business is the fastest-growing part of Apple and it is the principal reason for the above-average performance of Apple's stock these past several years. For too long, investors focused on the hardware business of Apple (laptops, iPhones, iPads, and the wearables: watches and AirPods), giving little credit to the services business. Indeed, when Berkshire first purchased Apple in 2016, the market assigned no value to the implied growth of the company. Once it became clear that Apple services was not only growing rapidly but also steadily becoming a bigger part of the company's total revenues (precisely because services was growing faster than hardware), attitudes about Apple's future growth rates changed. By 2020, more than one-third of Apple's enterprise value was attributed to its future growth.[50] Apple's highly profitable consumer electronics products, coupled with the rapidly growing and very high return on capital services business, combined to give the company unparalleled profitability.

In 2016, the year Berkshire purchased Apple, the company's return on equity was an impressive 37 percent. It reached 90 percent in 2020, and a staggering 147 percent in 2021. Just as impressive, Apple's return on net tangible assets has had a similar trajectory: starting with a 34 percent return in 2016, then reaching 150 percent return on equity by 2021.

How is a company able to achieve triple-digit returns on equity and net tangible assets? First, the rapid increase in returns, year-over-year, can be attributed to the rapid growth of Apple's services, which is a triple-digit return on equity-type business. The second reason, and one that is not fully appreciated, is the fact that Apple has required no tangible equity to operate its business.[51] The company's receivables, inventories, and fixed assets exceed its payables and accruals.

Tenet: Determine the Value

When Todd Finkle brought a group of his Gonzaga University students to visit Warren Buffett in Omaha, he asked, "How do you value a company?" Buffett replied, "The discounted cash flow method,"[52] the same methodology outlined by John Burr Williams, whom Buffett introduced to Berkshire Hathaway shareholders in 1992. Using a two-stage Gordon growth model to value Apple, based on an 8 percent growth rate for the first 10 years, followed by a 2 percent residual growth rate in perpetuity, discounted by 10 percent, Finkle found that Apple was near fair value.[53] Indeed, many dividend discount models that are used to value Apple have struggled to uncover a significant discount to fair value, a margin of safety, when analyzing Apple. Yet, the total return of Apple since year-end 2016 through June 30, 2023, is up 618 percent, for a 35 percent annualized return. Over the same time period the S&P 500 Index gained 123 percent for a 13 percent annualized return. Obviously, the market had mispriced Apple's common shares.

Charlie Munger is cited as saying he never saw Warren Buffett use a formal dividend discount model. Instead, he did most of the calculations in his head, then adjusted the valuation for extraneous elements including management's allocation of capital and other financial factors. We will report the rational capital allocation decisions of Tim Cook in the next section. Here we will examine two additional economic factors that have an enormous impact on valuation beyond what a standard dividend discount model would suggest is a company's intrinsic value.

First is the impact of intangible investing in determining a company's value. Michael Mauboussin, academician, author, and investment strategist, has written extensively on the concept of intangible investing.[54] Mauboussin points out the way a company is able to grow is by generating good returns on investments measured by profits. He reminds us that an investment can be either tangible or intangible. Tangible investments are fixed, hard assets that can be touched and felt. Think brick and mortar, equipment, and trucks. Intangible assets lack a physical existence, such as research and development costs, software, and the chemical compositions of pharmaceuticals.

The distinction between the two, Mauboussin explains, is that with tangible assets, only one company can use the asset at a time. But with intangible assets multitudes can use the asset at the same time. Those companies with intangible assets benefit from strong economies of scale. Think about software. Although it costs a lot to design the original software code, the cost per unit significantly drops as it is inexpensive to share. And millions of customers can use the new software at the same time.

What Mauboussin discovered is that companies that rely on intangible investing are able to grow faster than companies dependent on tangible assets. "As the overall mix of investments shifts from tangible to intangible," says Mauboussin, "we should expect to see faster growth rates for the winners than we have seen in the base rate data."[55] Now think about Apple. As its return on intangibles investments increased at a faster rate than its return on investment from tangibles, the growth rate of the company increased. This will remain true so long as the return from the company's intangible investing remains in high demand and avoids obsolescence. This is particularly relevant as the services part of Apple's business, which relies heavily on intangible investing, becomes a bigger and bigger part of the overall company.

Another important consideration about intangible investing is the accounting treatment of these investments versus tangible investments. Under generally accepted accounting principles (GAAP), born at the beginning of the industrial revolution, a company's cost for tangible investments is not expensed through the income statement, but rather is capitalized on the balance sheet as an asset then depreciated over the life of the tangible asset, sometimes 5, 10, or 20 years depending on the type of investment. Conversely, GAAP rules dictate a company's investment in intangibles must be expensed through the income statement and as a result doesn't appear on the balance sheet. As such, companies with high intangible investments typically trade at higher multiples of earnings and book value compared to a company that relies largely on tangible investments.

What is Apple's annual intangible investment? Approximately $30 billion, all expensed through the income statement and nowhere to be found on the balance sheet. However, the intangible investments do work to increase the intrinsic value of the company. For example, Apple is estimated to earn $95 billion in 2024, or $6.00 per share. At the end of 2023, the stock traded 31 times forward earnings (price-to-earnings ratio), far better than the 20 times earnings estimates of the S&P 500 Index. But if we capitalized the intangible investments and didn't expense them through the income statement, the company would generate $125 billion in income and earn $8.00 in earnings per share selling for 23 times earnings estimates. Even if you depreciated Apple's intangible investments with a five-year life, 2024 earnings would be $119 billion not $95 billion, and forward earnings estimates would be $7.62 per share not $6.00 per share. Apple then would trade at 24 times forward earnings multiple not a 31 times multiple.

Of course, intangible investments, particularly in the case of Apple, can be very profitable, adding to the intrinsic value of the company. But nowhere are Apple's value-creating intangible investments found in the customary GAAP analysis. As Warren Buffett has often counseled, when valuing a company, GAAP accounting is where you begin, not where you end. Mauboussin also points out that the intangible investments for companies in the Russell 3000, which encompasses the vast majority of all US equity stocks, were near $1.8 trillion in 2020, more than twice the level of tangible investing, which totaled $800 billion. For investors, it is important to understand that the stock market, on an accounting basis, is no longer a world where apples are routinely compared to apples.

A second important consideration is understanding the economic impact of return on capital as it relates to intangible investing. "Adjusting for intangible investments has a larger effect on some industries than others," explains Mauboussin. "It is the mix between tangible and intangible investments," he says, that "determines the magnitude of the impact."

Mauboussin points out the return on invested capital (ROIC), adjusting for intangible investing, is higher for industries such as pharmaceutical and biotechnology as well as internet software and services and internet retailing. One thing is for sure, Mauboussin writes, "capitalizing intangible investments lifts the ROIC"[56] for the company.

To better appreciate the valuation differences between companies with a high return on capital and those with a low return on capital, we need to return to Mauboussin. In 1961, finance professors Merton Miller and Franco Modigliani published a paper titled "Dividend Policy, Growth, and the Valuation of Shares." Mauboussin believes this paper "ushered in the modern era of valuation."[57] Miller and Modigliani asked a rather simple question: "What does the market *really* capitalize?" They measured earnings, cash flows, the future opportunities to create value, and dividends. What did they learn? Surprisingly, all these measures collapsed into the same model. The value of a stock, they determined, is the present value of the future free cash flows, just as described by John Burr Williams and seconded by Warren Buffett as the indisputable model for determining intrinsic value. But what was said next warrants our attention.

To help investors grasp the valuation impact for future cash flows, Miller and Modigliani offered a formula that breaks down a company into two parts. The value of a firm (business) is equal to a "steady-state value + future value creation." They define the steady-state value of a company as being equal to the net operating profit after tax (normalized) divided by the cost of capital plus additional cash. Mauboussin explains, "The steady-state value of a firm, calculated using the perpetuity method, assumes the current net operating after tax (NOPAT) is sustainable and that incremental investments will neither add nor subtract value."[58]

Turning to future value creation, Miller and Modigliani calculate a company's future value as the investments the company makes multiplied by its return on capital minus the cost of capital times the competitive advantage period over the cost of capital. Said differently, the positive future value creation of a business becomes the cash it produces over the time, but only if the cash return as a percentage return on the company's invested capital is above the cost of capital. Yes, this is a mouthful. But Miller and Modigliani are simply tabulating the same things Warren Buffett has stated on many occasions. The best business to own, the one that will create the most future value, is a company that generates high returns on incremental capital (above the cost of capital) and then reinvests the cash profits back into the company to continually generate a high return on capital for an extended period of time. It is the compounding effect of companies that generates high returns on capital that is most responsible for building wealth over time.

Next, Mauboussin helps us understand how Miller and Modigliani's future value creation relates to price-to-earnings multiples. The central thesis here is that a company that earns on investment above the cost of capital creates value. A company that earns on investment below the cost of capital destroys shareholder value. And a company that generates returns equal to the cost of capital neither creates nor destroys shareholder value no matter how fast or slowly it grows.[59]

Rarely do investors ever think a rapidly growing business can actually destroy their investment. But consider the following calculations: Assuming an 8 percent cost of capital, all equity financed for a period of 15 years, Mauboussin tells us a company that earns 8 percent on capital is worth a 12.5 price-to-earnings multiple. And no matter whether the company grows at 4 percent per year or 8 percent or 10 percent, its multiple remains the name, neither adding to or subtracting from shareholder value. But a company that earns only 4 percent return on invested capital against a cost of capital of 8 percent is worth only 7.1 times earnings at a 4 percent growth rate, or a 3.3 multiple for a 6 percent growth rate, and then summarily begins destroying shareholder value the faster it grows. Finally, a company that earns 16 percent on invested capital with an 8 percent cost of capital is worth 15.2 times earnings at 4 percent growth rate, 17.1 times at a 6 percent growth rate, 19.4 times at 8 percent growth rate, and 22.4 times at 10 percent growth rate.

Two observations are important to understand. First, a company that earns 100 percent return on invested capital (ROIC) is worth more than a company that earns 15 percent, which is the average ROIC of the S&P 500 Index. Why? Because the company that earns 100 percent return on capital has more money to reinvest back into the business. High return on invested capital acts as a turbocharger for the intrinsic value of a company as long as the incremental returns on investment remain substantially higher than the cost of capital.

The second consideration is the function of sales growth. As noted, if there are two companies earning the same return on capital, but one is growing faster than the other, then the market will more highly value the faster growing company.

Which begs the question: What is Apple worth if it grows at 8 percent earning over 100 percent on invested capital? The first lesson here is that a company with a seemingly high price-to-earnings ratio can actually be a terrific value proposition if its cash returns on capital exceed its cost of capital. And second, once a company earns above the cost of capital, the faster it grows the more valuable it becomes. In a nutshell, when a company earns above the cost of capital, sales growth becomes the toggle switch for determining the growth of intrinsic value.

Let's step back and think about the valuation of Apple. Yes, a standard dividend discount model of Apple's owner earnings growing at 8 percent might not reveal a deeply undervalued stock. But once you adjust for the investment of intangibles and calculate the return on capital of its investment, Apple appears undervalued. And if the services component of the company, which already creates the highest return on capital at the fastest rate, becomes an even bigger part of the business, it's not impossible that Apple's growth of intrinsic value could accelerate even more in the years ahead.

Tenet: Rational Management

Tim Cook joined Apple in 1998 serving as senior vice president for worldwide operations. When Steve Jobs, cofounder of Apple and periodic chairman and CEO of the company, passed away in 2011, Cook was named chief executive officer.

Whereas Steve Jobs's reputation as a leader was that of a tough taskmaster with a penchant for micromanagement, Cook's CEO approach is a more hands-off style; he encouraged and implemented a more collaborative culture at Apple. He once said his leadership focus is on people, strategy, and exaction. And "if you get those three right," he explained, "the world is a great place."[60]

When Tim Cook became CEO in 2011, the market cap of Apple was $350 billion. A dozen years later it was the world's first $3 trillion company. No doubt, Cook's experience and execution for Apple's worldwide operations was, and is, the chief reason why Apple has risen to become the most valuable company in the world. Managing a global technology company with global supply chains is no easy task. But there is another talent Cook possesses that is often overlooked but is just as important in leading to the rise in the value of Apple: the rational allocation of capital as it relates to repurchasing shares of stock, raising the dividend, and managing the balance sheet.

At year-end 2011, Apple had 26.3 billion common shares outstanding. As of September 30, 2023, the company had 15.7 billion shares outstanding. Before Tim Cook, Apple never had a systematic share repurchase program, but under Cook's leadership, the company has embarked on one of the most amazing corporate accomplishments in financial history.

In 11½ years, Apple has bought back 10.6 billion shares of stock, reducing the shares outstanding for the company by 40 percent. In dollar terms, the share repurchase program under Cook has retired $592 billion of stock. To give you an idea, $592 billion of Apple stock is larger than the $468 billion market capitalization of UnitedHealth Group, the ninth-largest company in the S&P 500 Index.[61]

Over this same time period, Apple has paid shareholders $140 billion in dividends, bringing the total return to shareholders, in dividends and repurchased stock, to $732 billion, nearly equal to the market capitalization of Berkshire Hathaway at $784 billion.

The return of $784 billion to shareholders occurred during a time when Apple became the first company to reach $1 trillion, $2 trillion, then $3 trillion in market cap. And if that's not enough, Apple finished the second quarter of 2023 with $110 billion in debt offset by $166 billion in cash, making the company essentially debt free with $56 billion in unencumbered cash on the balance sheet.

No company in history has ever come close to accomplishing the financial returns and objectives of Apple.

Tenet: Favorable Long-Term Prospects

When investors think about a company's long-term favorable prospects, it is best to judge (1) how "sticky" is the existing business, meaning how likely are existing customers to remain customers; (2) the opportunities to gain new customers in new markets with new products; and (3) how willing is management to continue funneling the rewards of the business back to shareholders, the owners of the company.

When asked why invest in Apple, Warren Buffett replied, "In effect we are betting on the ecosystem of Apple products led by the iPhone. And I see characteristics in that that make me think that it's extraordinary."[62] In his unique style, Buffett uses the term *ecosystem* to encapsulate Apple's ability to create competitive advantage by earning high rates of return for longer periods, thereby compounding shareholder wealth. In a word, Apple's ecosystem is Buffett's moat.

In the tech world, an ecosystem would comprise devices that work seamlessly together to enhance a digital experience. Apple's ecosystem is often referred to as a closed ecosystem in that the company has complete control of both the software (iOS system) and the hardware (Macs, iPhone, iPad). Apple's success in creating and strengthening its ecosystem is that it doesn't design around a single device but rather designs its products around the ecosystem. Apple's ability to maintain, develop, and extract value from its ecosystem is what had made it the world's most valuable company.

A distinguishing feature of digital ecosystems is the economic concept of increasing returns, the exact opposite of the law of diminishing returns we have followed for so long. In standard economic theory, that familiar law states that adding one more factor of production while holding constant other factors, namely demand, will at some point yield incremental lower returns per production unit. Said differently, the law of diminishing returns identifies a point at which the level of profits is less than the money invested. There is no more compounding of high returns on capital.

However, there are some companies that exhibit the law of *increasing* returns, meaning the tendency for that which is ahead to get further ahead and for that which loses advantage to lose further advantage. Diminishing returns are a feature of the brick-and-mortar world, whereas increasing returns are associated with the knowledge-based world.[63]

The principle of increasing returns is especially significant in the technology-digital industries. Companies that are experiencing increasing returns have certain attributes that further solidify their dominance within an industry. Collectively, those attributes create what is known as the *network effect*. People prefer to be connected to a larger network than to a smaller one. If there are two competing networks, one with 25 million members and one with 5 million members, a new member will tend to select the larger network because it is more likely to fulfill their need for connections to other members, offering more services and benefits.

A distinguishing trait of the network effect is that a product or service gains in value as more and more people use it. We might say that network effects are, in effect, demand-side economies of scale. So for network effects to take hold, it is important to get big fast. This thwarts the competition from becoming established.

What is interesting about studying network effects is understanding the powerful psychological forces that are in play once an individual joins a network. It begins with *positive feedback*. Positive experiences give us pleasure or satisfaction, and we want to relive them. Someone who has a positive experience when using a technology product (iPhone, iPad, Apple Watch) will have the tendency to return to the product. Another behavioral component of human psychology as it relates to technology investing is called *lock-in.* When we learn one way of doing something, we have little interest in learning another. Technology products, specifically software operating systems, can be difficult to master in the beginning. Once we have become proficient using a certain product or software, we fiercely resist changing to another. Closely related to lock-in is *path dependency*—whereby we become more comfortable repeating the same technological tasks. Consumers become satisfied with how they use technology, even if a competitor's product is deemed superior and less expensive.

All these factors—network effects, positive feedback, lock-in, and path dependency—result in high *switching costs*. Sometimes switching costs are literal, as when switching technologies and software costs so much money that customers can't be persuaded to change. But in many cases, any of those attributes, especially in combination with others, can create in customers a psychological dissuasion that is a form of high switching costs.

Now, with this being said, step back and think about the two billion Apple users of its products, one billion of whom also subscribe to Apple's services. How willing are they to dispose of their current products to incur the cost of a new and different product that will require them to learn a new operating system?

Warren Buffett taught us the best business with the best long-term prospects is called a *franchise*—a company that sells a product or service that is needed or desired and has no close substitute. Buffett also said he believed the next great fortunes would be made by investors who identify new franchises. With all we have learned about Apple's features and benefits, coupled with the psychological resistance that comes from switching products, there is a strong belief that Apple is the modern-day equivalent of Buffett's franchise factor.

Still, it is not enough simply to pacify existing customers when building a company's intrinsic value. Attention must also be paid to introducing newer, better products and services and attacking new markets. Apple has not only become a leading innovator of new electronic devices but it also has slavishly worked to introduce new and better versions of its existing products. Between 2007 and 2023, Apple released 38 different iPhone models, including the new iPhone 15 and iPhone 15 Pro in September 2023. It designed and improved 38 different iPad models, three generations of AirPods, and the Apple Watch, plus six different Mac laptops. And in 2024, Apple will begin selling the Apple Vision Pro, a mixed-reality headset, its first product in another major category since the Apple Watch in 2015.

Apple's services business, along with the App Store, continues to grow at double-digit rates. The services business generates hefty profit margins of 71 percent, roughly double Apple's hardware division. Lucas Maestri, Apple's chief financial officer, said, "The service business is important in many ways for us. It strengthens our ecosystem [and] it's important because it makes the overall business less dependent on the performance of our products."[64] When the sales of iPhones or iPads slow due to a slowing economy or a pause before new versions of the product are introduced, it is the services business that continues to motor Apple ahead. Not to be left behind, Apple has continued to work, quietly, on artificial intelligence (AI) tools that can compete with OpenAI and others. The company, not surprisingly, has built its own framework to create large language models for its ecosystem.

Setting aside new products, new services, and the advent of artificial intelligence, perhaps the biggest and most exciting near-term opportunity for Apple is new markets. At the end of 2023 the Americas represented 42 percent of Apple's revenues, Europe 25 percent, China 20 percent, and the rest of Asia Pacific 13 percent. Buried at the bottom of the Asia Pacific market is India, which had accounted for just 2 percent of Apple's revenue with a run rate of about $6 billion. But not for long. India is the world's most populated country, the world's largest democracy, and by 2027, it is forecast to become the third-largest economy in the world, behind the US and China. On April 18, 2023, Apple opened its first Apple Store in Mumbai and two days later its second store in New Delhi. India is the most important opportunity for Apple during the next 15 years, with economic potential compared to that of China 15 years ago.

Last, Apple shareholders stand to benefit from all the favorable long-term prospects for the company but can also take comfort that Tim Cook will continue to channel the rewards of being an Apple shareholder back to its owners. One year after introducing a $90 billion stock buyback program in 2022, Apple announced as part of its financial results for the second quarter of 2023, another repurchase program. "Given our confidence in Apple's future and the value we see in our stock," said Maestri, "our Board has authorized an additional $90 billion for share repurchases."[65]

Errors of Omission and Second Chances

Buffett met Jeff Bezos soon after Amazon went public. In 2003, Berkshire owned $459 million in Amazon bonds. At the time Buffett bought only three things via the internet: *The Wall Street Journal*, online bridge, and books from Amazon. "I don't know if Amazon is going to weigh 150 pounds or 300 pounds," said Buffett, "but one thing I do know is that they are not anorexic. Here is a guy [Bezos] who took something that is right in front of us—selling books—and put it together with new technology to create, in a couple of years, one the biggest brand names in the world."[66]

Fifteen years later, Buffett was still singing Bezos's praise. It is Olympic for someone to build from scratch a business that became the biggest in the world. Bezos, Buffett noted, had done it twice, first with online retailing and then later with Amazon Web Services (AWS), the world's largest on-demand cloud computing platforms for individuals, companies, and governments on a metered pay-as-you-go basis. "I have always admired Jeff," Buffett said. "I've been an idiot for not buying. I always thought he was special, but I didn't realize you could go from books to what happened here. He had vision and executed in in an incredible way."[67]

Charlie Munger was more reserved. "We are a bit older than most," said Munger, "and we are not as flexible as others." Buffett added that he and Munger grew up studying John Rockefeller and Andrew Carnegie, two of the 20th century's greatest industrialists and richest men in history. They could have never predicted someone could build a trillion-dollar business generating billions in earnings with so little capital employed. It was unimaginable.

At the same meeting, Munger gave himself a pass for not buying Amazon, but he said he "felt like a horse's ass for not buying Google." Now called Alphabet, Google went public in 2004 at $85 per share and today is one of the world's largest companies, worth over $1 trillion. For years, Buffett and Munger watched GEICO send checks to Google to pay for the clicks consumers hit on the search engine to learn about GEICO insurance. "We just sat on our hands," Munger said, his version of what Buffett sometimes calls errors of omission. Then he added, "Maybe Apple is our atonement."[68]

The Value of Retained Earnings

In the 1980 Berkshire Hathaway Annual Report, Buffett states, "*The value to Berkshire Hathaway of retained earnings is not determined by whether we own 100%, 50%, 20% or 1% of the business in which they reside. Rather, the value of those retained earnings is determined by the use to which they are put and the subsequent level of earnings by that usage.*"[69]

In general, italics are widely used for emphasis—to draw attention to some particular part of text, to ensure it stands out from surrounding sentences. But Buffett doesn't often use italics when writing his chairman's letter, so when he does, it's important. It behooves us, therefore, to read carefully anything he italicizes and then import his words into our own thinking.

In this report, Buffett began with a short tutorial on GAAP as it relates to the consolidation of sales, expenses, and earnings of businesses under different ownerships. In admittedly simplistic terms, Buffett explained that for businesses in which Berkshire owns greater than 50 percent of the shares, the proportional earnings of each business flow directly into Berkshire's reported operating earnings. However, in noncontrolled businesses (less than 20 percent owned), it is only the dividends received (if paid) that Berkshire gets to report.

Buffett described the year 1980 as "unusual" for Berkshire for one simple reason: it was the first year "to produce an unusual result. The large increase in our [noncontrolled] holdings [common stocks], plus the growth of earnings experienced by those partially owned companies—earnings that these companies retained last year (not paid as dividends) exceeded the total reported annual operating earnings of Berkshire Hathaway."[70]

Said differently, the proportional retained earnings of Berkshire Hathaway's common stock portfolio was higher than the earnings of Berkshire's wholly owned businesses. The dramatic increase in the prosperity of Berkshire's insurance operations, the result of rapid growth in insurance policies, meant that Buffett had greatly enlarged the common stock portfolio on the back of increasing premiums—the insurance float. As a result, and because of GAAP accounting, Buffett pointed out this "only allows less than half of our earnings 'iceberg' to appear above the surface, in plain view." In a sign of things to come for Berkshire, Buffett forewarned that "within the corporate world such a result is quite rare; in our case it is likely recurring."[71]

Buffett next reassured Berkshire shareholders there was no need to be alarmed: "Because Berkshire's concentration of resources in the insurance field produces a corresponding concentration of its assets in [common stocks], many of these companies pay out relatively small portions of their earnings in dividends. This means that only a small portion of their earnings power is recorded in our own current operating earnings."

But fear not, said Buffett. "While our reported operating earnings reflect only the dividends received from such companies [commons stocks], our economic well-being is determined by their earnings, not their dividends."

To illuminate his point, he told Berkshire shareholders, "If a tree grows in the forest partially owned by us, but we don't record the growth in our financial statement, we still own part of the tree."[72] Forty years later, Buffett was preaching the same sermon for the benefit of new Berkshire shareholders and older shareholders alike: the value of retained earnings.

In the 2019 Berkshire Hathaway Annual Report, Buffett introduced Edgar Lawrence Smith. A Harvard-educated economist and then an investment manager, at the brokerage firm Low, Dixon & Company, Smith fully accepted the then-dominant view that bonds were the better long-term investment than stocks. But all that changed when he began writing the book for which we know him today: *Common Stocks as Long Term Investments,* published in 1924. In it, Smith revealed he had been unable to find any 20-year period within which a diversified portfolio of common stocks did not generate better returns than a similar diversified portfolio of bonds. At the time, this was a truly radical idea, for it was universally agreed that long-term bonds were superior to stocks, and it gained Smith a great deal of attention.

John Maynard Keynes, the well-known English economist and philosopher, was among the many who reviewed the book. Clearly impressed, he soon thereafter invited Smith to join the prestigious Royal Economic Society. In the review, Keynes wrote:

> I have kept until last what is perhaps Mr. Smith's most important and certainly most novel point. Well-managed industrial companies do not, as a rule, distribute to the shareholders the whole of their earned profits. In good years, if not all years, they retain a part of their profits and put them back into the business. Thus *there is an element of compound interest* operating in favor of a sound industrial investment. Over a period of years, the real value of the property of a sound industrial is increasing at a compound interest, quite apart from the dividends paid out to the shareholders."[73]

"And with that sprinkling of holy water," said Buffett, "Smith was no longer obscure."[74]

Buffett admitted that he was baffled why the idea of compounding retained earnings, which can lead to increasing shareholder value, seems totally lost on investors. Buffett wrote: "After all, it was no secret that mind-boggling wealth had earlier been amassed by such titans as Carnegie, Rockefeller, and Ford, all of whom had retained a huge portion of their business earnings to fund growth and produce ever greater profits. Throughout America, there had long been small-time capitalists who became rich following the same playbook."[75]

For over 65 years, Warren Buffett has steadfastly pointed out there is no difference in his mind between investing in common stocks and owning 100 percent of a company: "Charlie and I do not view [Berkshire's portfolio of common stocks] as a collection of stock market wagers—dalliances to be terminated because of downgrades by 'the street,' an earnings miss, expected Federal Reserve actions, possible political developments, forecasts by economists, or whatever else might be the subject *du jour*."[76]

At Berkshire Hathaway, there is no investing difference, intellectually speaking, between owning See's Candies and Apple, other than See's Candies does not have a stock price and its earnings are 100 percent tallied by Berkshire, compared to Apple, which has a stock price but its earnings are not additive to Berkshire's GAAP earnings per share. Buffett explains further: "As I have emphasized before, Charlie and I view Berkshire's holdings of marketable securities as a collection of *businesses*. Although we don't control the operations of our common stock holdings nor get accounting benefit (with the exception of dividends), we do share proportionately in their long-term prosperity."[77]

"What's out of sight," said Buffett, "should *not* be out of mind: Those unrecorded retained earnings are usually building value—*lots* of value—for Berkshire." It's a lesson that is often overlooked by individual investors who own common stocks, particularly those who don't stick around long enough to benefit from the compounding effect of retained earnings. "As we have pointed out [before]," explained Buffett, "retained earnings have propelled American business throughout our country's history. What worked for Carnegie and Rockefeller has, over the years, worked its magic for millions of shareholders as well."[78]

CHAPTER 5

Managing a Portfolio of Businesses

Warren Buffett does not practice portfolio management, at least not in the traditional sense. Contemporary portfolio managers are acutely aware of the number of stocks they own, the weightings of each stock, industry and sector diversification, and the up-to-the-minute performance of their portfolio relative to a performance benchmark. Most portfolio managers equally weight the dollar amount of their individual stocks. They are also focused on how much money they have invested in various industries including consumer cyclicals, consumer staples, health care, financials, technology, industrials, energy, materials, and utilities. Buffett knows all these statistics, too, but he does not waste time thinking about it.

Hollywood has given us a visual cliché of the modern-day portfolio manager at work. Phone stuck to their ear, eyes glued to a computer screen watching intensely the red and green flashes of ever-changing prices. Showing pained expressions whenever one of those computer blinks shows even a minuscule drop in a stock price. Warren Buffett is far from that kind of frenzy. Soft-spoken, he moves with the calm that comes with great confidence. He has no need to watch multiple computer screens; the minute-by-minute changes in the market are of no interest to him. Buffett does not think in minutes, hours, days, weeks, or months, but in years. He doesn't need to constantly monitor hundreds of companies, because his common stock portfolio contains only a select few. "We just focus on a few outstanding companies," he once said.[1] This approach, called *focus investing*, greatly simplifies the task of portfolio management and increases the probability of generating above-average, market-beating returns.

Focus investing is a remarkably simple idea, and yet, like most simple ideas, it rests on a complex foundation of interlocking concepts. In this chapter, we look more closely at the effects focus investing produces. The goal here is to give you a new way of thinking about portfolio management, the one described by Warren Buffett. Fair warning: In all likelihood, this unique approach to portfolio management is the opposite of what you have always been taught about investing in the stock market.

Portfolio Management Today: A Choice of Two

The current state of portfolio management is locked into a tug-of-war between two competing strategies: (1) active portfolio management and (2) index investing.

Active portfolio managers constantly buy and sell stocks. A typical mutual fund owns over 100 stocks with portfolio turnover ratios north of 100 percent, meaning that most mutual funds are buying and selling their entire portfolios every year. This frenetic buying and selling is an attempt to keep their clients satisfied, because on any given day a client is likely to ask, "How is my portfolio doing; is it beating the market?" If the answer is "yes," clients typically leave their money with the portfolio manager. If not, a portfolio manager risks losing clients and assets under management.

Index investing, by contrast, is a buy-and-hold approach. It involves assembling and then holding a broadly diversified portfolio of stocks deliberately designed to mimic the behavior of a specific benchmark, such as the Standard & Poor's 500 Index. In that example, the investor would end up owning 500 companies.

Active portfolio managers argue that, by virtue of their superior stock-picking skills, they can outperform an index fund.

Index strategists, for their part, have history on their side. The latest statistics reveal that over a three-year period, 79 percent of active mangers underperform their benchmarks; 88 percent over five years; and 93 percent over 10 years.[2] Active portfolio managers with high investment management fees and high transactions costs from constantly buying and selling stocks have a high hurdle to overcome in order to beat the market—even before they get a payoff from stock selection. Index investors with low transaction costs and rock-bottom management fees have demonstrably fewer expenses. But take note of this: Even though an index fund, with minimum expenses, will never do much worse than the index it mimics, it also can never beat the market.

From the investor's point of view, the underlying attraction of both strategies is the same: minimize risk through diversification. By holding a large number of stocks representing many industries and sectors of the market, investors hope to create a warm blanket of protection against the horrific loss that could occur if they had all their money in one area of the market that suffered a disaster. In a normal period (so the thinking goes), some stocks in a diversified portfolio will go down and others will go up, and let's keep our fingers crossed that the latter compensates for the former.

We have all heard the mantra of *diversification* for so long that we have become intellectually numb to its inevitable results: mediocre investment returns. Although it is true that both active and index portfolios offer diversification, in general neither strategy generates exceptional performance. The questions investors must ask themselves are, Am I satisfied with average returns? Can I do better?

What does Warren Buffett say about the ongoing debate regarding index versus active portfolio management strategy? Given these two choices, Buffett unhesitatingly recommends indexing, especially if the hypothetical investor is nervous about the inherent short-term price volatility of most stocks, or might know very little about the economics of the businesses they own, or both. "By periodically investing in an index fund," said Buffett, "the know-nothing investor can actually outperform most investment professionals."[3]

However, Buffett is quick to point out there is a third alternative, a very different kind of active portfolio management strategy that significantly increases the odds of beating the market.

A Third Choice: Focus Investing

In Berkshire Hathaway's 1991 Annual Report Warren Buffett explained how he approaches portfolio management: "If my universe of business possibilities was limited, say, to private companies in Omaha, I would, first, try to assess the long-term economic characteristics of each business; second, assess the quality of the people in charge of running it; and third, try to buy into a few of the best operations at a sensible price. I certainly would not wish to own an equal part of every business in town. Why, then, should Berkshire take a different tack when dealing with larger universe of public companies?"[4]

The portfolio management approach at Berkshire Hathaway is called *focus investing*, and its essence can be stated quite simply: Choose a few outstanding businesses that are likely to produce above-average economic returns over the long haul, concentrate the bulk of your portfolio in the common shares of these businesses, and have the fortitude to hold steady during periods of short-term market volatility.

The Warren Buffett Way tenets, if followed closely, inevitably lead the investor to good companies that make sense for a focus portfolio. "Charlie and I are *not* stock pickers," said Buffett. "We are business pickers. We own publicly traded stocks based on our expectations about their long-term *business* performance, not because we view them as vehicles for adroit purchases and sales."[5] That crisp description of the key difference between a "business picker" versus a "stock picker" is critical to understanding why someone would choose to manage a focus portfolio versus a broadly diversified portfolio.

Thirty years ago, Warren Buffett wrote, "We continually search for large businesses with understandable, enduring and mouth-watering economics that are run by able and shareholder-oriented managements. This focus doesn't guarantee results: We both have to buy at a sensible price and get business performance from our companies that validates our assessment. But this investment approach—searching for superstars—offers us our only chance for real success."[6]

Buffett then confessed, "Charlie and I are simply not smart enough, considering the large sums we work with, to get real results by adroitly buying and selling portions of far-from-great businesses. Nor do we think many others can achieve long-term investment success by flitting from flower to flower. Indeed, we believe that according the name 'investors' to institutions that trade actively is like calling someone who repeatedly engages in one-night stands a romantic."[7]

Remember Buffett's advice to a "know-nothing" investor: to stay with index funds? What is more interesting is what he said next: "If you are a *know-something* investor, able to understand business economics and to find five to ten sensibly priced companies that possess important long-term competitive advantages, conventional diversification makes no sense for you. It is apt simply to hurt your results and increase your risk. I cannot understand why an investor of that sort elects to put money into a business that is his 20th favorite rather than simply adding that money to his top choices—the businesses he understands the best and that present the least risk, along with the greatest profit potential."[8]

In Buffett's opinion, investors are better served if they concentrate on a few spectacular investments rather than jumping from one mediocre idea to another. He believes that his success can be traced to a few outstanding investments. If, over his career, you eliminate one dozen of Buffett's best decisions, his investment performance would be no better than average. To avoid becoming average while increasing the odds of generating above-average investment results, Buffett recommends that "an investor should act as though he had a lifetime decision card with just twenty punches on it. With every investment decision his card is punched, and he has one fewer available for the rest of his life."[9] If investors were restrained in this way, Buffett figures that they would wait patiently until a great opportunity surfaced.

There is another demerit associated with conventional diversification. It greatly increases the chance you will have purchased a company without knowing much about the business. Buffett references John Maynard Keynes, economist and one of the first focus investors, on this point. Buffett wrote, "John Maynard Keynes, whose brilliance as a practicing investor matched his brilliance in thought, wrote a letter to a business associate, F. C. Scott, on August 15, 1934, that says it all." Buffett quoted from Keynes' letter:

> As time goes on, I get more and more convinced that the right method in investment is to put fairly large sums into an enterprise which one thinks one knows something about and in the management of which one thoroughly believes. It is a mistake to think that one limits one's risk by spreading too much between enterprises about which one knows little and has no reason for special confidence. . . . One's knowledge and experience are definitely limited and there is seldom more than two or three enterprises at any given time in which I personally feel myself entitled to put *full* confidence."[10]

Philip Fisher, whose impact on Buffett's thinking has been duly noted, was also well known for his focus portfolios. He always preferred owning a small number of outstanding companies that he understood well rather than owning a large number of them, many of which he understood poorly. Fisher began his investment counseling business shortly after the 1929 stock market crash, and he remembers how important it was to produce good results. "Back then, there was no room for mistakes. I knew the more I understood about the company the better off I would be."[11] As a general rule, Fisher limited his portfolio to fewer than 10 companies, of which three to four often represented 75 percent of the total investment.

"It never seems to occur to [investors], much less their advisors," Fisher wrote in *Common Stocks and Uncommon Profits*, "that buying a company without having sufficient knowledge of it may be even more dangerous than having inadequate diversification."[12] At age 91,

Managing a Portfolio of Businesses 169

Fisher had not changed his mind. "Great stocks are extremely hard to find," he said. "If they weren't, then everyone would own them. I knew I wanted to own the best of them or none at all."[13] You could summarize Fisher's portfolio management approach as "based on an unusual but insightful notion that less was more."[14]

Fisher's influence on Buffett can be seen in his belief that when you encounter a handsome, profitable investment, the only reasonable course is to make a large investment. Buffett echoed this thinking, writing in 1978, "Our policy is to concentrate our holdings. We try to avoid buying a little of this or that when we are only lukewarm about the business or its price." Instead, he explained, "When we are convinced as to the attractiveness, we believe in buying worthwhile amounts."[15] He later said, "With each investment you make, you should have the courage and conviction to place at least 10 percent of your net worth in the stock."[16]

Over the years, we can cite several occasions when Buffett bet not only 10 percent of his portfolio on a single stock but also, in some cases, significantly more. In 1963, he invested 25 percent of the Buffett Limited Partnership's assets in American Express, which netted $20 million in profits. In 1974, he invested more than 20 percent of Berkshire Hathaway's stock portfolio in the Washington Post Company. By 1976, he invested 25 percent of the portfolio in GEICO's common and preferred shares. In 1989, he invested $1 billion in the Coca-Cola Company, representing slightly over 30 percent of Berkshire's portfolio. Then, in 2018, perhaps Warren Buffett's most aggressive purchase was the $35 billion investment in Apple, which represented more than 20 percent of Berkshire's $172 billion portfolio. Hard to fathom any other portfolio manager would have made such a large single bet. Nor that any other portfolio manager with $172 billion under management would own only 15 major positions, as was the case for Berkshire's common stock portfolio at year-end 2018.

To this, Buffett responds, "The strategy we've adopted precludes our following standard diversification dogma. Many pundits would therefore say the strategy must be riskier than that employed by conventional investors. We disagree. We believe that a policy of concentration may well *decrease* risk if it raises, as it should, both the intensity with which an investor thinks about a business and the comfort level he must feel with its economic characteristics before buying into it."[17]

In addition to managing a concentrated portfolio, much of Warren Buffett's success is attributed to his portfolio inactivity. He is content not purchasing or selling a single share of Berkshire's major holdings throughout the year. "Lethargy bordering on sloth," he once quipped, "remains the cornerstone of our investment style."[18] He thus nimbly reminds us that hyperactive investing is the pickpocket that reduces an investor's return. High portfolio turnover ratios increase transaction costs and increase taxes paid which, in turn, works to reduce the compounding effect of buying and holding great companies. As we will learn, a carefully concentrated portfolio, in combination with a low-turnover discipline, works best for building long-term wealth.

The Superinvestors of Buffettville

Although Warren Buffett has been a dedicated focus investor since launching the Buffett Partnership in 1956, I believe it can be useful to examine the performance returns and portfolio attributes of other like-minded focus investors including Charlie Munger; Bill Ruane, who managed the Sequoia Fund; and Lou Simpson, who managed the investment portfolio at GEICO.[19] And, of course, Warren Buffett himself. Each ran concentrated, low-turnover portfolios. From their performance records there is much we can learn about focus investing. But before we start this investigation, let us begin with the very first focus investor.

John Maynard Keynes as Investor

Most people recognize John Maynard Keynes for his contributions to economic theory. What they may not know is that in addition to being a great macroeconomic thinker, Keynes was a legendary investor. Proof of his investment prowess can be found in the performance record of the Chest Fund at King's College in Cambridge.

Managing a Portfolio of Businesses 171

Prior to 1920, King's College investments were restricted to fixed-income securities. However, when Keynes was appointed the second bursar, in late 1919, he persuaded the trustees to begin a separate fund that would contain only common stocks, currencies, and commodity futures. This separate account became the Chest Fund. From 1927, when he was named first bursar, until his death in 1946, Keynes had sole responsibility for this portfolio.

In 1938, Keynes prepared a full policy report for the Chest Fund, outlining his investment principles:

1. A careful selection of a *few* [emphasis mine] investments having regard to their cheapness in relation to their probable actual and potential *intrinsic* value over a period of years ahead and in relation to alternative investments at the time;
2. A steadfast holding of these fairly large units through thick and thin, perhaps for several years, until either they have fulfilled their promise or it is evident that they were purchased on a mistake;
3. A *balanced* investment position, i.e., a variety of risks in spite of individual holdings being *large* [emphasis mine], and if possible opposed risks.[20]

My reading of Keynes' investment policy suggests he was a focus investor. He purposely limited his stocks to a select few and relied on fundamental analysis to estimate the value of his investments relative to price. His preference was to manage a low-turnover, big-bet portfolio. But he also recognized the importance of diversifying his risks. His strategy was to invest in high-quality, predictable businesses with a variety of economic outlooks.

How well did Keynes perform? A quick study of Table 5.1 reveals his stock selection and portfolio management skills were outstanding. During the 18-year period, the Chest Fund achieved an average annual return of 13.2 percent compared to the UK market return, which was flat. Considering the time period included both the Great Depression and World War II, we can say that Keynes's performance record was extraordinary.

Table 5.1 John Maynard Keynes: Annual Investment Performance History

Year	Chest Fund (%)	UK Market (%)
1928	0.0	0.1
1929	0.8	6.6
1930	−32.4	−20.3
1931	−24.6	−25.0
1932	44.8	−5.8
1933	35.1	21.5
1934	33.1	−0.7
1935	44.3	5.3
1936	56.0	10.2
1937	8.5	−0.5
1938	−40.1	−16.1
1939	12.9	−7.2
1940	−15.6	−12.9
1941	33.5	12.5
1942	−0.9	0.8
1943	53.9	15.6
1944	14.5	5.4
1945	14.6	0.8
Average Return	13.2	−0.5
Standard Deviation	29.2	12.4
Minimum	−40.1	−25.0
Maximum	56.0	21.5

Even so, the Chest Fund endured some painful periods. In three separate years (1930, 1938, and 1940), the portfolio declined significantly more than the overall UK market. From the large swings in the Fund's fortunes, it is obvious that the Fund must have been more volatile than the market.[21] Indeed, if we measured the standard deviation of the Chest Fund, we find it was almost two and a half times more volatile than the general market. Without a doubt, investors in the Fund received a "bumpy ride" but, in the end, they outscored the market by a large margin.

Lest you think Keynes, with his macroeconomic background, possessed market timing skills, take further note of his investment policy:

> We have not proved able to take much advantage of a general systematic movement out of and into ordinary shares as a whole at different phases of the trade cycle. As a result of these experiences I am clear that the idea of wholesale shifts is for various reasons impracticable and indeed undesirable. Most of those who sell too late and buy too late, and do both too often, incur heavy expenses and develop too unsettled and speculative a state of mind, which, if it is widespread has besides the grave social disadvantage of aggravating the scale of the fluctuations.[22]

Buffett Partnership, Ltd.

The Buffett Partnership operated between 1957 and 1969, and its returns were both remarkable and somewhat abnormal. Remarkable in that Buffett creamed the Dow Jones Industrial Average's average annual return by 22 percentage points net return to partners over the period. Abnormal in that he beat the Dow 13 consecutive years without one negative yearly return and, to boot, was able to achieve these returns with less volatility. Note that in Table 5.2, Buffett's standard deviation, which is another way to express volatility, was lower than the Dow's. In his typical self-effacing way, Buffett remarked, "I think that any way you figure it, it has been satisfactory."[23]

How did he do it? How did he manage to avoid the volatility that is associated with focused portfolios? Two possible explanations come to mind. First, he owned stocks whose prices moved in dissimilar fashion, although I am sure his objective was not to purposely construct a low-variance portfolio, but rather a portfolio that was designed to be economically diverse. Another possible explanation, which is far more likely, is that Buffett's careful and disciplined approach to purchasing only

Table 5.2 Buffett Partnership, Ltd.: Annual Investment Performance History

	Annual Percentage Change	
Year	Overall Partnership (%)	Dow Jones Industrial Average (%)
1957	10.4	−8.4
1958	40.9	38.5
1959	25.9	20.0
1960	22.8	−6.2
1961	45.9	22.4
1962	13.9	−7.6
1963	38.7	20.6
1964	27.8	18.7
1965	47.2	14.2
1966	20.4	−15.6
1967	35.9	19.0
1968	58.8	7.7
1969	6.8	−11.6
Average Return	30.4	8.6
Standard Deviation	15.7	16.7
Minimum	6.8	−15.6
Maximum	58.8	38.5

stocks that demonstrated a significant discount to their intrinsic value worked to limit his downside price risk while giving the partnership all the upside benefits.

Charles Munger Partnership

Warren Buffett is often called the world's greatest investor, and that title is richly deserved. However, the outstanding record that Berkshire Hathaway has earned over the years comes not only from Buffett but also from the wise counsel of his business partner and vice chairman, Charlie Munger. Although Berkshire's investment performance is assigned to its chairman, we should never forget that Charlie was an outstanding investor himself. Shareholders who

Table 5.3 Charlie Munger Partnership: Annual Investment Performance History

	Annual Percentage Change	
Year	Overall Partnership (%)	Dow Jones Industrial Average (%)
1962	30.1	−7.6
1963	71.7	20.6
1964	49.7	18.7
1965	8.4	14.2
1966	12.4	−15.8
1967	56.2	19.0
1968	40.4	7.7
1969	28.3	−11.6
1970	−0.1	8.7
1971	25.4	9.8
1972	8.3	18.2
1973	−31.9	−13.1
1974	−31.5	−23.1
1975	73.2	44.4
Average Return	24.3	6.4
Standard Deviation	33.0	18.5
Minimum	−31.9	−23.1
Maximum	73.2	44.4

have attended Berkshire's annual meetings or have read Charlie's thoughts in various interviews realize both the breadth and depth of his intellect.

Charlie Munger was trained as a lawyer and, at the time he and Buffett met, had a thriving law practice in Los Angeles. However, Buffett convinced Charlie to take up investing, and the results of his talents can be found in Table 5.3. "His portfolio was concentrated in very few securities and therefore, his record was much more volatile," Buffett explained, "but it was based on the same discount-from-value approach."

Charlie was a value investor who favored better businesses over cheap stocks. But he would only look at companies that were selling below their intrinsic value. "He was willing to accept greater peaks and valleys in performance," said Buffett, "and he happens to be a fellow whose psyche goes toward concentration."[24]

Notice that Buffett does not use the word *risk* in describing Charlie's performance. Using the standard investment management definition of risk (price volatility), it could be said that Charlie's partnership was extremely risky, with a standard deviation almost twice that of the market. But beating the average annual return of the market by 18 percentage points was the act not of a risky individual, but that of an astute investor who was able to focus on a few outstanding stocks that were selling below intrinsic value.

Sequoia Fund

Warren Buffett first met Bill Ruane in 1951, when both were taking Ben Graham's security analysis course at Columbia University. The two classmates stayed in touch, and Buffett watched Ruane's investment performance over the years with admiration. When Buffett closed his partnership in 1969, he contacted Ruane. "I asked Bill if he would set up a fund to handle all of our partners, so he set up the Sequoia Fund."

Both men knew it was a difficult time to start a mutual fund, but Ruane plunged ahead. The stock market was splitting into a two-tier market. Most of the hot money was gravitating towards the "nifty fifty," popular names such as IBM, Polaroid, and Xerox, leaving classic value stocks far behind. Although, as Buffett pointed out, comparative performance for value investors was difficult in the beginning, "I am happy to say that my partners, to an amazing degree, not only stayed with him but added money, with happy results."[25]

The Sequoia Fund was a true pioneer, the first mutual fund run on the principles of focus investing. The early public records of Sequoia's holdings demonstrated clearly that Ruane and his partner, Rick Cuniff, managed a tightly focused, low-turnover portfolio. On average, Sequoia owned between 6 and 10 companies that represented well over 90 percent of the portfolio. Even so,

Managing a Portfolio of Businesses   177

the economic diversity of the portfolio was, and continued to be, broad. Ruane often pointed out that even though Sequoia was a focused portfolio, it owned a variety of businesses, including commercial banks, pharmaceuticals, and automobile and property casualty insurance.

Bill Ruane's point of view was, in many ways, unique among mutual fund managers. Generally speaking, most investing begins with some preconceived notion about portfolio management and then fills in the portfolio with various stocks from different industries and sectors. At Ruane, Cuniff, and Company, they began with the idea of selecting the best businesses and then let the portfolio form around those selections.

Selecting the best possible companies, of course, requires a high level of research; here again, Ruane, Cuniff and Company stood apart from the rest of the industry. The firm built a reputation as one of the brightest shops in money management. It eschewed Wall Street's broker-fed research reports and, instead, relied on its own intensive company investigations. "We don't go in much for titles at our firm," Ruane once said, "[but] if we did my business card would read 'Bill Ruane, Research Analyst."

Such thinking is unusual on Wall Street, explained Ruane: "Typically, people start out their career in an 'analyst' function but aspire to get promoted to the more prestigious 'portfolio management' designation, which is considered to be a distinct and higher function. To the contrary, we have always believed that if you are a long-term investor, the analyst function is paramount and the portfolio management follows naturally."[26]

How well did this unique approach serve the fund's shareholders? Table 5.4 outlines the investment performance of Sequoia Fund from 1971 through 1997.

During this period, Sequoia earned an average annual return of 19.6 percent compared to the 14.5 percent of the S&P 500. Similar to other focus portfolios, Sequoia achieved this above-average return with a slightly bumpier ride. During this period, the standard deviation of the stock market (which, you remember, is one way to express price volatility) was 16.4 percent compared to Sequoia's

Table 5.4 Sequoia Fund, Inc.: Annual Investment Performance History

Year	Sequoia Fund (%)	S&P 500 (%)
1971	13.5	14.3
1972	3.7	18.9
1973	−24.0	−14.8
1974	−15.7	−26.4
1975	60.5	37.2
1976	72.3	23.6
1977	19.9	−7.4
1978	23.9	6.4
1979	12.1	18.2
1980	12.6	32.3
1981	21.5	−5.0
1982	31.2	21.4
1983	27.3	22.4
1984	18.5	6.1
1985	28.0	31.6
1986	13.3	18.6
1987	7.4	5.2
1988	11.1	16.5
1989	27.9	31.6
1990	−3.8	−3.1
1991	40.0	30.3
1992	9.4	7.6
1993	10.8	10.0
1994	3.3	1.4
1995	41.4	37.5
1996	21.7	22.9
1997	42.3	33.4
Average Return	19.6	14.5
Standard Deviation	20.6	16.4
Minimum	−24.0	−26.4
Maximum	72.3	37.5

20.6 percent. Some might call that higher risk, but given the care and due diligence at Ruane, Cuniff, and Company in selecting companies, the conventional definition of risk (that it equals price volatility) does not apply here.

Lou Simpson: GEICO

In addition to Berkshire Hathaway acquiring the automobile insurer GEICO, Buffett was fortunate to acquire the talents of Lou Simpson to manage GEICO's investment portfolio. We took note of Simpson's qualifications in Chapter 4. Similar to Buffett, Simpson was a voracious reader who ignored Wall Street research, preferring instead to spend his time reading annual reports. His common stock selection process was similar to Buffett's. He purchased only high-return businesses that were run by able managers and were available at reasonable prices. Simpson has something else in common with Buffett. He focused his portfolio on a few stocks. GEICO's billion-dollar equity portfolio customarily owned fewer than 10 stocks.

Between 1980 and 1996, the equity returns in GEICO's portfolio achieved an average annual return of 24.7 percent compared to the market's return of 17.8 percent (see Table 5.5). "These are not only terrific figures," said Buffett, "but, fully as important, they were achieved in the right way. Lou consistently invested in undervalued common stocks that, individually, were unlikely to present him with a permanent loss and that, collectively, were close to risk free."[27] Once again, in Buffett's mind, the estimate of risk has nothing to do with stock price volatility. It is based on the certainty an individual company will, over time, produce a handsome profit. Simpson's performance and investment style fit neatly with Buffett's way of thinking. "Lou takes the same conservative concentrated approach to investments that we do at Berkshire," said Buffett, "and it is an enormous plus for us to have him on board."[28]

Keynes, Buffett, Munger, Ruane, and Simpson: It is clear that the Superinvestors of Buffettville have a common intellectual approach to investing. They are united in their belief that the way to reduce risk is to buy stocks only when a margin of safety (that is, the favorable discrepancy between the intrinsic value of a company and its stock price) is present. They also believe that concentrating their portfolio on a limited number of these high-probability events not only reduces risk but also helps to generate returns far above the market rate of return.

Table 5.5 Lou Simson, GEICO: Annual Investment Performance History

	Annual Percentage Change	
Year	GEICO Equities (%)	S&P 500 (%)
1980	23.7	32.3
1981	5.4	−5.0
1982	45.8	21.4
1983	36.0	22.4
1984	21.8	6.1
1985	45.8	31.6
1986	38.7	18.6
1987	−10.0	5.1
1988	30.0	16.6
1989	36.1	31.7
1990	−9.1	−3.1
1991	57.1	30.5
1992	10.7	7.6
1993	5.1	10.1
1994	13.3	1.3
1995	39.7	37.6
1996	29.2	37.6
Average Return	24.7	17.8
Standard Deviation	19.5	14.3
Minimum	−10.0	−5.0
Maximum	57.1	37.6

Still, when we point out these successful focus investors, many remain skeptical. Perhaps the success is based on their close professional relationship. But these investors picked different stocks. Buffett started managing his portfolio in 1956. Munger followed in 1962, and although they each owned Blue Chip Stamps, the bulk of their respective portfolios were different. Munger didn't own what Ruane owned. Ruane didn't own what Simpsons owned, and nobody owned what Keynes owned.

Well, that may be true, say the skeptics, but you only offered five examples of focus investors. Five observations are not enough to draw a statistically meaningful conclusion. In an industry that had thousands of portfolio managers, five success stories could simply be random chance.

Fair enough. But if we were to eliminate any notion that the five Superinvestors of Buffettville are nothing more than statistical aberrations, we needed to examine a wider field. Unfortunately, there were not that many focus investors to study. So how did we proceed? By going inside a statistical laboratory to design a universe of 12,000 portfolios.

Three Thousand Focus Investors

Using the Compustat data base of common stock returns, we isolated 1,200 companies that displayed measurable data, including revenues, earnings, and a return on equity from 1979 through 1986.[29] We then asked the computer to randomly assemble, from these 1,200 companies, 12,000 portfolios of various sizes:

- ☐ 3,000 portfolios containing 250 stocks
- ☐ 3,000 portfolios containing 100 stocks
- ☐ 3,000 portfolios containing 50 stocks
- ☐ 3,000 portfolios containing 15 stocks

At this point we had 3,000 observations; mathematicians define the data set as being statistically significant. Next, we calculated the average annual return of each portfolio in each group over two time periods—10 years and 18 years—and plotted the distribution of these returns as shown in Figures 5.1 and 5.2, respectively. Then, we compared the returns of the four portfolio groups to the overall stock market, defined as the Standard & Poor's 500 Index (S&P 500) for the same time periods. From all this, one key finding emerged. In every case, when we reduced the number of stocks in a portfolio, we began to increase the probability of generating returns that were higher than the market's rate of return.

Let's look a little deeper, starting with the 10-year time frame (Figure 5.1). All four portfolio groups had an average yearly return

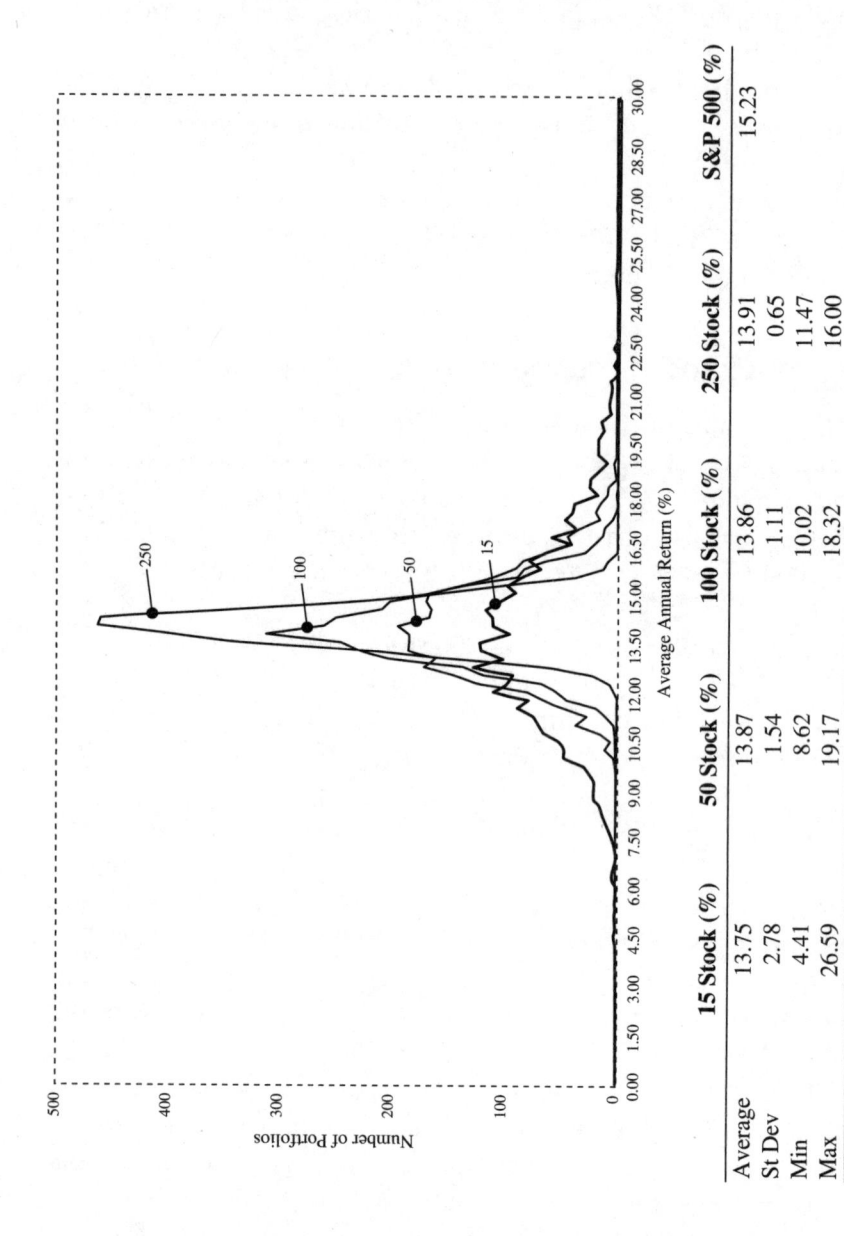

	15 Stock (%)	50 Stock (%)	100 Stock (%)	250 Stock (%)	S&P 500 (%)
Average	13.75	13.87	13.86	13.91	15.23
St Dev	2.78	1.54	1.11	0.65	
Min	4.41	8.62	10.02	11.47	
Max	26.59	19.17	18.32	16.00	

Figure 5.1 10-Year Period (1987–1996) Annual Average Return

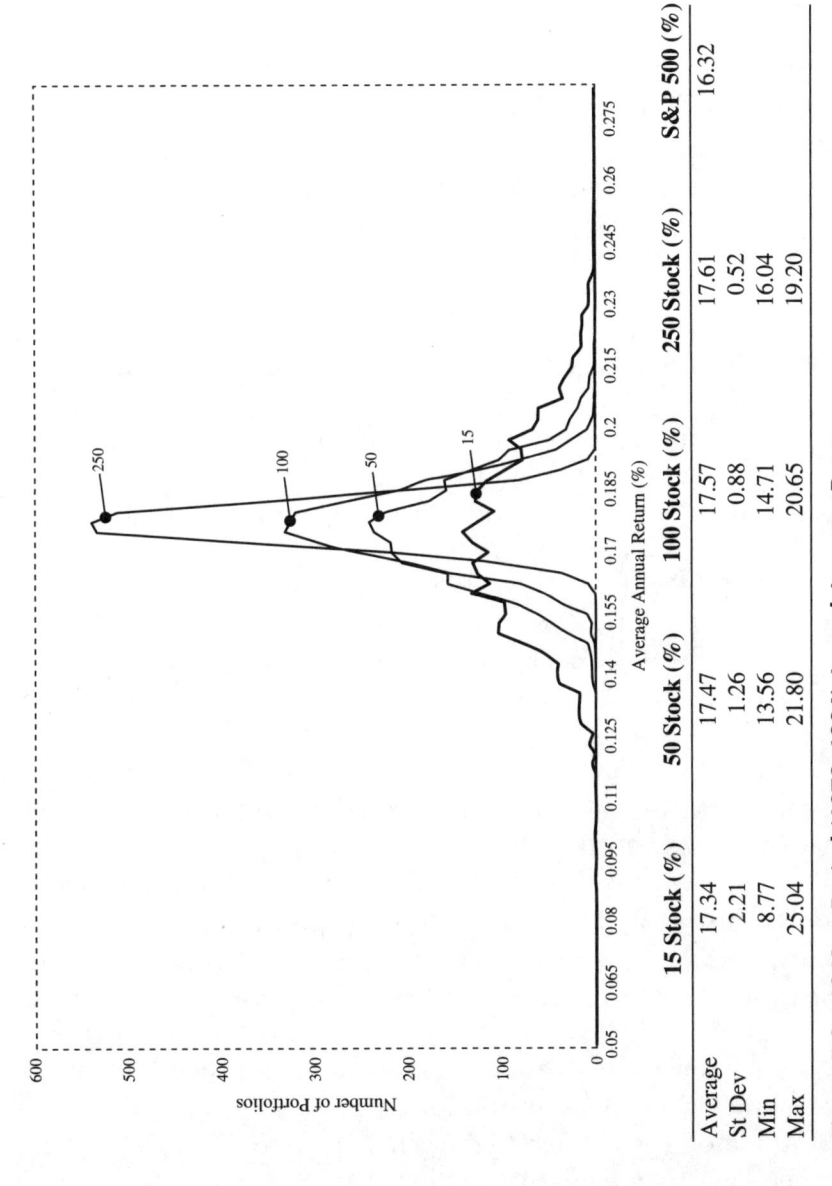

	15 Stock (%)	50 Stock (%)	100 Stock (%)	250 Stock (%)	S&P 500 (%)
Average	17.34	17.47	17.57	17.61	16.32
St Dev	2.21	1.26	0.88	0.52	
Min	8.77	13.56	14.71	16.04	
Max	25.04	21.80	20.65	19.20	

Figure 5.2   18-Year Period (1979–1996) Annual Average Return

of about 13.8 percent. The S&P 500 average return for the same time period was somewhat higher at 15.2 percent. Keep two important points in mind: The S&P 500 is a capitalization-weighted index dominated by the largest companies, and the time period under consideration was one in which large capitalization stocks performed particularly well. In our study, the portfolios were equally weighted, and they included not only large capitalization stocks but small and midsize companies as well. What we can say is that the four groups of "laboratory" portfolios performed approximately on par with the broad market.

This study starts to get more interesting when we look at the minimum/maximum numbers—the best-performing and worst-performing portfolios in each group. Here's what we discovered:

☐ Among the 250-stock portfolios, the best return was 16.0 percent and the worst was 11.4 percent.
☐ Among the 100-stock portfolios, the best return was 18.3 percent and the worst was 10.0 percent.
☐ Among the 50-stock portfolios, the best return was 19.1 percent and the worst was 8.6 percent.
☐ Among the 15-stock portfolios, the best return was 26.5 percent and the worst was 4.4 percent.

Of special note, in the fourth group, the 15 focused stock portfolios, and *only* in this group, were the best returns substantially higher than the S&P 500.

The same relative trends were found in the longer (18-year) period (Figure 5.2). The smaller, focused portfolios showed much higher highs and lower lows than the larger, diversified portfolios. These results lead us to two inescapable conclusions:

☐ You have a much higher chance of doing better than the market with a focus portfolio.
☐ You also have a much higher chance of doing worse than the market with a focus portfolio.

Managing a Portfolio of Businesses

To reinforce the first conclusion for the skeptics, we found some remarkable statistics when we sorted the 10-year data:

- Out of 3,000 250-stock portfolios, 63 beat the market.
- Out of 3,000 100-stock portfolios, 337 beat the market.
- Out of 3,000 50-stock portfolios, 549 beat the market.
- Out of 3,000 15-stock portfolios, 808 beat the market.

I submit this is strong evidence that the probabilities of beating the market go up as the number of stocks in a portfolio goes down. With a 250-stock portfolio, your chances of beating the market were 1 in 50. With a 15-stock portfolio, you had a 1-in-4 chance of outperforming the market.

Another important consideration: In our study, we did not factor in the effect of management fees and the impact of trading expenses. Obviously, when the portfolio turnover ratio is high, so are the costs. If these realized expenses had been included in the data, the annualized returns of the portfolios would have shifted to the left side of the graph, making it even harder to beat a market rate of return.

The second conclusion simply reinforces the critical importance of intelligent stock selection. It is no coincidence that the Superinvestors of Buffettville were also talented business pickers. If you had not picked the right companies your underperformance would have been striking. Having said this, we suggest the outsized returns earned by the Superinvestors was made possible by their willingness to focus their portfolios on their best businesses.

A Better Way to Measure Performance

Joseph Nocera, a writer for *Fortune* magazine, observed the obvious inconsistencies between what professional money managers recommend for their clients—"buy and hold"—and what those same mangers do with their own portfolios—buy-sell, buy-sell, buy-sell. Reinforcing his personal observations of this double standard,

Nocera quoted Morningstar's Don Phillips who said, "There is a huge disconnect between what the [money management] industry does and what it tells investors to do."[30]

The obvious question becomes: If investors are counseled to wisely buy and hold, why do managers frenetically buy and sell stocks each year? The answer, said Nocera, "is that the internal dynamics of the industry make it impossible for portfolio managers to look beyond [the] short term."[31] Why? Because the business of professionally managing portfolios has turned into a senseless short-term game of who has the best performance on any given day.

There is substantial pressure on portfolio managers to generate eye-catching short-term performance numbers. These numbers, not surprising, attract a lot of attention. Every three months, leading publications post the quarterly performance rankings of mutual funds. The funds that have done the best in the past three months move to the top of the list and are praised by financial commentators. Investors are constantly on the lookout for top-ranked portfolio managers who have the "hot hand." Never mind the academic evidence that reveals a portfolio manager's streak of *short-term* performance is no better than what chance would dictate.[32]

In short, the fixation on short-term performance dominates the money management industry. We are not in an environment where portfolio managers are measured over the long term. In many ways, we have become enslaved to a marketing machine that stresses short-term results over long-term returns, which all but guarantees underperformance. Caught in a vicious circle, there appears to be no way out. But, as we have learned, there *is* a way to improve investment performance. The cruel irony is that the portfolio management strategy most likely to provide above-average returns over time appears incompatible with how we have customarily judged performance—with an emphasis on the short term.

The Tortoise and the Hare

V. Eugene Shahan, a Columbia University Business School alumnus, wrote an article titled, "Are Short-Term Performance and

Value Investing Mutually Exclusive?" Shahan took on the same question that we are now asking: How appropriate is it to measure a money manager's skill on the basis of short-term performance?

Shahan noted that, with the exception of Buffett himself, many of the portfolio managers described as the "Superinvestors of Graham-and-Doddsville" were undeniably skilled and undeniably successful. And they all faced periods of short-term underperformance. In a money-management version of the tortoise and the hare, Shahan wrote, "It may be another of life's ironies that investors principally concerned with short-term performance may very well achieve it, but at the expense of long-term results."[33]

The same is true of the Superinvestors of Buffettville. Table 5.6 shows that they struggled through several difficult periods. Only Buffett, again, went through the performance derby with the Buffett Partnership unscathed.

John Maynard Keynes, who managed the Chest Fund for 18 years, underperformed the market one-third of time. Indeed, his underperformance of the market during the first three years he managed the fund put him behind the market by 18 percentage points.

The story was similar for the Sequoia Fund. Over the marking period, Sequoia underperformed 37 percent of the time (see Table 5.7). Similar to Keynes, Ruane had difficulty coming of age.

"Over the years," wrote Bill Ruane, "we have periodically qualified to be the Kings of Underperformance. We had the blurred vision to start the Sequoia Fund in the early 1970s and suffered the

Table 5.6 Superinvestors of Buffettville: Performance Percentage over Time

	Number of Years of Performance	Number of Years of Underperformance	Underperformance Years as a Percentage of All Years
Keynes	18	6	33
Buffett	13	0	0
Munger	14	5	36
Ruane	27	10	37
Simpson	17	4	24

Table 5.7 Superinvestors of Buffettville: Underperformance Over Time

	Number of Consecutive Years Underperformed the S&P 500
Keynes	3
Buffett	0
Munger	3
Ruane	4
Simpson	1

Table 5.8 Superinvestors of Buffettville: Worst Relative Performance

	Worst Relative Performance During the Period of Underperformance (%)
Keynes	−18
Buffett	N/A
Munger	−37
Ruane	−36
Simpson	−15

Chinese water-torture of underperforming the S&P four straight years." By the end of 1974, Sequoia was a whopping 36 percentage points behind the market (see Table 5.8).

"We hid under our desk, didn't answer the phones and wondered if the storm would ever clear."[34] The storm did clear. By the end of 1976, Sequoia was 50 percent ahead of the market over the five-and-one-half-year period, and, by 1978, Sequoia had gained 220 percent versus the S&P 500 Index, which gained 60 percent.

Even Charlie Munger couldn't escape the inevitable performance bumps of focus investing. Over 14 years, Munger underperformed, on an annual basis, 36 percent of the time. Like other focus investors, he had a string of bad luck. From 1972 to 1974, Munger fell behind the market by 37 percentage points. Over 17 years, Lou Simpson underperformed four years, or 24 percent of the time. His worst relative performance occurred during a one-year period when he was 15 percentage points behind the market.

Table 5.9 Focus (15-Stock) Portfolios—10-Year Data (1987–1996)

Number of Years Outperform/ Underperform S&P 500	Number of Portfolios	Percentage Total
10–0	0	0.00
9–1	1	0.12
8–2	20	2.48
7–3	128	15.84
6–4	272	33.66
5–5	261	32.30
4–6	105	13.00
3–7	21	2.60
2–8	0	0.00
1–9	0	0.00
0–10	0	0.00

Incidentally, we saw the same trends when analyzing the performance results of our laboratory focus portfolios (see Table 5.9). Of the 3,000 focus portfolios holding 15 stocks, 808 beat the market during the 10-year periods of time (1987–1996). Yet of those 808 winners, an astonishing 97 percent of the focus portfolios endured some period of underperformance—4, 5, 6, even 7 years out of 10.

What do you think would have happened to Keynes, Munger, Ruane, and Simpson if they were rookie portfolio mangers starting their career in today's environment, in which the importance of one year's performance is overemphasized? They would have likely been canned, to their clients' profound loss. Yes, following the argument that the focus strategy does sometimes mean enduring several years of underperformance, we run into a very real problem. How can we tell, using only price performance as our sole measure, whether we are observing a very bright portfolio manager who is having a poor year (or even a poor three years) but who will do well over the long haul from an inept portfolio manager who is starting a very long road of underperformance? If all we use to judge by is price performance, we can't.

Academics and researchers have invested considerable energy trying to determine which money managers, which strategies, have the best chance of beating the market over time. The *Journal of*

Finance has published several articles based on studies by prominent university professors, all asking the same basic question: Is there a pattern to mutual fund performance? Together, these academicians brought considerable intellectual weight and data analysis to the problem, but their findings failed to produce a perfect answer.

Four of these studies dealt with the term *persistence*—the tendency of investors to choose funds with the best recent track records because they believe a fund manager's record is an indication of future performance. This creates a kind of self-fulfilling momentum in which this year's money follows the top-performing mutual fund. When this momentum is measured in one-year units (picking next year's winner by buying last year's winner), we describe this as the "hot hands" phenomenon. It is all a matter of trying to predict which mutual funds will do well in the near future by observing what they did in the near past. Can it be done? That was what these studies attempted to discover.

In two separate studies, Mark Cahart of the University of Southern California School of Business Administration and Burton Malkiel of Princeton were unable to find any meaningful correlation between persistence and future performance.[35] In the third study, three professors from the John F. Kennedy School of Government at Harvard University (Darryll Hendricks, Jayendau Patel, and Richard Zeckhauser) examined 15 years of data and concluded that there appears to be no guarantee that buying this year's "hot hand" manager ensures owning next year's "hot hand" mutual fund.[36]

Working separately, these academics came to the same conclusion: There appears to be no significant evidence available that will help investors locate next year's top performers by relying on previous years' performance. Bouncing from one hot fund to the next does nothing to aid investors in building their net worth. Not when *hot* is defined by price performance. Even so, and despite the overwhelming academic evidence, investors continue to use price-only performance statistics to make decisions.

The fourth *Journal of Finance* study, written by Amit Goyal, a finance professor at Emory University, and Sunhil Wahal, a finance professor at Arizona State University, moves from the theoretical observations of performance persistence to the material mistakes made by those that actually make recommendations for portfolio managers. Goyal and Wahal analyzed 6,260 institutional portfolios managed by 1,475 investment management firms between 2001 and 2004. They discovered that the consultants in charge of hiring and firing portfolio managers followed a rather simple approach. They fired managers who had, in the most recent past, underperformed their benchmark and consistently hired managers who outperformed their benchmarks. There was only one problem with this simple metric: It wasn't a smart decision. In subsequent years, many of the managers who were fired ended up outperforming the new managers hired to replace them.[37]

Each year, investors step back to evaluate the performance of their portfolio managers. Managers that outperformed are ranked at the top; those that underperformed sit at the bottom. You would think the decision to replace a manager would be a thoughtful exercise—evaluating *outcomes* (performance returns), along with understanding the investment *process*, the strategies that drove returns. But, unfortunately, this is not the case.

It is not that outcomes don't matter; of course they do. But the obsession of wanting only winners each and every year inevitably puts investors' portfolios in harm's way. It forces investors to become performance chasers, which leads to buying a strategy only after it works and avoiding strategies that have lagged. But without understanding how a strategy drove the results, an investor could easily buy a strategy that employs a bad process but stumbled into good performance. The technical term is *dumb luck*. Conversely, good investment processes sometimes experience bad outcomes, what are called *bad breaks*,[38] a fact we have noted by examining the returns of the Superinvestors of Buffettville.

Robert Rubin, former banking executive and US Treasury Secretary, said it best: "Any individual decision can be badly thought through, and yet be successful, or exceedingly well thought through but be unsuccessful. But over time, more thoughtful decision-making will lead to better results, and more thoughtful decision-making can be encouraged by evaluating how well they were made rather than an outcome."[39]

We can well imagine what Warren Buffett might make of these academic studies. For him, the moral of the story is clear: We have to drop our insistence on price as the only measuring stick, and we have to break ourselves of the counterproductive habit of making short-term judgments.

But if price is not the best measuring stick, what are we to use instead? "Nothing" is not a good answer. Even the buy-and-hold portfolio managers don't recommend keeping your eyes shut. We have to find another benchmark for measuring performance. Fortunately, there is one, and it is the cornerstone of how Buffett judges the performance of his common stock holdings and the performance of his operating units at Berkshire Hathaway.

Alternative Performance Benchmarks

Warren Buffett once said he "wouldn't care if the stock market closed for a year or two. After all it closes every Saturday and Sunday and that hasn't bothered me yet."[40] Now it is true that "an active trading market is useful, since it periodically presents us with mouth-watering opportunities," said Buffett. "But by no means is it essential."[41]

To fully appreciate this statement, you need to think carefully what Buffett said next: "A prolonged suspension of trading in securities we hold would not bother us any more than does the lack of daily quotations for World Book or Fechheimer [two Berkshire Hathaway wholly owned companies]. Eventually our economic fate will be determined by the economic fate of the businesses we own, whether our ownership is partial [in the form of common shares] or total."[42]

If you owned a business and there was no daily quote to measure its performance, how could you determine your progress? Likely you would measure the growth in sales and earnings, or perhaps the improvement in operating margins, or changes in returns on equity. You would simply let the economics dictate whether the intrinsic value of your business is increasing or declining. In Buffett's mind, the litmus test for measuring the performance of a private company is no different than measuring the performance of a publicly traded company. Buffett explains: "Charlie and I let our marketable equities tell us by their operating results—not by their daily, or even yearly, price quotations—whether our investments are successful. The market may ignore our business success for a while, but it eventually will confirm it. As Ben [Graham] said: "In the short run, the market is a voting machine, but in the long run it is a weighing machine. The speed at which a business's success is recognized, furthermore, is not that important as long as the company's intrinsic value is increasing at a satisfactory rate."[43]

Look-Through Earnings

To help shareholders appreciate the value of Berkshire Hathaway's common stock portfolio, Buffett, in the 1990 Berkshire Annual Report, introduced the term *look-through earnings*. Berkshire's look-through earnings are the sum of the operating earnings of its wholly owned businesses, plus the retained earnings of its common stock investments, less an allowance for the tax that would have had to be paid if the retained earnings were actually reported by Berkshire. Retained earnings of Berkshire's common stock holdings, remember, are a portion of the company's annual earnings that are not distributed to shareholders in the form of dividends but are reinvested back into the company.

The notion of look-through earnings was originally devised by Buffett for the benefit of Berkshire shareholders to help them appreciate the value creation that occurs when a company retains part of its earnings to reinvest back into the business. Buffett reminded shareholders that Berkshire's share of retained earnings that accrue from its common stock holdings may be "forgotten" because they are not GAAP reported but they are, nonetheless, noteworthy as they work to increase Berkshire's underlying intrinsic value.

Look-through earnings are also a thoughtful guidepost for focus investors who seek to understand the economic progress of their portfolio when, as will happen from time to time, the share price of their stocks disengages from the financial returns of their underlying businesses. Buffett concurs: "We also believe that investors can benefit from focusing on their own look-through earnings. To calculate these, they should determine the underlying earnings attributed to the shares they hold in their portfolio and total these."

Buffett continues: "The goal of each investor should be to create a portfolio (in effect, a "company") that will deliver him or her the highest possible look-through earnings a decade or so from now."

Importantly, said Buffett, "I've told you that over time look-through earnings must increase at about 15% annually if our intrinsic value is to grow at the rate."[44] In this way, Buffett's recommendation is for investors to take their common stock portfolio and imagine they are running their own mini-Berkshire Hathaway.

According to Buffett, since 1965 (the year Buffett took control of Berkshire Hathaway), the company's look-through earnings have grown at almost an identical rate of the market value of Berkshire. However, the two have not always moved in lockstep. There have been many occasions when earnings moved ahead of prices (when Ben Graham's famous Mr. Market was unduly depressed). At other times, prices moved far ahead of earnings (when Mr. Market was uncontrollably enthused). What is important to remember is that the relationship works over time. Most important, counseled Buffett, "An approach of this kind will force the investor to think about the long-term business prospects rather than short-term market prospects, a perspective that will likely improve results."[45]

Berkshire's Measuring Stick

When Buffett considers adding an investment, he first looks at what he already owns to see whether the new purchase is any better. What Berkshire owns today is an economic measuring stick used to compare possible acquisitions—wholly owned businesses or common stocks. "What Buffett is saying is something very useful to practically any investor," said Charlie Munger. "For an ordinary individual, the best thing you already have should be your measuring stick." What happens next is one of the most critical but widely overlooked secrets to increasing the value of your portfolio. "If the new thing [you are considering purchasing] isn't better than what you already know is available," explained Munger, "then it hasn't met your threshold. This screens out 99 percent of what you see."[46]

You already have at your disposal, with what you own, an economic benchmark—a measuring stick. You can define your own personal economic benchmark in several different ways, for example, sales growth, look-through earnings, return on equity, or margin of safety. When you buy or sell a company in your portfolio, you have either raised or lowered your economic benchmark. The job of a good portfolio manager, someone who is a long-term owner of securities and believes future stock prices eventually match with underlying economics, is to find ways to raise the benchmark. "That's an enormous thought observer," said Munger, "and it's not taught at the business schools by and large."[47]

If you step back and think for a moment, the S&P 500 Index is a measuring stick. It is made up of 500 companies, and each has its own economic returns. To outperform the S&P 500 over time—to raise your own benchmark—you have to assemble and manage a portfolio of companies whose economics are superior to the average weighted economics of the index.

You should not be lulled into thinking that just because a focus portfolio lags the stock market on a price basis from time to time, you are excused from the ongoing responsibility of performance scrutiny. Employing an economic benchmark, you will, despite the vagaries of the market, still have to defend your individual picks. Granted, a focus portfolio manager should not become a slave to the stock market's whims, but you should always be thoughtfully aware of all the economic stirrings of the companies in your portfolio. After all, if a focus investor hasn't got the economics right in the portfolio, it is unlikely Mr. Market will ever find an occasion to handsomely reward the selection.

Two Good Reasons to Move Like a Sloth

Focus investing is necessarily a long-term approach to investing. If we were to ask Buffett what he considers an ideal holding period, he would answer "forever"—as long as the company continues to generate above-average economics and management allocates the earnings of the company in a rational manner. "Inactivity strikes us an intelligent behavior," explained Buffett. "Neither we nor most business managers would dream of feverishly trading highly profitable subsidiaries because a small move in the Federal Reserve's discount rate was predicted or because some Wall Street pundit has reversed his views on the market. Why, then should we behave differently with our minority positions in wonderful businesses? The art of investing in public companies successfully is little different from the art of successfully acquiring subsidiaries. In each case you simply want to acquire, at a sensible price, a business with excellent economics and able, honest management."

Then coming back to monitoring the economics of what you own, Buffett tells us, "Thereafter, you need only monitor whether these qualities are being preserved."[48]

If you own a mediocre company, you require turnover because, without it, you end up owning, for the long term, the economics of a subpar business. But if you own a superior company, the last thing you want to do is to sell it. Here's Buffett:

> When carried out capably, a [focus, low-turnover] investment strategy will often result in its practitioner owning a few securities that will come to represent a very large portion of his portfolio.
>
> This investor would get a similar result if he followed a policy of purchasing an interest in, say, 20 percent of the future earnings of a number of outstanding college basketball stars. A handful of these would go on to achieve NBA stardom, and the investor's take from them would soon dominate his royalty stream. To suggest that this investor should sell off portions of his most successful investments simply because they have come

to dominate his portfolio is akin to suggesting that the Bulls trade Michael Jordan because he has become so important to the team.[49]

This sloth-like approach to money management might appear quirky to those accustomed to actively buying and selling stocks on a regular basis, but it does have two important economic benefits, in addition to growing capital at an above-average rate:

☐ It works to reduce transaction costs.
☐ It increases after-tax returns.

Each advantage by itself is extremely valuable; their combined benefit is enormous.

Reduce Transaction Costs

On average, mutual funds generate greater than 100 percent portfolio turnover ratios each year. The turnover ratio describes the amount of activity in a portfolio. For example, if a portfolio manager sells and rebuys all the stocks in the portfolio once a year, the turnover ratio is 100 percent. Sell and rebuy everything twice a year, and you have 200 percent turnover. But if a manager sells and rebuys only 10 percent of the portfolio in a year (implying an average 10-year holding period), the turnover ratio is a lowly 10 percent.

In a review of 3,560 domestic stock funds, Morningstar, the Chicago-based researcher of mutual funds, discovered that funds with low turnover ratios generated superior returns compared to funds with higher turnover ratios. The Morningstar study found that, over a 10-year period, mutual funds with turnover ratios of less than 20 percent were able to achieve returns 14 percent higher over the time period than funds with turnover ratios of more than 100 percent.[50]

This is the result of one of those "common-sense" dynamics that is so obvious it is easily overlooked: Hyperactive trading adds brokerage costs, which works to lower your net returns.

After-Tax Returns

Low-turnover funds have another important economic advantage: the positive effect of postponing capital gains taxes. Ironically, turnover, which is supposed to increase your returns, also increases your tax liability. When a portfolio manager sells a stock and replaces it with another stock, the idea is the trade will enhance the fund's return. But selling a stock, in many cases, means that a capital gain is realized. So each new pick going forward has the burden of outperforming the capital gains tax associated with the stock it replaced plus generating a return better than the market.

If you have a tax-free account (Individual Retirement Account or a 401k plan), you do not pay taxes on the gain from a sale. But if you own stocks in your personal taxable account, any realized gain triggers a capital gains tax. The more stocks sold, if profitable, the higher the tax bill.

Even when year-end performance of your mutual fund or personal portfolio shows a competitive return, by the time you have paid the taxes on the gains realized, your net after-tax return may drop your total return to below the benchmark return. Investors need to ask whether the return provided by their actively managed portfolio or mutual funds is high enough to pay the taxes owed and still generate a return higher than the benchmark.

Except in the cases of nontaxable accounts, taxes are the biggest expense that investors face. They are higher than brokerage commissions and higher than the management fee, an expense ratio for running the portfolio. In fact, taxes have become one of the principal reasons why portfolios generate poor returns. "That is the bad news," according to Robert Jeffrey and Robert Arnott. They are the authors of an article that appeared in the *Journal of Portfolio Management*, "Is Your Alpha Big Enough to Cover Its Taxes?" "The good news," they wrote, "is that there are strategies that can minimize these typically overlooked tax consequences."[51]

In a nutshell, the key strategy involves another of those commonsense notions that is often underappreciated: the enormous value of the unrealized gain. When a stock appreciates in price *but is not sold,* the increase in the value is an unrealized gain. No capital gains tax is owed until the stock is sold. If you leave the gain in place, your money compounds more forcefully as you are compounding a larger unrealized capital gain.

Overall, investors, too often, have underestimated the enormous value of this unrealized gain—what Buffett calls an "interest-free loan from the Treasury." To make his point, Buffett asks us to imagine what happens if you buy a $1 investment that doubles in price each year. If you sell the investment at the end of the first year, you will have a net gain of $.66 (assuming you are in the 34 percent tax bracket). In the second year, you reinvest $1.66 and it doubles in value by year-end. If the investment continues to double each year, and you continue to sell, pay the tax, and reinvest the proceeds, at the end of 20 years you would have a net gain of $25,200 after paying taxes of $13,000. If, however, you purchased a $1 investment that doubled every year and was not sold until the *end* of 20 years, you would gain $692,000 after paying taxes of approximately $356,000.

A cold look at the numbers makes a couple of observations clear. You end up with a great deal more profit if you don't take your gain each year but just let your money compound. At the same time, your lump-sum tax bill at the end of 20 years will take your breath away. That may be one reason people instinctively, but incorrectly, feel it's better to convert the gain each year and thereby keep the taxes under control. What most investors fail to comprehend is the enormous difference in compounding unrealized gains over time versus paying smaller capital gains taxes each year.

For their article, Jeffrey and Arnott calculated the point at which turnover begins to negatively affect the portfolio. The answer, surprisingly, is counterintuitive. The greatest tax damage to the portfolio occurs at the outset of turnover and then diminishes as turnover increases. Jeffrey and Arnott wrote, "Conventional wisdom thinks any turnover in the range 1 percent and 25 percent is categorically low and inconsequential, and anything greater than 50 percent as being high and presumably of considerable consequence; the reality is just the opposite."[52]

The Jeffrey-Arnott study shows that, at a 25 percent turnover ratio, the portfolio incurs 80 percent of the taxes that would be generated by a portfolio turnover ratio of 100 percent. They conclude that it is more important to be mindful of turnover ratios in the lower range than in the higher range. To achieve high after-tax returns, investors need to keep their average annual portfolio turnover ratios somewhere in between 0 and 20 percent.

What strategies lend themselves best to low turnover ratios? One approach is a passive, low-turnover index fund. Another is an actively managed focused, low-turnover portfolio. "It sounds like premarital counseling advice," wrote Jeffrey and Arnott, "namely, to try to build a portfolio that you can live with for a long, long time."[53]

High Active-Share Investing

In 1978, Warren Buffett let it be known his portfolio approach was to concentrate his common stock positions, believing it was more profitable to buy worthwhile amounts as opposed to buying a little of this or that. In 1999, we wrote about the benefits of focus investing.[54] Today, academicians are fully engaged. The most notable thinkers on concentrated portfolios are K. J. Martijn Cremers and Antii Petajisto. But it is no longer called focus investing. It is now referred to as *high active-share investing*.

In 2009, Cremers and Petajisto, at the time both at the International Center of Finance at the Yale School of Management, coauthored a landmark paper on portfolio management, "How Active Is Your Fund Manager?" First a definition. Active share is the percentage amount of a portfolio that is different from the performance benchmark, calculated by tabulating the differences in names and weights in a portfolio compared to a benchmark. A portfolio with no names in common with a benchmark has an active share of 100 percent. A portfolio that has exactly the same holding and weights as the benchmark will have an active share of 0 percent. If a portfolio has an active share of 75 percent, then 25 percent of its holdings are identical to the holdings of the benchmark and 75 percent of the holdings are different.

Cremers and Petajisto examined 2,650 mutual funds from 1980 to 2003. What did they discover? Those portfolios with high active-share defined as 80 percent or higher, beat their benchmark indices by a range of 2.0 percent to 2.7 percent before fees and 1.5 percent to 1.6 percent after fees.[55] In addition, those funds with low active share, commonly referred to as closet indexers because they are actively managed portfolios that closely resemble the benchmark, were unable to outperform the index after expenses.

It is now understood that portfolios with the highest active share outperform their benchmark while portfolios with the lowest active share underperform. Today, active share is considered a predictor of fund performance.

On a side note, Cremers and Petajisto pointed out that tracking error volatility, which measures the standard deviation of the difference between the portfolio manager's return and the index return, does not predict future returns. Whether a manager has a portfolio with low tracking error or high tracking error only implies what price actions are occurring in the portfolio, not how different the portfolio looks compared to the benchmark.

In a follow-up paper, Cremers, along with Ankur Pareek at the Rutgers Business School, wrote an article for the *Journal of Financial Economics* titled "Patient Capital Outperformance: The Investment Skill of High Active Share Managers Who Trade Infrequently." Here the authors examined the results of portfolios that were both high active share and low turnover—in other words, focus portfolios managed by and for buy-and-hold investors. They found that "among high active share portfolios—whose holding differed substantially from their benchmark—only those with patient strategies (with holding durations over two years—implying turnover ratios less than 50 percent) on average outperformed." Importantly, they discovered high active-share portfolios with high turnover ratios actually underperformed the market.[56]

Collectively, Cremers, Petajisto, and Pareek have made it clear that the worst portfolio management strategy is a widely diversified portfolio that trades a lot. The best approach for beating the market is to own high active-share portfolios run by mangers who buy and hold stocks, exactly the same type of portfolio Warren Buffett manages for Berkshire.

"In investment management today," said Charlie Munger, "everybody wants to not only win, but to have the yearly outcome path never diverge very much from the standard path except on the upside. From the viewpoint of a rational consumer, the whole system is bonkers and it draws a lot of talented people into socially useless activity." The fear of so-called tracking error (performance that is too far away from the market's return) has, according to Munger, "hobbled the industry."[57]

What we have learned is that strong short-term performance does not necessarily identify superior portfolio managers any more than weak short-term performance excludes them. The time horizon we customarily use to judge ability is simply too short to draw any meaningful conclusions. However, using alternative economic benchmarks such as look-through earnings is a thoughtful approach for investors to gauge one's progress, particularly when stock prices deviate from expected returns.

We have also learned that low turnover ratios translate into higher returns in two simple, obvious ways. First, fewer transactions mean lower trading costs. Second, don't overlook the value of unrealized capital gains. Focus investing not only gives you the opportunity to generate market-beating returns but also the best opportunity to compound unrealized gains into major profits.

"The Berkshire system is not bonkers," explained Charlie Munger. "I'd say that Berkshire Hathaway is adapting to the nature of the investment problem as it really is."[58]

CHAPTER 6

It's Not That Active Management Doesn't Work

At the 1997 Berkshire Hathaway Annual Meeting, Charlie Munger posed an important question to shareholders. The Berkshire style of investing "is so simple," he said, "but it is not widely copied." Ever the philosopher, he added, "I don't know why our approach is not taught at great universities or largely practiced at other institutional money management firms. It's a very interesting question," he mused. "If we are so right, why are so many imminent places so wrong?"[1]

Why indeed? In a world where investors are drawn to outperforming strategies, why are there so few Berkshire copycats? Yes, there are a select few, but as a percentage of the global money management industry the number of firms that follow Berkshire's approach to investing is minuscule.

Unhappy investors increasingly complain that active portfolio management costs too much, trades too much, and underperforms too much. Many have switched to passive index investing. Others have embraced alternative high-cost approaches including quantitative algorithmic hedge funds, private equity, and venture capital investing with its promises of riches but dubious outcomes. All told, hundreds of billions of dollars have been liquidated from active, long-only portfolio managers seeking better investment returns.

But, as we will learn, it's not that active management doesn't work. *It is the strategies used by most active managers that don't work.* How investors came to this crossroad, frustrated and disillusioned, is worth taking the time to understand.

If you asked people what they know about the history of investing, I would suspect most would begin by recounting the infamous stock market crash of 1929. The Roaring Twenties, the decade following World War I, was a period of double-barreled economic activity: great wealth building and speculation. The latter of these culminated in the biggest stock market crash in US history.

Others might answer that US investing actually began on May 17, 1792, when 24 stockbrokers gathered under a buttonwood tree outside 68 Wall Street to sign an agreement, later known as the Buttonwood Agreement, that founded what is now the New York Stock Exchange. But history buffs would tell you in that in actuality, the clock of investing began with the Amsterdam Stock Exchange in 1602. An invention of the Dutch East India Company, the exchange not only allowed joint stock companies to attract capital from investors, but also allowed investors to buy and sell their shares. So, in all, the history of modern investing is about 425 years old.

Today, that which passes for the standard investment management approach, called Modern Portfolio Theory, is barely 40 years old. We can trace the root of that theory back to 1952, some 70 years ago, although, as you might remember, for the first 30 years no one outside academia gave it much thought.

High Priests of Modern Finance

Modern Portfolio Theory (MPT) assumes investors are risk averse and that given the choice of two portfolios with the same expected return, an individual will always prefer the less risky one. Understanding this, investors can build an optimal portfolio of stocks and bonds that reflects their risk tolerance, defined as the emotional wherewithal to withstand price volatility. As we will see, MPT is about the bounciness of a stock price and the individual's ability to handle bad news. To say this in other, blunter terms, the driving force for the standard investment management approach is the paramount objective of solving a psychological discomfort—an objective deemed more important than achieving higher investment returns.

Central to MPT is the belief that the portfolio's overall risk and return is more important than the risk and return of an individual investment. In other words, in MPT the whole becomes more important than the individual parts. Over the years numerous strategies have been developed to guide investors toward their goals with a minimum of angst. But as we will discover, all those strategies fail to find the answer to reaching that goal because they emphasize the wrong question.

MPT puts investors' emotional well-being ahead of investment returns, which are given second place on the priority list. Thus grounded in this definition of risk tolerance, standard active portfolio management cannot, as a general rule, outperform passive index funds. No value is added. No wonder investors are turning sour on active management.

By mis-prioritizing what is critical for outperformance, MPT has sowed the seeds of its own demise. It is a theory built on straw legs that today is wobbling as investors rush to take money away.

The question of how we got into this self-defeating mindset starts with Harry Max Markowitz, born in Chicago on August 24, 1927. By all accounts he was a fine young man. Played the violin and studied hard. His interest included physics, mathematics, and philosophy. It was said that his hero was David Hume, the Scottish philosopher, and that his favorite essay was "Skeptical Doubts Concerning the Operations of Understanding" in which Hume drew a distinction between the "relation of ideas" and "matters of fact."[2]

Markowitz attended the University of Chicago—the only college he applied to—where he earned a bachelor's degree in liberal arts and continued graduate studies in economics. As a graduate student, Markowitz gravitated to the Cowles Commission for Research and Economics, embedded at the University of Chicago. Alfred

Cowles had established the commission in 1932. Having subscribed to several investment services, none of which had predicted the 1929 stock market crash, Cowles set about to determine whether market forecasters could actually predict the future direction of the market. In one of the most detailed studies ever conducted, the commission analyzed 6,904 forecasts between 1929 and 1944; the results, Cowles noted in a model of understatement, "failed to disclose the evidence of ability to predict the future course of the stock market."[3]

When it came time to decide on a topic for his doctoral dissertation, Markowitz chose as his financial advisor Professor Jacob Marschak, a recent director of the Cowles Commission. One afternoon, Markowitz was sitting outside Marschak's office when he introduced himself to an older, distinguishing-looking gentleman sitting nearby. In the casual conversation that ensued, the gentleman mentioned that he was a stockbroker and suggested that Markowitz might consider writing his dissertation on the stock market. When Markowitz mentioned the idea to his advisor, Marschak enthusiastically agreed—and then reminded his student that Alfred Cowles was himself interested in markets.[4]

Jacob Marschak's field of expertise was economics, not the stock market, so he directed Markowitz to Marshall Ketchum, dean of the Graduate School of Business and coeditor of the *Journal of Finance*. Ketchum, in turn, sent Markowitz to the university library to read *The Theory of Investment Value* by John Burr Williams, which you may recognize as the same book that Warren Buffett studied to better help him determine a company's intrinsic value.[5]

Markowitz was instantly intrigued. He was fascinated by Williams' net present value (NPV) model for valuing stocks but was left perplexed. Markowitz believed Williams' suggestion to use the NPV model would logically drive an investor to own a portfolio of just a few stocks, possibly only one. Surely, no sensible investor would only own one or two stocks, he thought. The uncertainty of what could happen in the world would argue against taking such risk.

Going deeper, Markowitz could not see how Williams was controlling for risk, despite the fact that Williams had aligned his thinking on risk with Ben Graham's idea of a margin of safety. In the preface of Williams' book, he advised the reader to select stocks that were selling below net present value and avoid stocks selling at prices above it. Williams wrote, "Investment value, defined as the present worth of future dividends, or future coupons and principal, is of practical importance to every investor because it is the *critical* value above which he cannot go in buying and holding, without added risk."[6]

Other than this, Williams did not expound on risk management. Even so, it is puzzling why Markowitz made no reference to Williams' recommendation to buy stocks below value in order to manage risk. Nonetheless, Markowitz was consumed with the idea investors should be interested in risk as well as return. The theory he ultimately developed, with refinements from others, is that risk to investors is wholly a function of the volatility of stock prices. That understanding of "investment risk" became the first leg of MPT.

In March 1952, "Portfolio Selection" by Harry Markowitz, a graduate student in search of his PhD, appeared in the *Journal of Finance*. Markowitz would receive his doctorate in economics two years later. The article was not long—only 14 pages—and, by the standards of academic journals, it was unremarkable; only four pages of text (graphs and mathematical equations consume the rest) and only three citations: John Burr Williams, *The Theory of Investment Value* (1938); John Richard Hicks, *Value and Capital* (1939); and James Victor Uspensky, *Introduction to Mathematical Probability* (1937). From Markowitz's standpoint, it didn't take volumes to explain what he believed was a rather simple notion: risk and return are inextricably linked. As an economist, he believed it was possible to quantify the relationship between the two and thus determine the degree of risk that would be required for various levels of return.

To illustrate his point, Markowitz simply drew a trade-off graph with the expected return on the vertical axis and the risk on the horizontal axis. A simple line drawn from the bottom left to the top right is referred to as the efficient frontier, a staple of MPT. Each point on the line represents an intersection between the potential reward and the corresponding level of risk. The most efficient portfolio is one that gives the highest return for a given level of risk. An inefficient portfolio exposes the investor to a level of risk without a corresponding level of expected returns. The goal for an investor, said Markowitz, was to match portfolios to his or her tolerance for taking risk while limiting or avoiding inefficient portfolios.

Variance: Quantifying Risk and Return

However, the slippery slope that Markowitz introduced was the idea that the best measure of risk is variance, which is price volatility. In the first paragraph of his paper, Markowitz wrote, "We consider the rule that the investor does (or should) consider expected return as a desirable thing and the variance of the return an *undesirable thing* [italics mine]."[7] Markowitz went on to say, "This rule has many sound points, both as a maxim for, and hypothesis about, investment behavior. We illustrate geometrically relations between beliefs and choice of portfolios according to the 'expected returns–variance returns' rule."[8] Markowitz notes that the "terms 'yield' and 'risk' frequently appear in financial writings but are not always used in precision." He suggested, that "if the term 'yield' were replaced with 'expected yield' or 'expected return,' and 'risk' by 'variance of return,' little change of apparent meaning would result."[9]

If you stop and think about Markowitz's reasoning, it was a gigantic leap, and arguably pretentious, for a 25-year-old graduate student to assert that which is undesirable (the unpleasantness of price volatility) is in fact *risk*, without any corresponding economic explanation or evidence that an asset that has high variance actually leads to permanent capital loss. It is also noteworthy that Markowitz ignored the issue of a company's value as it relates to a stock price, which as we know is the centrality of Ben Graham's approach to investing. Nowhere does Markowitz equate risk to capital loss—only to price variance.

It is not clear why Markowitz did not cite, nor did his advisor or the dissertation committee suggest he make reference to, the leading textbook at the time, *Security Analysis*. In 1951, just one year earlier than the publication of Markowitz's paper, the third edition of Graham and Dodd's masterwork had been published. Neither did Markowitz reference Graham's *The Intelligent Investor*, at the time a popular investment book that had been widely reviewed three years earlier. Graham had made the important point that there is a difference between short-term quotational loss and permanent capital loss. In these two separate cases, Markowitz ignored the viewpoints of John Burr Williams and Benjamin Graham as they related to risk management.

The bedrock of Markowitz's theory of risk is the way assets behave, pricewise. According to Markowitz, the risk of the portfolio depends on the price variance of its holdings with no mention of the financial risk to the value of the underlying company. With each step in Markowitz's thinking, he moved further away from understanding the value of stocks and closer toward constructing a portfolio solely on the price volatility of its underlying stocks. Hence, the primary objective of Markowitz's approach became an exercise in managing a portfolio of prices rather than a portfolio of businesses.

Initially, Markowitz's approach suggested the riskiness of a portfolio is simply the weighted average variance of all its individual stocks. Although the variance may provide a gauge to the riskiness of an individual stock, the average of two variances (or 100 variances) will tell you very little about the riskiness of a two-stock (or a 100-stock) portfolio. To measure the riskiness of the entire portfolio, Markowitz introduced the formula for "covariance" to portfolio management.

Covariance measures the direction of a group of stocks. Two stocks exhibit high covariance when their prices, for whatever reason, tend to move together. Two stocks that move in opposite direction are said to have low covariance. In Markowitz's thinking, the risk of a portfolio is not the variance of the individual stocks but the covariance of the holdings. The more stock prices move in the same direction, the riskier the portfolio. Conversely, a portfolio of low-covariance stocks is less risky. According to Markowitz, constructing a low-covariance portfolio should be an investor's primary goal. As we know, the objective of Warren Buffett's business-driven approach is *not* to build a portfolio on low volatility and low covariance but to invest in individual businesses (stocks) that generate high economic returns, each unto themselves.

Sharpe: Defining Volatility

In 1959, Markowitz published his first book, *Portfolio Selection: Efficient Diversification of Investment*, based on his PhD dissertation. Two years later, a young PhD student named William Sharpe approached Markowitz, who was then working on linear programming at the RAND Institute. Sharpe was in need of a dissertation topic and one of his professors at UCLA had suggested tracking down Markowitz. The next year, 1963, Sharpe's dissertation was published: "A Simplified Model of Portfolio Analysis." While fully acknowledging his reliance on Markowitz's ideas, Sharpe suggested a simpler method that would avoid countless covariant calculations.

It was Sharpe's contention that all securities bear a common relationship to some underlying base factor. For any specific security this factor could be a stock market, the gross domestic product, or some other price index, as long as it was the single most important influence on the behavior of the security. Using Sharpe's theory, an analyst would need only to measure the relationship of the security to the dominant base factor. It greatly simplified Markowitz's approach.

According to Sharpe, the base factor for stock prices, the single greatest influence on their behavior, was the stock market itself. Also important, but less influential, were industry groups and unique characteristics about the stock. Sharpe's argument was that if the price of a particular stock is more volatile than the market as a whole, then the stock will make the portfolio more variable and therefore more risky. Conversely, if a stock price is less volatile than the market, then adding this stock will make the portfolio less variable, less volatile, and less risky. The volatility of the overall portfolio, based on Sharpe's methodology, could be determined easily by the simple weighted average volatility of the individual securities.

Sharpe's volatility measure was given a name—beta factor. Beta is described as the degree of correlation between separate price movements: the market as a whole and an individual stock. Stock prices that rise and fall exactly with the market are assigned a beta of 1.0. If a stock rises and falls twice as much as the market, its beta is 2.0; if a stock's move is only 80 percent of the market's move, the beta is 0.8. Based solely on this information, Sharpe was able to ascertain the weighted average beta of a portfolio. His conclusion, perfectly in line with Markowitz's view of price variance, was that any portfolio with a beta greater than 1.0 will be more risky than the market, and any portfolio with a beta less than 1.0 will be less risky.

What would a young Warren Buffett make of the earliest teachings of MPT? Let's think back for a minute. When Harry Markowitz was researching and writing his paper "Portfolio Selection" in 1951, Buffett was enrolled at Columbia University, sitting for Ben Graham's spring investment seminar. When William Sharpe published his dissertation in 1963, Buffett was in the seventh year managing the Buffett Partnership, posting outstanding investment results. At the time, Markowitz and Sharpe were both warning about the dangers of stock price volatility as something an investor should guard against. For his part, Buffett, with lessons learned from Ben Graham, was actually *attracted* to price volatility, knowing that a big drop in the price of a stock may have the potential to increase the rate of return of his investment. For a concrete example, think back to Buffett's purchase of American Express for the Buffett Partnership during the salad oil scandal. While Markowitz and Sharpe sought to promote their theories of risk as volatility, Buffett was firmly planted in a different direction.

What is Warren Buffett's opinion of MPT? In Berkshire Hathaway's 1975 Annual Report, Buffett distilled his thoughts on risk and price volatility. The year before, Buffett had purchased the Washington Post Company. At the time, it was Berkshire's largest equity investment. By year-end 1974, the stock market was down 50 percent in the midst of a brutal bear market. The share price of the Washington Post Company declined with everything else;

however, Buffett remained steadfast and calm. Writing in the annual report he said, "Stock market fluctuations are of little importance to us—except as they may provide buying opportunities—but business performance is of major importance. On this score we have been delighted with the progress made by practically all of the companies in which we have significant investments,"[10] the Washington Post Company included.

Years later, in a 1990 lecture at Stanford Law School, Buffett fully laid out his thinking on price volatility as a measurement for risk. He began, "We bought the Washington Post Company at a valuation of $80 million in 1974. If you'd asked any one of 100 analysts how much the company was worth when we were buying it, no one would have argued about the fact it was worth $400 million." Buffett continued, "Now, under the whole theory of beta and modern portfolio theory, we would have been doing something riskier buying stock for $40 million than we were buying it for $80 million, even though it's worth $400 million—because it had more volatility. With that, they lost me."[11]

Warren Buffett has always perceived a drop in share price as an opportunity to make additional money, not something to avoid. The way Buffett conceptualizes investing, after you determine a company's intrinsic value, a drop in share price *reduces* your risk as defined by the margin of safety. "For owners of a business—and that's the way we think of shareholders—the academic's definition of risk is far off the mark, so much so that it produces absurdities."[12]

Buffett: Business-Driven Investing

Warren Buffett has a different definition of risk. For him, risk is the possibility of harm or injury. And that, he says, is a factor related to the intrinsic value of a business, not the ongoing short-term price behavior of the market. In Buffett's view, harm or injury comes from misjudging the primary factors that determine the future profits of your business: (1) "the certainty with which the long-term economic characteristics of the business can evaluated"; (2) "the certainty with which management can be evaluated, both as to its ability to realize the full potential of the business and to wisely employ its cash flows"; (3) "the certainty with which management can be counted on to channel the rewards from the business to the shareholders rather than to itself"; and (4) "the purchase price of the business."[13]

The fault line that separates MPT from Buffett's business-driven investing approach is the difference in how an investor who owns public securities thinks about risk versus how a private business owner thinks about risk. One has to wonder why does an individual who owns publicly traded common stocks behave differently from an individual who owns the entire business. Buffett would say just because a business has a daily price does not justify the perverse behavior of the owner to panic over short-term price volatility when their economic interests are long term.

Importantly, Warren Buffett tells us risk is inextricably linked to an investor's time horizon. If you buy a stock today, he explains, with the intention of selling it tomorrow, then you have entered into a risky transaction. The odds of predicting whether share prices will be up or down in a short period are the same as the odds of predicting a coin toss—you will lose half the time. However, says Buffett, if you extend your time horizon out several years, the possibility that a stock is a risky transaction declines meaningfully, assuming of course that you have made a sensible purchase in the first place. "If you ask me the risk of buying Coca-Cola this morning and selling it tomorrow morning," said Buffett, "I'd say that's a very risky transaction."[14] However, in Buffett's mind, there was little risk when he bought Coca-Cola in 1998 with the thought of holding it for 10 years, no matter how the stock market performed in the subsequent time period.

The best we can say about the Modern Portfolio Theory concept of risk is that it is applicable for short-term investors but meaningless for long-term investors. The MPT's definition of risk—how much a stock price bounces around the overall bounciness of the market—is relevant for someone who treats their investment portfolio like a money market account, flinching whenever their portfolio's net asset value drops below $1.

But this begs the question, why would an investor be short-term reactive if their investment goals and objectives are long term? We can make a good argument that managing a portfolio to minimize short-term price volatility has the unhappy effect of suboptimizing long-term investment returns. Second, and more problematic, an investor who obsesses over the short-term price dips is more likely to embrace speculative habits, frenetically buying and selling stocks in a vain attempt to keep their portfolio from declining in price. Warren Buffett as usual puts it succinctly: "If the investor fears price volatility, erroneously viewing as it as a measure of risk, he may, ironically, end up doing some very risky things."[15]

"To invest successfully," said Buffett, "you need not understand beta [or] modern portfolio theory. You may, in fact, be better off knowing nothing of these." He then weighs in: "That, of course, is not the prevailing view at most business schools, whose finance curriculum tends to be dominated by such subjects. In our view, investment students need only two well-taught courses: 'How to Value a Business' and 'How to Think About Market Prices.'"[16]

Business-driven investors look on price volatility occurring in the stock market as a periodic opportunity, nothing else. Otherwise, they rarely give stock price variance much thought, if at all. In a nutshell, business-driven investors do not obsess over ever-changing stock prices. Instead they choose to focus on the economic progress of the companies they own. "In business schools," said Buffett, "volatility is almost universally used as a proxy for risk. Though this pedagogic assumption makes for easy teaching, it is dead wrong. Volatility is *far* from synonymous with risk. Popular formulas that equate the two terms lead students, investors, and CEOs astray."[17]

Lesson learned: Just because a business-driven investor operates in the stock market does not mean they have to worship at the altar of MPT.

The second leg of MPT is portfolio diversification. In his paper "Portfolio Selection," Markowitz said the reason he rejected John Burr Williams' net present value rule, which he called the *expected return rule,* was "that it never implied the superiority of diversification." Markowitz then added, in no uncertain terms, that an investor must reject the idea of a concentrated portfolio. In his view, because error rates do occur, a diversified portfolio is always preferable to a nondiversified one. But not just any diversified portfolio. "It is necessary to avoid investing in securities with high covariances."[18] Markowitz believed investors should diversify across industries because firms in different industries, especially industries with different economic characteristics, have lower covariances than firms within an industry.

Markowitz's definition of risk as price volatility is what drives his decision-making about portfolio management. For those who adhere to MPT, the paramount consideration when managing a portfolio is calculating the best way of reducing price risk. The goal of achieving above-average investment returns is definitely secondary. We have already taken note of Warren Buffett's ideas regarding portfolio management in Chapter 5, and it is the polar opposite of MPT. It's worth repeating: MPT's primary objective for portfolio management is to dampen a bumpy ride in the stock market, not to achieve outstanding investment returns. Buffett often quips, "I would rather have a 15% bumpy ride than a smooth 10% return."[19] No wonder the standard investment approach, practiced by so many, is unable to beat the market.

The best thing Warren Buffett can say about MPT's recommendation for portfolio management is that "diversification serves as a protection against ignorance." He went further: "If you want to make sure that nothing bad happens to you relative [to] the market, you should own everything." As you might remember, Buffett's advice for "know-nothing investors" is to own an index fund. "There is nothing wrong with that," he said. "It's a perfectly sound approach for somebody who doesn't know how to analyze businesses." But that protection comes with a price. According to Buffett, "Modern Portfolio Theory will tell you how to do average. But I think almost anybody can figure out how to do average by fifth grade."[20]

Rethinking Modern Portfolio Theory

The intertwined threads of MPT woven by Markowitz and Sharpe during the 1950s and 1960s consumed the interests of theorists and academic journals, but Wall Street paid no attention. However, all this changed in October 1974 with the culmination of the worst bear market since the Great Depression.

Without question, the 1973–1974 bear market shook the confidence of the old guard, the stock market establishment. The financial damage was just too deep and widespread to wave off. Star portfolio managers who rose to fame touting the "nifty-fifty" stocks of the late 1960s disappeared, leaving behind the rubble that was their portfolio. The self-inflicted wounds caused by years of senseless speculation were simply too grave to ignore.

"No one emerged unscathed," said Peter Bernstein, head of Bernstein-Macaulay, a wealth management firm that personally managed billions of dollars of individual and institutional portfolios, including numerous pension funds. According to Bernstein, employees found the decline in their pension assets alarming. Many wondered if they could afford to retire. This distress, which reverberated throughout the world of finance, called for a change in how professionals managed their clients' accounts.[21]

"The market disaster of 1974 convinced me that there had to be a better way to manage investment portfolios," said Bernstein. "Even if I could have convinced myself to turn my back on the theoretical structure that the academics were erecting, there was too much of it coming from universities for me to accept the view of my colleagues that it was 'a lot of baloney.'" Peter Bernstein soon became the founding editor of the *Journal of Portfolio Management*. There, he said, "my goal was to build a bridge between the gown and the town: to foster a dialogue between the academicians and the practitioners in language they could both understand and thereby enrich the contributions of both."[22]

Thus for the first time in history, our financial destiny rested not on Wall Street or even in the hands of business owners. As the financial industry moved forward in the late 1970s and into the early 1980s, the investment landscape would be defined by university professors. From the ivory towers, they became known as the high priests of modern finance.

Although Bernstein's intention "to foster a dialogue between the academicians and the practitioners" was well meaning, the fact remained that the two groups were speaking different languages. MPT was founded by academics, outside observers of the stock market who believed stock price volatility was the demon that must be defeated. Everything else, including portfolio management and its subsequent investment returns, is submissive to this goal. Conversely, business-driven investors are the insiders, the practitioners who own businesses or at least think of stocks as business ownership. Their charge is not to defeat stock price volatility but to outwit it so as to enhance their investment return. We can say with certainty, business-driven investing is the philosophical antithesis of MPT.

But business-driven investing is not the antichrist. Business-driven investors did not cause the 1973–1974 bear market. No, that debacle lies at the feet of speculators who masked themselves as investors. Glamming for the performance returns of the "nifty-fifty" stocks, these speculators had no idea what value they were receiving for the price being paid. It's been said, "When you use the word 'value' and it means something besides 'price' you probably have to spell it out."[23] But the speculators who blew up the stock market in 1974 had no interest in hearing the message of value investing, much less trying to understand it.

Some observers thought the value camp would take back the reins from these reckless speculators and help drive the stock market back on the tracks. But their numbers were few and their attention was diverted. Into the breach, by default only, the high priests of modern finance emerged. When Peter Bernstein said there was too much research to ignore, I don't think he fully appreciated how deep and wide the teachings of MPT had reached into academia. Dissertation committees at the major universities were constantly anointing new disciples (PhDs), who would soon become the new cardinals (professors), and whose ultimate self-interest drove them to solicit more disciples. PhD dissertations circled MPT and became fodder for a growing library of professional journals all spouting the same message.

Looking back, we can see that the tidal wave of academic research that was crashing down on Wall Street occurred at a fortuitous time. As the dust settled from the 1973–1974 bear market, a new bull market was being planted. Investors, as they customarily do after enough time has lapsed, returned to the stock market in droves.

Investment firms were rapidly being organized, and everything was on the table. Investment objectives were being rewritten. Risk-tolerance questionnaires were invented. More than half the questions asked how the investor felt about price volatility. The more risk averse the answers, the more conservative was the portfolio recommendation. Trading strategies were outlined. Standards of performance were agreed on and ratified by advisors and clients.

Modern Portfolio Theory was easily scalable, which had the effect of speeding up its takeover of the money management industry. A leviathan had been created, quiet at first but now unleashed, and it was preaching low price volatility, broadly diversified portfolios, and conservative returns. And before most fully recognized what was occurring, MPT had taken root, becoming the standard approach for investment management that has lasted to this day.

Efficient Market Hypothesis

The Efficient Market Hypothesis, alternatively referred to as the Efficient Market Theory and closely associated with Modern Portfolio Theory, is the third leg of the stool that holds up modern finance. Although several academicians have written about efficient markets, including the economist Paul Samuelson, the person most credited with developing a comprehensive theory of stock market behavior is Eugene Fama.

Born in Boston in 1939, Fama attended Malden Catholic High School, where he became an honoree of the school's Athletic Hall of Fame, lettering in football, basketball, and baseball. In 1960, he graduated magna cum laude from Tufts University with a degree in romance languages, then moved to the University of Chicago for graduate study, earning both an MBA and PhD in economics and finance.

Fama began studying the change in stock prices the minute he arrived in Chicago. An intense reader, he absorbed all the written work on stock market behavior then available, but it appears he was especially influenced by Benoit Mandelbrot, a French mathematician. Mandelbrot was a maverick. He spent 35 years at IBM's Thomas J. Watson Research Center before moving to Yale, where at the age of 75, he became the oldest professor in the university's history to receive tenure. Along the way, Mandelbrot received more than 15 honorary degrees.

Mandelbrot developed the field of fractal geometry (he coined the term) and applied it to physics, biology, and finance. A fractal is defined as a rough or fragmented shape than can split into parts, each of which is at least a close approximation of its original full self. Examples of fractals include snowflakes, mountains, rivers and streams, blood vessels, trees, ferns, and even broccoli. In studying finance, Mandelbrot argued that because stock prices fluctuate so irregularly, they would never oblige any fundamental or statistical research; furthermore, the pattern of irregular price movements was bound to intensify, causing large and intense shifts.

Like Harry Markowitz and William Sharpe, Eugene Fama was a newcomer to finance, a graduate student looking for a dissertation topic who was neither an investor in the market nor the owner of a business. Instead, also like Markowitz and Sharpe, he was an academician through and through. Even so, his PhD dissertation, "The Behavior of Stock Prices," caught the attention of the finance community. The paper was published in 1963 and later excerpted in the *Financial Analysts Journal* and *The Institutional Investor*.

Fama's message was very clear: stock prices are not predictable, because the market is too efficient. Essentially, an efficient market is one in which at any given time stock prices reflect all available information and trade at exactly their fair value. In an efficient market, as soon as market information becomes available, a great many smart people (Fama called them *rational profit maximizers*) aggressively apply the information in a way that causes prices to adjust simultaneously before anyone else can profit. Predictions about the future, therefore, have no place in an efficient market because share prices adjust too quickly.

Market Efficiency: In Theory

In May 1970, Fama wrote an article for the *Journal of Finance* titled "Efficient Capital Markets: A Review of Theory and Empirical Work." In it, he proposed there were three different types of market efficiency: strong form, semi-strong form, and weak form. The strong form of market efficiency states that all information, whether public or private, is accounted for in the current stock price. The semi-strong form believes that information in public use is immediately reflected in the price of the stock but there is a possibility private information, something that is not publicly available, could help investors boost their returns above the market return. The weak form of market efficiency says that today's stock prices simply reflect all past prices, which are widely available, so no further analysis is needed.

In 1984, Columbia Business School hosted a conference to celebrate the 50th anniversary of the first publication of *Security Analysis*. Warren Buffett was asked to present Ben Graham's value investing approach. Michael Jensen, a finance professor from the University of Rochester, argued on behalf of the Efficient Market Hypothesis. Jensen, along with other academicians—all disciples of Eugene Fama—believed the market quickly and accurately priced stocks, hence active management was a waste of time. No one could beat the stock market. Buffett, not surprisingly, believed otherwise and offered evidence in a speech titled "The Superinvestors of Graham-and-Doddsville."[24]

Buffett began by recapping the central argument of the EMT: The stock market is efficient, all stocks are priced correctly, and therefore anyone who beats the market over the long term is simply lucky. Maybe so, he said, but I know some folks who have done it, and their success can't be explained away simply by random chance.

Still, to give the must-be-luck argument its fair hearing Buffett asked the audience to imagine a coin-flipping contest in which 225 million Americans bet $1 on their guess. After each flip, the losers dropped out and the winners kept the pot to advance to the next round. After 10 events, there would be 220,000 winners left who, by letting their winnings ride, would have gained $1,064. After another 10 tosses, there would be 215 winners, each with $1 million.

Now, Buffett continued, the academicians, analyzing this national contest, would point out that the coin-tossers demonstrated no exceptional skill. The event could just as easily be replicated, they would protest, with a group of 225 million coin-flipping orangutans.

Slowly building his case, Buffett then granted the statistical possibility that, by sheer chance, the orangutans might get the same result. But imagine, he asked the audience, if 40 of the 215 winning animals came from the same zoo. Wouldn't we want to ask the zookeeper what he feeds his now very rich orangutans?

The point, said Buffett, is that whenever a high concentration of anything occurs in one specific area, something unusual may be going on at that spot, and bears investigation. And what if—here comes the clincher—the members of this one unique group are defined not by where they live but by whom they learned from.

And thus we come to what Buffett called the "intellectual village" of Graham and Doddsville. All the examples he presented that day were centered on individuals who managed to beat the market consistently over time—not because of luck but because they all followed the principles learned from the same source: Benjamin Graham and David Dodd.[25]

Market Efficiency: In Practice

If the EMT is correct, there is no possibility, except random chance, that any person or group could outperform the market, and certainly no chance that the same person and group could consistently do so over the long term. Yet, the investment returns of the Graham-Newman Corporation between 1926 and 1956, plus the "Superinvestors of Graham-and-Doddsville" and the "Superinvestors of Buffettville" are prima facie evidence that it *is* possible to outperform the market. What does that say about the EMT?

"Proponents of the theory have never seemed interested in discordant evidence," said Buffett. "Apparently, a reluctance to recant, and thereby demystify the priesthood, is not limited to theologians."[26]

We could talk all day about why EMT is not defensible, but the many reasons can easily be summarized into three broad issues.

- Investors are not always rational. Extensive research in behavioral finance, including Prospect Theory and Myopic Loss Aversion, suggests that investors do not always possess rational expectations.
- Investors do not process financial information correctly. This problem is especially evident, and especially critical, when the issue has to do with the all-important task of determining intrinsic value. Too many investors rely on shortcuts here, and a favorite one is price-to-earnings ratios. Yes it's easy. It's also wrong. Using simple price-to-earnings ratios will not, by itself, yield an accurate estimate of intrinsic value. That takes some work: first, apply owner earnings to a discounted cash flow model, then adjust the intrinsic value calculation for return on invested capital and sales growth.
- Performance yardsticks that emphasize short-term returns over long-term returns incite bad behavior in both portfolio managers and investors.

What drove proponents of the Efficient Market Hypothesis to continually argue the stock market was efficient was the apparent lack of evidence that few investors, if any, could beat the market. And those that did were simply dismissed as random outcomes. However, they didn't stop to consider this critical truth: *The reason why most investors don't beat the market lies not in market efficiency but in the inept strategies used by most investors.*

Warren Buffett's problem with the EMT rests on one central point: It makes no provision for investors who analyzed all the information, gained a competitive advantage by doing so, then acted rationally in executing an investment decision. Buffett elaborates, "As a corollary, professors who taught EMT said that someone throwing darts at stock tables could select a stock portfolio having prospects just as good as one selected by the brightest, most hard-working analyst."

Buffett expands further. "Amazingly, EMT was embraced not only by academics, but many investment professionals and corporate managers as well."

Then in one of Buffett's most insightful observations about EMT, he wrote, "Observing correctly that the market was *frequently* efficient, they went on to conclude incorrectly that it was *always* efficient. The difference between these propositions is night and day."[27]

On a side note, Paul Samuelson, a US economist and early proponent of the Efficient Market Hypothesis, was an early investor in Berkshire Hathaway. In an article written for the *Wall Street Journal* titled "From a Skeptic: A Lesson on Beating the Market," Jason Zweig pointed out that Samuelson invested in Berkshire Hathaway at an average price of $44 per share in 1970, the same year he won the Nobel Prize. Samuelson learned about Warren Buffett and Berkshire Hathaway from Conrad Taff, a private investor who attended Columbia Business School and studied with Ben Graham. Although Taff trumpeted Buffett's track record, it appears that Samuelson was most attracted to the idea of compounding money tax-free because Berkshire didn't pay a dividend.

"Professor Samuelson," wrote Zweig, "who for years had been blasting the mediocrity of most fund managers knew lightning had struck. He soon began buying shares [of Berkshire], adding more over the years."[28] According to his son, Samuelson bequeathed his shares of Berkshire to his children and grandchildren and various charities. If he had kept the Berkshire shares they would have been worth over $100 million. "Professor Samuelson believed the same [as I do]," said Buffett. "Markets are efficient but not perfectly efficient."[29]

Nonetheless, MPT and the EMT are still religiously taught in business schools, a fact that gives Buffett no end of satisfaction: "Naturally, the disservice done students and gullible investment professionals who have swallowed EMT has been an extraordinary service to us and other followers of Graham."

Buffett wryly observed, "In any sort of contest—financial, mental, or physical—it's an enormous advantage to have opponents who have been taught it's useless to even try. From a selfish standpoint, we should probably endow chairs to ensure the perpetual teaching of EMT."[30]

Here, now, is a summary of the major differences between the two major competing investment paradigms.

The *standard approach to investing* accepts MPT as its guiding principles. It believes variance—price volatility—is almighty. Hence, all investment decisions, from an investor's goal to portfolio management, is driven by how a person emotionally handles the bounciness of stock prices. Portfolios are broadly diversified to minimize the variance of returns, while portfolio turnover ratios (how much buying and selling occurs) are elevated in an attempt to keep variance in check. And not too far removed from high-turnover portfolios is an unrelenting goal to achieve short-term price performance. In the standard approach to investing, short-horizon arbitrage is the game.

In *business-driven investing* the guiding principle is the economic returns of stocks, that is, the businesses you own. The long-term compounding growth of intrinsic value is almighty. Stock price volatility, the variance of returns, is an afterthought. Business-driven portfolios are focused, high active share, with low turnover ratios in order to benefit from the economic compounding. Short-term price performance is not considered useful as a meaningful gauge of progress. Instead, business-driven investors favor the long-term economic progress, the look-through earnings of the businesses they own. Business-driven investors frequently quote Ben Graham's famous dictum: "In the short run, the market is a voting machine but in the long run it is a weighing machine."[31]

In the standard approach, investors are in a constant frenetic chase for "votes." In the business-driven approach, investors are less anxious. Instead, they keep a careful eye on the economic "weights" of what they own, knowing full well the scales will eventually balance. In business-driven investing, long-horizon arbitrage is the game.

One last advantage business-driven investors have above all others—and it's critically important—is a crystal-clear understanding of the differences between investment and speculation. They were taught by the best.

Investment and Speculation: Understanding the Difference

The great financial thinkers, including John Burr Williams, John Maynard Keynes, Benjamin Graham, and Warren Buffett, have all taken turns explaining the differences between investment and speculation. This tug-of-war between the two approaches is nothing new. However, the persistent confusion over the differences is a mental mistake that, too often, can be fatal for many investors. Graham rightly warned that the greatest danger an investor faces is not so much speculation, an attitude that has been around for hundreds of years, but acquiring speculative habits without realizing they have done so. And in doing so, an investor ends up with a speculator's return, believing they were investing.

In John Burr Williams' *The Theory of Investment Value*, Chapter III, Section 7, "Investors and Speculators," he writes, "To gain by speculation, a speculator must be able to foresee price changes. Since price changes coincide with changes in marginal opinion, he must in the last analysis be able to foresee *changes in opinion*."

John Maynard Keynes was like-minded. Writing in his last and most important book, *The General Theory of Employment, Interest, and Money*, Keynes describes "the term *speculation* [as] the activity of forecasting the psychology of the market, and the term *enterprise* [as] the activity of forecasting the prospective yield of assets over their life."

Forecasting the "psychology of the market," which requires "foreseeing changes in opinion," caused Keynes to introduce an interesting analogy to describe the behavior of many investors. In his book, Keynes creates a fictitious beauty contest in which the contestants are challenged to select the six prettiest faces from 100 photographs spread across the pages of a newspaper. The trick is not to select the faces the individual finds the prettiest, "but those which he thinks likeliest to catch the fancy of the other competitors, all of whom are looking at the problem in the same point of view."[32]

Keynes believed a similar contest was at work in the stock market: "It is not a case of choosing those [faces] that, to the best of one's judgement, are really the prettiest, nor even those that average opinion genuinely thinks the prettiest. We have reached the third degree where we devote our intelligence to anticipating what the average opinion expects the average opinion to be. And there are some, I believe, who practice the fourth, fifth, and higher degrees."[33]

You might think Keynes' beauty contest is a game played amongst naive individual investors who should know better than to speculate. Or better yet, the rational behavior of institutional investors works in quick fashion to correct the mistakes of ignorant individual investors. But, alas, no. In Keynes' opinion,

> The energies and skill of the professional investor is mainly occupied otherwise. For most of these persons are, in fact, largely concerned, not with making superior long-term forecasts of the probable yield of an investment over its whole life, but with forecasting changes in the conventional basis of valuation a short time ahead of the general public. They are concerned, not with what an investment is really worth to a man who buys it for "keeps," but with what the market will value it, under the influence of mass psychology, three months or a year hence.[34]

Not surprisingly, Warren Buffett's opinion on the differences between investing and speculation is identical to those of Graham, Williams, and Keynes. According to Buffett, "If you're an investor, you're looking at what the asset—in our case, businesses—will do. If you're a speculator, you're primarily forecasting on what the price will do independent of the business."[35]

If you are not thinking about what the asset produces, he warns, you are leaning toward speculation. Then in no uncertain terms, Buffett wrote, "If you focus on the prospective price change, what the next fellow will pay for it, you are speculating."[36]

Similar to Keynes, Buffett was highly suspicious of the motivations of institutional investors, the supposedly smart money in the market. He writes, "You might think that institutions, with their large staffs of highly paid and experienced investment professionals, would be a force for stability and reason in financial markets. They are not: stocks heavily owned and constantly monitored by institutions have often been among the most inappropriately valued."[37]

Because financial markets are ultimately moved by investors, institutional and retail alike, academicians have long been interested in the psychological theories of mob-like behavior. Ben Graham offered a story to help illustrate the irrational behavior of a good many investors, a story that Buffett later shared with Berkshire's shareholders in the 1995 Annual Report. It seems that an oil prospector, moving to his heavenly rewards, was met at the gates by St. Peter with bad news. "You're qualified for residence," said St. Peter, "but as you can see, the compound reserved for oil men is packed. There's no way to squeeze you in." After thinking for a moment, the prospector asked if he might say just four words to the present occupants. That seemed harmless to St. Peter, so the prospector cupped his hand and yelled, "Oil discovered in hell." Immediately the gates to the compound opened and all the oil men marched out to head for the nether regions. Impressed, St. Peter invited the prospector to move in and make himself comfortable. The prospector paused. "No," he said, "I think I will go along with the rest of the boys. There might be some truth to the rumor after all."[38]

It is perplexing to Buffett, with so many well-educated, experienced professionals working on Wall Street, there is not a more logical and rational force in the stock market. After all, business managers cannot determine their share prices. They can only hope, by releasing corporate information, to encourage investors to act rationally. The wild swings in share prices, Buffett notes, have more to do with the "lemming-like" behavior of institutional investors than with the aggregate economic returns of the company they own.

A quick science lesson. Lemmings are small rodents indigenous to the tundra region and are well known for their periodic mass exodus to the sea. Every three or four years, something odd happens. For a variety of reasons, the number of lemmings in the pack increases until a panic-like reaction takes hold; then they plunge themselves into the sea and perish. The behavior of lemmings is not fully understood. Zoologists have a number of theories, but what is generally agreed on is the *crowding* and *competition* among lemmings induces an alteration in their behavior.

Certainly, the institutional market for clients and assets is crowded. And, no doubt, the competition among institutional investors is intense, which, in turn, invokes a strategy to generate the highest rate of return for clients in the shortest period of time—an approach that wins assets.

John Maynard Keynes weighs in: "The battle of wits to anticipate the basis of conventional valuation a few months hence, rather the prospective yield of an investment over a long term of years, does not even require gulls amongst the public to feed the maws of the professional; it can be played by professionals amongst themselves."

He rightly observes that "the professional investor is forced to concern himself with the anticipation of impending changes in the news or the atmosphere, of the kind which experience shows that mass psychology of the market is most influenced."[39]

Writing more than a century ago, Keynes laments that "investment based on genuine long-term expectation is so difficult today as to be scarcely practicable. He who attempts it must surely lead much more laborious days than he who tries to guess better than the crowd how the crowd will behave."

Finally, Keynes observes even though it is the long-term investor who best promotes the value of markets, it is sadly unfair that it is the long-term investor who receives the most criticism: "For it is the essence of his behavior [the long-term investor] that he should be eccentric, unconventional and rash in the eyes of average opinion. If he is successful, that will only confirm the general belief in his rashness; and if in the short run he is unsuccessful, which is very likely, he will not receive much mercy."

Then Keynes added what would become one of his most famous quotes: "Worldly wisdom teaches that it is better for reputation to fail conventionally than to succeed unconventionally."[40]

In *The Intelligent Investor*, Ben Graham sought to distinguish the differences between *timing* and *pricing* in the stock market: "By timing, we mean the endeavor to anticipate the action of the stock market. By pricing, we mean the endeavor to buy stocks when they are quoted below fair value and to sell them when they rise above such value."

Graham then unequivocally states, "We are sure that if he [investor] places his emphasis on timing, in the sense [of] forecasting, he will end up as a speculator and with a speculator's financial results."

In concert with Keynes, Graham adds, "Timing is of great psychological importance for the speculator because he wants to make his profit in hurry. The idea of waiting a year before his stock moves up is repugnant to him. But a waiting period, as such, is of no consequence to the investor."[41]

To give encouragement, Graham adds, "A serious investor is not likely to believe that the day-to-day or even month-to-month fluctuations of the stock market makes him richer or poorer."

He then notes one important fact: "The true investor scarcely ever *is forced to sell* his shares, and at all other times he is free to disregard the current price quotation."

Forewarning the investor, Graham wrote, "The investor who permits himself to be stampeded or unduly worried by unjustified market declines in his holdings is perversely transforming his basic advantage into a basic disadvantage. That man would be better off if his stocks had no market quotation at all, for he would then be spared the mental anguish caused him by *other persons'* mistakes of judgment."[42]

The biggest challenge for the proponents of business-driven investing is how to survive in a world hostile to their success. With all the demerits earned by MPT, Efficient Market Hypothesis, and the persistence of speculation over investing, you would think the stranglehold these approaches have on the money management industry would loosen. But more time is needed. Until then, business-driven investors will have to get comfortable living in a parallel universe.

Investing in a Parallel Universe

At the beginning of Ben Graham's career, he was firmly planted in the idea that temperament was a key component to successful investing. He came to understand that the temperament of the business person was the cornerstone for profitable investing in contrast to the flighty opinions of speculators. Even so, he was constantly dismayed why an individual who became a successful business owner would embrace speculative actions when it came to buying common stocks that were in fact a partial ownership of a company. For Graham, it was difficult to understand why an investor who had received the financial benefits that came from owning a business would choose instead to speculate with their investment just because there was a stock market, a place where individuals could buy and sell their ownership interests in a business.

The tug-of-war between these points of view was a matter of deep concern for Graham. Throughout his life, he made note of the losing battle, and in 1973, he wrote, "The development of the stock market in the recent decades has made the typical investor more dependent on the course of the price quotation and less free than formerly to consider himself merely a business owner."[43] It seemed to him that the news of the moment—any moment—obscured the more important financial data that would determine one's long-term prospects.

It is no surprise that Warren Buffett, Graham's most famous student, adopted the same thinking. Viewing stocks as businesses has been the cornerstone of Buffett's approach for more than 70 years. So, we are left with a conundrum. The father of financial analysis and the world's greatest investor are telling us the same thing: The daily quotations of the stock market are unnecessary for an investor to be successful. Indeed, for most investors they can cause more harm than good. At the same time, investors around the world are consumed with what is happening in the stock market. Every day, they watch financial news programs and carry their mobile phones loaded with real-time quotes, especially the upticks and downticks of their personal holdings.

Ben Graham and Warren Buffett barely thought about the market. The vast majority of investors can think of nothing else.

As a mental exercise, imagine this for a moment. How would you change your behavior if there was no daily stock market pricing? What if the stock market was open only once a year? On that one day, and only then, investors could buy and sell common stocks. For the other 364 days of the year, the only stock-specific information would be quarterly financial reports and any other news deemed material for the owners of the company.

In this hypothetical world, we would inhabit a new financial dimension. It's a place we will call the *investment zone*. Everything you would need to know about buying and selling stocks can be found in the investment zone. Lessons can be learned; an education can be obtained. All the necessary ingredients for becoming a successful investor are available for those who are willing to cross over from the market zone to the investment zone. But if you do, you will not be alone. It is a world where Warren Buffett has lived since 1956.

When Buffett buys common stocks for Berkshire Hathaway he doesn't think in terms of stock prices. For him, stocks are an abstraction. "We approach a transaction," he said, "as if we are buying into a private business"—the entire business. Furthermore, once he has purchased shares in a company, Buffett does not have in mind some future date or a higher price at which he would sell the stock. "We are willing to hold a stock indefinitely so long as we expect the business to increase in intrinsic value at a satisfactory rate."[44]

When Warren Buffett invests in a common stock, he sees a business. Most investors see only a stock price. They spend far too much time and effort watching, predicting, and anticipating prices changes and far too little time understanding the business they now own a part of. Buffett believes the investor and the businessperson should look at the company in the same way, because they essentially want the same thing. The businessperson wants to buy the entire company; the investor wants to buy portions of the company. Both will profit from the growth of intrinsic value of the business they own.

Admittedly, Warren Buffett has a distinct advantage not available to most other investors. Simultaneously owning common stocks and privately owned companies gives him a hands-on perspective. "Can you explain to a fish what it's like to walk on land?" he asked. "One day on land is worth a thousand years of talking about it and one day running a business has exactly the same kind of value."[45] Over the years, Buffett has experienced success and failure in his business ventures and has applied to the stock market the lessons he learned. Most other investors have not been given the same unique education. While they were busy trying to forecast the stock market, Buffett studied income statements and balance sheets, capital reinvestment requirements, and the cash-generating capabilities of his companies. Along the way he had an opportunity to learn from the managerial talents of the companies Berkshire owned.

It is impossible to overstate this: *The bedrock to becoming a successful investor is a purposeful detachment from the stock market.* Mentally, investors must put on blinders so that the stock market does not absorb their attention during every waking moment. It is no longer your primary focus. It is secondary at best, only to be acknowledged periodically when market prices gyrate wildly up and down. That is the only sensible time when a business owner should turn their attention to the stock market, and then only to gauge where there might be a profitable opportunity to buy or sell shares of a business. But all other times, the daily, weekly, monthly news about the stock market is of little interest.

Think of it this way: The market zone is a carnival full of different actors playing different games with different time horizons. Some are investors, some are traders, but most are speculators. And almost all are easily distracted by the endless streaming of financial news telling all who will listen how best to proceed. But business-driven investors mentally distance themselves from this noise. Their game does not change. When the stock the market is speeding up and everyone is blindly, fanatically racing for short-term performance, there invariably comes a point when the business owner simply slows down. And in doing so, sees everything. All that is required is to not forget the lessons learned in the investment zone taught by Warren Buffett.

Whenever they are in the market zone, it is imperative that business-driven investors not allow themselves to be pulled into the vortex of short-term noise. They must never lose sight of this truth: They are managing a portfolio of value-creating companies, all of them compounding their intrinsic value over time.

Warren Buffett and Charlie Munger "believe in the discipline of mastering the best that other people have figured out." Munger once said, "I don't believe in just sitting down and trying to dream it all up yourself. Nobody is that smart."[46]

Buffett agrees. "I've mainly learned by reading," he said. "So I don't think I have any original ideas. Certainly, I talk about reading Graham. I've read Phil Fisher. So I've gotten a lot of ideas myself from reading." He goes on, "You can learn a lot from other people. In fact, I think if you learn basically from other people, you don't have to get too many ideas on your own. You can just apply the best of what you see."[47]

Gaining knowledge is a journey. Warren Buffett and Charlie Munger took much of their wisdom from people who came before them, shaped it into their own mosaic of understanding, and now generously offer it to others—that is, to others who are willing to do their own homework and learn all they can, with a fresh, vigorous, open mind.

"It's extraordinary how resistant some people are to learning anything," said Munger. "What's really astounding," Buffett added, "is how resistant they are even when it's in their self-interest to learn." Then, in a more reflective tone, Buffett continued, "There is just an incredible resistance to thinking or changing. I quoted Bertrand Russell one time, saying, most men would rather die than think. Many have. And in the financial sense, that's very true."[48]

CHAPTER 7

Money Mind

It's the first Saturday in May 2017, and for those who follow Warren Buffett, that means just one thing: the annual Berkshire Hathaway shareholder meeting. In the investment world, there is nothing quite like it.

For five straight hours (not counting a one-hour lunch break), Warren Buffett and Charlie Munger, chairman and vice chairman of Berkshire Hathaway, answer questions from shareholders in the audience and from financial journalists on behalf of their readers and viewers. No attempt is made to vet the questions ahead of time, and every one is answered fully with candor, warmth, and the gentle wit that is the trademark of both men. There is nothing on the head table but water glasses, cans of Coke, See's candy, peanut brittle, and two microphones; no notes, no briefing books; just two men happy to answer questions and talk about their ideas.

The morning session begins as usual.[1] There's a question about driverless trucks and the threat it might become to Burlington Northern Santa Fe (BNSF) Railway or GEICO. Another question is about Berkshire's reinsurance deal with American International Group and a discussion about technology stocks. Buffett is asked about the competitive nature of the airline industry, then his thoughts on Coca-Cola and Kraft Heinz.

Then toward the end of the morning session, a shareholder asks the 28th question, addressed to both Buffett and Munger.

"The two of you have largely avoided the capital allocation mistakes by bouncing ideas off of one another. Will this continue long into Berkshire's future?" Although on the surface the question is about capital allocation, its focus is clearly on succession and who will be making capital allocation decisions many years from now.

Buffett responds first. "Any successor that's put in at Berkshire, capital allocation abilities and proven capital allocation abilities are certain to be the uppermost in the board's mind." Buffett points out that CEOs of a great many companies get to the top from a variety of backgrounds, including sales, legal, engineering, or manufacturing. But once in a leadership role, the CEO has to be able to make the decisions on capital allocation. "Berkshire would not do well," Buffett adds, "if somebody was put in who had a lot of skills in other areas but really did not have an ability to allocate capital."

And then, his next remark makes me sit upright in my chair:

> I've talked about it as being something I call a Money Mind. People can have 120 IQs or 140 IQs or whatever it may be, and some of them have minds that are good at one kind of thing and some of them another. They can do all kinds of other things that most mortals can't do. But I have also known very bright people who do not have Money Minds, and they can make very unintelligent decisions. That skill [capital allocation] isn't the way their wiring works. So we do want somebody and hopefully they've got a lot of talent. But we certainly don't want somebody if they lack a Money Mind.[2]

A Money Mind. I had never heard Buffett say those words before. At that moment I knew that after all those years studying Warren Buffett I was only half right.

I have never met anyone who disagreed with Warren Buffett's investment principles. Those principles became the investment tenets in *The Warren Buffett Way*, and when applied to a focused, low-turnover portfolio strategy the returns are impressive. Whenever I asked someone if they would like to invest in the same way, the answer was almost always, "yes." But as time passed, I discovered that some investors who had chosen to invest like Warren Buffett were struggling. The gap between knowing the stock you own is a business and having the emotional wherewithal to withstand the short-term push and pull of the stock market was, for many, too wide. I came to understand there was a big difference between knowing the path and walking the path.

But on that Saturday morning sitting with my fellow shareholders, I began to realize what was needed to help people invest successfully had less to do with the investment tenets and more to do with achieving the right mindset. Although Ben Graham and Warren Buffett had for years written about the importance of temperament, I had pushed this aside in favor of sharpening my pencil to figure out what a business was worth. The harder it became for people to invest in the stock market, the more I sharpened my pencil. Then, on that eventful Saturday morning in Omaha, I finally realized I had discounted the most important advice.

Let me be clear. Applying the Warren Buffett investment tenets to a few selected stocks harbored in a low-turnover portfolio is, without question, the right approach for achieving above-average returns. However, applying the investment tenets without being well anchored, temperamentally speaking, runs the risk of leaving one's portfolio adrift in the pounding waves of the stock market. Without question, temperament and investment tenets are inextricably connected. One does not work without the other.

Money Mind: In his usual precise way, Warren Buffett gives us a memorable name for a complex notion. That easy-to-remember phrase describes, at one level, a way of thinking about the major questions such as investing wisely. At another level, it summarizes an overall mindset for the modern financial world. It also identifies a person who has made a commitment to learning and facing down irrelevant noise. At a still deeper level, the profound philosophical and ethical constructs at the core of a Money Mind tell us a great deal about the person—a person who is quite likely to be successful in many aspects of life. Including investing.

Sportsman, Teacher, Artist

Remember the clever business ventures Warren Buffett achieved as a young boy? Pretty amazing for someone so young, and a fascinating preview to the adult he would become. But one thing we didn't cover was his passion for playing games. At age six, Buffett became a race promoter—marble races, that is. He would summon his sisters to the bathroom, where they would each line up a marble on the back edge of the bathtub filled with water. With the click of his stopwatch they all cheered for their marble racing to the stopper, where young Warren would declare the winner. Along with his childhood friend Bob Russell, Buffett invented numerous games: one required recording license plate numbers of passing cars and another involved counting how many times an individual letter of the alphabet would appear in that day's *Omaha World-Herald*. And like all boys in Omaha, he loved baseball and University of Nebraska football. What connected all his childhood games together was competition. Buffett *loved* to compete.

Buffett the Sportsman

Today, as most people know, Buffett is an enthusiastic bridge player. It has been said that his motivation for buying his first computer was so he could play bridge online late into the night without having to leave home. "I always say I wouldn't mind going to jail if I had three cellmates who played bridge."[3] Many have noted the similarities of playing bridge and investing. Both are games of probabilities where confidence in decision-making is key. And the best part—both games keep dealing new hands. The puzzle solving never stops. But make no mistake, said Warren, "Investing is the best game."[4]

Investing is not a physical challenge, but it is a game nonetheless, a thinking game. And like all games, investing is a competition and those who play have a strong desire to win. Sports psychologists divide athletes into two groups: product-oriented or process-oriented. The product-oriented athletes, as you might guess, are singularly focused on winning. They can think of nothing else. By contrast, the process-oriented athletes see their sport on a much broader scale. They find rewards in the activity itself, what some refer to as "for the love of the game." In addition, process-oriented athletes are dedicated to self-improvement and the deeper satisfaction that comes from striving for the team.[5]

Investing is also a game of process and outcome. Appreciating the process in sports or investing means acknowledging the journey, not just results. Great investors like Warren Buffett understand and appreciate the long journey that is investing. They don't limit themselves to calculating short-term gains or losses as the sole measuring stick of their ability. Buffett's investment process is for the sake of something far greater than one day's scorecard.

What investors have in common with athletes is that both seek to achieve excellence. Investors, like athletes, are pragmatic, adaptive, and willing to change their habits and routines to improve their chances to win. In order to do so, investors, again like athletes, are perpetually interested in gaining knowledge.

Buffett the Teacher

There are two types of knowledge—*knowledge of acquaintance* and *knowledge about*. Knowledge of acquaintance comes from the *experiencer*, the person who actually has had the experience of gaining the specific knowledge. In this case Warren Buffett is the experiencer. His observations about investing are grounded in his experiences, the acts of buying private companies as well as common stocks. Separately, *knowledge about* is validated by a larger catalog of knowledge, what is called *shared experience*.[6] It was the philosopher and psychologist John Dewey who recommended a social and interactive process of learning. He believed the best education involved learning by doing. However, he also believed that to be effective, an educational experience required interaction between the student and the environment. As such, the student benefits by interacting with the shared experience, the greater catalog of knowledge.

Berkshire Hathaway is a shared experience. Some have referred to it as the *University of Berkshire*.[7] It was made so by Warren Buffett's commitment to his shareholders. It began in 1973, when Buffett sent an invitation to Berkshire's shareholders to spend a few hours asking him questions about the company and investing in general. That year, a dozen shareholders showed up in the employee cafeteria at National Indemnity. Each year, more and more shareholders made the trip to Omaha for the annual shareholder meeting, forcing Buffett to find ever bigger venues to host everyone. Today, the Berkshire meeting is held at the city's largest facility, the Omaha Convention Center and Arena, to which nearly 40,000 investors make the pilgrimage each year.

Berkshire's annual shareholder retreat has become known as the Woodstock of Capitalism. It includes not only the Saturday shareholder meeting but also several investment conferences held before and after the meeting. Berkshire's "students" who come to Omaha each year gather in groups from early in the morning to late into the evening. The conversations about Berkshire and investing never stop. At the shareholder meeting there is a library of books about all things Berkshire. The magnum opus is the Berkshire Hathaway Letters to Shareholders from 1965 to 2022: 57 years' worth of the chairman's letters written by Warren Buffett, 906 pages in all.

What the University of Berkshire has accomplished is to combine the "knowledge of acquaintance" with "knowledge about." A financial journalist once asked Buffett if he expected Berkshire to outperform the market over the next few years. The journalist posed the question as a hypothetical: might his own son do just as well by investing in the broader S&P 500 Index fund. "I think your son will learn more," Buffett the experiencer replied, "by being a shareholder of Berkshire."[8]

Today, virtual learning at the University of Berkshire is available for shareholders and investors who live around the world. Berkshire students can watch videos of Warren Buffett and Charlie Munger on Yahoo Finance. There is the Warren Buffett Archive on CNBC.com. It contains the full Berkshire Hathaway Shareholder Meetings dating back to 1994. YouTube is also stocked full of videos of both Buffett and Munger. There is even a video of Warren Buffett's first-ever television interview in 1962, at the young age of 32.

That Buffett became a teacher is not surprising. His father, his hero, was a teacher in both church and in government. Ben Graham, Buffett's mentor, taught for over 30 years at Columbia University. His partner, Charlie Munger, became a thought leader who expanded the concept of investing into far-reaching ideas across several disciplines. As a teacher, Munger happily shared his thoughts on the importance of achieving worldly wisdom. Buffett himself taught his first class at Omaha University soon after returning from Columbia in 1951. Next, he schooled his partners in the Buffett Partnership for 13 years. And for almost six decades he has educated the Berkshire faithful.

The US philosopher William James believed the best teachers grounded their lessons in the idea of *association*. "Your pupils, whatever else they are," said James, "are at any rate little pieces of associating machinery."[9] In practical pedagogical terms, James explained, this meant teaching by comparing one thing to another. That might seem an abstract notion of education theory, but it has very real application in the investment world. When Ben Graham said investing was "most intelligent when it is most *businesslike*," he was teaching by association. When Warren Buffett said investors should think about stocks as ownership interests in a business, he too was teaching by association. Common stocks that were surreal for many investors suddenly made sense. The purpose of teaching, James wrote, is not to shock one's students but "to shape them towards optimistic and hygienic conclusions."[10] Business-driven investing, as outlined by Warren Buffett, is a grand example of William James' "healthy minds"—his characterization of those who have an attitude toward life that is open, engaged, and optimistic.

In his monograph *Talk to Students*, William James included an essay titled "A Certain Blindness" in which he explored the meaning of life. "Whenever a process of life communicates an eagerness to him who lives it, their life becomes genuinely significant." This eagerness, he wrote, can appear in various activities: sports, art, writing, and reflective thought. But "wherever it is found, there is *zest*, the tingle, the excitement of reality."[11]

Zest is defined as having great enthusiasm and energy. For James, "zest is the vibrant inside of human meaning."[12] When describing Warren Buffett, the name surely applies. Everyone who has made contact with him is instantly connected to his energy, optimism, humor, and boundless enthusiasm.

In the first edition of *The Warren Buffett Way*, I concluded the book with this final paragraph. "He is genuinely excited about coming to work every day. 'I have in life all I want right here,' said Buffett. 'I love every day. I mean, I tap dance in here and work with nothing but the people I like.'"[13] Thirty years later, nothing has changed. I guess you could say *Tap Dancing to Work* is a metaphor for "zest." It is also the title of a wonderful book by Carol Loomis, which catalogs 86 articles about Warren Buffett over a span of 46 years, many of them by Carol herself. "When you finish this book," she wrote, "you will see the arc of Warren's business life."[14] And what a life it has been.

Buffett the Artist

"I feel very good about my work," said Buffett. "When I go into the office every morning, I feel like I'm going to the Sistine Chapel to paint. What could be more fun? It's like an unfinished painting. If I want to paint blue or red on the canvas, I can do it."[15] If Berkshire is the canvas, then the capital is the pigment that the artist Warren Buffett applies with his brush.

The Sistine Chapel ceiling is one large fresco that depicts nine separate scenes from the Book of Genesis. The stunning fact about this majestic work, in addition to its sublime beauty, is that it was created by one person, working alone, under extremely difficult conditions. When Buffett compares his own endeavors to Michelangelo, it is not from braggadocio; his personal humility is deeply held and widely known. I see it rather as a reflection of Buffett's broad interests in many areas of achievement. In that regard, considering

Berkshire's history as one mammoth fresco is simply one more metaphor—a teaching tool Buffett particularly relishes.

The Berkshire fresco would depict many scenes, many challenges, many events. It would be difficult for anyone, even Buffett, to single out one scene in that fresco that is the most famous. It is even a challenge to tabulate the nine most important scenes that make up the Berkshire Hathaway financial masterpiece. So many people, companies, and investments large and small have made an impact on Berkshire. But making sense of all those influences and painting the combined scene is largely the work of one man. Johann Wolfgang von Goethe once said, "Without having seen the Sistine Chapel, one cannot form a truer picture of what one person is capable." In much the same way, we cannot really form an appreciation of Berkshire's story without seeing it as a piece of art from the hand of one individual. And once you have, you come away saying to yourself, "It's astonishing, it astonishes. One of us did that."[16]

The art critic Lance Esplund wrote, "We forget in art, it is not the destination that matters and engages us, but the journey." The journey in art is the same as what is known as "the process" in long-term investing. It is said that looking at art requires a comfortable chair. Why a chair? Because to properly look at art we need to be comfortable, patient, and undistracted. "Then, like artists," explained Esplund, "we might discover that we have moved beyond the art of looking, to the art of finding—the art of seeing."[17]

The decision to purchase a company is very much like an art appreciation class. An investor examines the qualities that classify all great works of business art: the products and services a company provides and its competitive position, the financial returns it generates, and management that decides how to allocate capital. Investing—true investing—is an exploration of the art forms of a business.

When investors *look* at a stock, most quickly tabulate the financial facts without ever *seeing* the important question—how did this occur? And only by asking those questions do you have any real chance of truly understanding and ultimately achieving the insight about what the future answers may be. Just as a painting is too complex to be fully understood with a quick glance, so too is a company. No one can fully understand a company simply by tallying a few accounting factors, passing comments, or flighty opinions.

William James said, "The greatest use of life is to spend it on something that will outlast it."[18] At the end of Steve Jordon's book, *The Oracle of Omaha*, Warren Buffett says this about Berkshire: "I've spent my lifetime working on it. I believe Berkshire's as permanent as you can come up with."[19] The original company, Berkshire Cotton Manufacturing, was incorporated in 1889. Buffett took control in 1965. We can say the original Berkshire is 135 years old, although the modern version is a bit younger at 59, which is still very old compared to the average life span of most large companies.

Corporate longevity lies at the heart of understanding valuation as well as judging a company's long-term sustainable competitive advantage. The survival rate for most companies is not very long. Between 1965 and 2015, only half of the global companies with a market capitalization of at least $250 million survived longer than 10 years. Those that survived and grew up to become members of the Fortune 500 had a somewhat longer life span, but not by much. Today, the implied survival rate for the largest companies is, on average, only 16 years.[20]

The key to understanding corporate longevity is to recognize it is highly correlated to change, what Joseph Schumpeter called the "perennial gale of destruction." What we know is short corporate lives are associated with rapid innovation. When the "rate of change is accelerating, corporate longevity is shrinking."[21]

Now think about all the economic changes that have occurred over the last 250 years. The first—the Industrial Revolution—began in 1771 when Arkwright's water-powered cotton spinning mill opened in Cromford, England. The second, in 1829, the Age of Steam and Railways, was launched with the test of the Rocket steam engine for the Liverpool–Manchester railway. The third is the Age of Steel, Electricity, and Heavy Engineering. It began when Bessemer's steel processing plant opened in Pittsburgh in 1875. The fourth is identified as the Age of Oil, the Automobile, and Mass Production. It began in 1908 when the first Model T rolled out of the Ford assembly plant in Detroit. Today, we are in the midst of the Age of Information and Telecommunications. It began in 1971 in Santa Clara, California, when Intel unveiled the microprocessor.[22] The economic disruption that has occurred since the late 18th century has been astonishing.

Michelangelo's Sistine Chapel ceiling is more than 500 years old. Could Berkshire survive five centuries? Hard to imagine. Even so, despite Schumpeter's creative destruction that has occurred over the last 250 years, the one thing that has not been disrupted is the mathematical constant e—compound interest. So perhaps it is not out of bounds to imagine Berkshire could last another 100 years or longer, outliving every major company in the world.

Berkshire Hathaway: An American Institution

"Berkshire is now a sprawling conglomerate," wrote Buffett, "constantly trying to sprawl further."[23] It began as a "one-trick pony," he said, "beholden to a doomed textile business. And then came a stroke of good luck: National Indemnity became available in 1967."[24] That purchase moved Berkshire Hathaway into the insurance business. Since then, Berkshire's total float (money from premiums available for investment) has grown from $8.6 million to $165 billion, making the company the world's leader of insurance float.

Today, Berkshire owns dozens of companies, but it is largely motored by what Buffett calls "our four giants."[25] The number-one giant has been and continues to be the collection of insurance companies, which provides massive amounts of float for Buffett to invest. The third largest giant is BNSF (Burlington Northern Santa Fe), the largest freight railroad in the United States with 32,500 miles of track spread across 28 states powered by nearly 8,000 locomotives. The fourth largest giant is BHE (Berkshire Hathaway Energy), which Berkshire first purchased in 2000. At that time the company earned $122 million. Twenty years later, BHE generated $4 billion in profits.

What about Berkshire's second largest giant? Not to be left out, the runner-up is Apple, a company Buffett said that "happens to be the better business than any we own."[26] Although only the dividends paid by Apple ($878 million annually) are accounted for in Berkshire's GAAP earnings, the value of Apple's retained earnings, not reported by Berkshire, is immense. Berkshire owns 915 million shares of Apple's common stock worth $162 billion, an ownership interest representing 5.9 percent of the company. Lest you think owning 5.9 percent of a company is not substantive for Berkshire's economic well-being, every 0.1 percent of Apple's earnings in 2022 amounted to $100 million of earnings owned, but not reported, by Berkshire. Said differently, owning 5.9 percent of Apple means Berkshire is, in de facto, the beneficiary of $5.9 billion in earnings, much of which the company retained and directed to buying back Apple stock, thereby increasing Berkshire's ownership in the company without Berkshire having to spend a penny.

Berkshire's unique structure, "the ability to buy *pieces* of a wonderful business—a.k.a. common stocks—is not a course of action open to most managements," said Buffett. As noted, throughout its history, Berkshire has been in the enviable position of being able to purchase wholly owned businesses as well as the common shares of publicly traded companies. He continues: "The businesses we are offered by the stock market every day—in small pieces, to be sure—are often far more attractive than the businesses we are concurrently being offered in their entirety."

In addition, Buffett points out, "The capital gains realized from owning common stocks has enabled Berkshire to make certain large acquisitions that otherwise would have been beyond our financial capabilities."

Finally, he goes on to say, "The world is Berkshire's oyster—a world offering us a range of opportunities far beyond those realistically open to most companies."[27] True indeed, but this is also worth remembering: The opportunities in the stock market available for Berkshire are also available for individual investors.

The long journey since the time Berkshire bought National Indemnity has been "a bumpy road," said Buffett, "involving a combination of *continuous* savings by our owners (retained earnings), the power of compounding, our avoidance of *major* mistakes and—most important of all—the American tailwind." Buffett confessed, "America would have done fine without Berkshire. The reverse is *not* true."[28]

Warren Buffett is unabashedly bullish on the United States of America. He has never been shy to express his belief that the United States offers tremendous opportunity to anyone who is willing to work hard. Conventional wisdom holds that it is the young who are the eternal optimists and as you get older pessimism begins to tilt the scale. But Buffett appears to be the exception. And I think part of the reason is that for more than eight decades he has invested in the US stock market.

Since March 11, 1942, it has been 82 years since Warren Buffett bought his first shares of stock. "I was 11, and I went all in, investing $114.75 I had been accumulating since age six. What I had bought was three shares of Cities Services preferred stock. I had become a capitalist, and it felt good."[29]

Writing in the 2016 Berkshire Hathaway Annual Report, Buffett pointed out "America's economic achievements have led to staggering profits for stockholders. During the 20th century, the Dow-Jones Industrial advanced from 66 to 11,497, a 17,320% gain." Now think about all the economic, political, and military challenges the United States faced over those 100 years.

Buffett believes that "American business—and consequently a basket of stocks—is virtually certain to be worth far more in the years ahead. Innovation, productivity gains, entrepreneurial spirit, and abundance of capital will see to that. Ever-present naysayers may prosper by marketing their gloomy forecasts. But heaven help them if they act on the nonsense they peddle."

He added, "Many companies, of course, will fall behind, and some will fail. Winnowing of that sort is a product of market dynamism. Moreover, the years ahead will occasionally deliver major market declines—even panics that will affect virtually all stocks."[30]

Buffett then counseled: "During such scary periods, you should never forget two things: First, widespread fear is your *friend* as an investor, because it serves up bargain purchases. Second, *personal fear is your enemy.* It will also be unwarranted. Investors who avoid high and unnecessary costs and simply sit for an extended period with a collection of large, conservatively financed American businesses will almost certainly do well."[31]

Then in one of his most famous protestations, Buffett reminds his shareholders: "It's been a terrible mistake to bet against America, and now is not that time to start. America's golden goose of commerce and innovation will continue to lay more and larger eggs. And, yes, America's kids will live far better than their parents did."[32]

In *The Republic,* Plato recognizes four virtues: *prudence, justice, fortitude,* and *temperance.* They are called the cardinal virtues because Plato regarded them as the basic qualities required for leading a morally fit life. The word *cardinal* is not a reference to the Cardinals in the Roman Catholic Church. Rather it comes from Latin, the root word being a "door hinge." As such, the cardinal virtues were thought to be pivotal for someone to live a moral life. Prudence is defined as acting with care for the future. Prudent investing is the cornerstone of thoughtful investing. Those who believe in justice know how to recognize what is appropriate and well deserved, a critical skill for evaluating investment performance. Fortitude is defined as having courage in the face of adversity. We all know the importance of holding steadfast in volatile stock markets. Last, Plato defined temperance as *soundmindedness,* which he believed was the most important of all virtues. *Soundmindedness*—that marvelous word—may be the perfect descriptor for the Money Mind. Together, the four cardinal virtues are the linchpins for long-term investing.

Those who have studied Warren Buffett's life can see a person who lives a virtuous life, not only in the game of investing but also in the grander scheme of life. As we all know, Buffett's charity is unmatched. He has pledged to give away 99 percent of his net worth to charitable organizations and foundations. In 2023, Buffett donated $4.6 billion in Berkshire Hathaway stock to five charities including the Bill and Melinda Gates Foundation, the Susan Thompson Foundation, the Howard G. Buffett Foundation, the Sherwood Foundation, and the NoVo Foundation. Since 2006, Buffett has given away over $50 billion in Berkshire stock, more than his net worth of $43 billion at the end of 2006 and made possible by the continued capital appreciation of his Berkshire Hathaway shares. Today, Warren Buffett still owns $112 billion in Berkshire stock, which means he will return over $160 billion of his wealth back to society. Nothing in history compares.

Today, Berkshire Hathaway is in transition. In 2018, Buffett announced Ajit Jain, CEO of National Indemnity, would become vice chairman of insurance operations at Berkshire and Greg Abel, CEO of Berkshire Hathaway Energy, would become vice chairman of the non-insurance operations. Since then, it has been disclosed that when the time comes it will be Greg Abel who will become CEO of Berkshire Hathaway. Howard Buffett, Warren's oldest son, is in position to assume the chairman's role when called on. Last, Todd Combs and Ted Wechsler, who joined Berkshire Hathaway in 2011 and 2012, respectively, are now managing a portion of Berkshire's investment portfolio. The necessary people are in place when the day comes that Warren Buffett is no longer answering shareholder questions at the annual shareholder meeting.

Even so, many question whether Berkshire will endure without Warren Buffett. "People say Warren Buffett is so special that Berkshire can't survive losing him," said Lawrence Cunningham, professor and author of several books on Buffett and Berkshire Hathaway. "But I say Berkshire is so special that it can survive without him, thanks to the culture of permanence he cultivated."[33] Cunningham believes the permanence of Berkshire resides in its culture. Susan Decker, a member of Berkshire Hathaway's board of directors, agrees. When asked if she thought Berkshire was sustainable after Warren Buffett, Decker replied in the affirmative: "It is about the culture." And long-time friend Carol Loomis, who has edited the Berkshire Hathaway's Chairman's Letter for decades, echoed, "It's the people."[34]

With all that Warren Buffett has professionally achieved, arguably his greatest accomplishment was breathing life into a culture that became Berkshire Hathaway. At the heart of the company is a community of owner partners, managers, and employees who above all else seek to rationally allocate capital. This primary objective is what fuels the engine that motors Berkshire Hathaway. Why would anyone think this could not continue many more decades into the future? When asked whether his eventual exit will halt this nearly six decades of success, Warren Buffett simply replied, "The reputation belongs to Berkshire now."[35]

Appendix A

Berkshire's Performance Versus S&P 500 Index (1965–2022)

Table A.1 Berkshire's Performance Versus S&P 500 Index (1965–2022)

Year	Annual Percentage Change in Per-Share Market Value of Berkshire	in S&P 500 with Dividends Included
1965	49.5	10.0
1966	(3.4)	(11.7)
1967	13.3	30.9
1968	77.8	11.0
1969	19.4	(8.4)
1970	(4.6)	3.9
1971	80.5	14.6
1972	8.1	18.9
1973	(2.5)	(14.8)
1974	(48.7)	(26.4)
1975	2.5	37.2
1976	129.3	23.6
1977	46.8	(7.4)
1978	14.5	6.4
1979	102.5	18.2
1980	32.8	32.3
1981	31.8	(5.0)
1982	38.4	21.4
1983	69.0	22.4
1984	(2.7)	6.1
1985	93.7	31.6
1986	14.2	18.6
1987	4.6	5.1
1988	59.3	16.6
1989	84.6	31.7

(Continued)

Table A.1 (Continued)

Year	Annual Percentage Change in Per-Share Market Value of Berkshire	in S&P 500 with Dividends Included
1990	(23.1)	(3.1)
1991	35.6	30.5
1992	29.8	7.6
1993	38.9	10.1
1994	25.0	1.3
1995	57.4	37.6
1996	6.2	23.0
1997	34.9	33.4
1998	52.2	28.6
1999	(19.9)	21.0
2000	26.6	(9.1)
2001	6.5	(11.9)
2002	(3.8)	(22.1)
2003	15.8	28.7
2004	4.3	10.9
2005	0.8	4.9
2006	24.1	15.8
2007	28.7	5.5
2008	(31.8)	(37.0)
2009	2.7	26.5
2010	21.4	15.1
2011	(4.7)	2.1
2012	16.8	16.0
2013	32.7	32.4
2014	27.0	13.7
2015	(12.5)	1.4
2016	23.4	12.0
2017	21.9	21.8
2018	2.8	(4.4)
2019	11.0	31.5
2020	2.4	18.4
2021	29.6	28.7
2022	4.0	(18.1)
Compounded Annual Gain — 1965–2022	19.8%	9.9%
Overall Gain — 1964–2022	3,787,464%	24,708%

Note: Data are for calendar years with these exceptions: 1965 and 1966, year ended 9/30; 1967, 15 months ended 12/31.

Appendix B

Berkshire's Common Stock Portfolios (1977–2021)

Table B.1 Berkshire Hathaway 1977 Common Stock Portfolio

Number of Shares	Company	Cost	Market Value
934,300	The Washington Post Company	$ 10,628	$ 33,401
1,969,953	GEICO Convertible Preferred	19,417	33,033
592,650	Interpublic Group of Companies	4,531	17,187
220,000	Capital Cities Communications, Inc.	10,909	13,228
1,294,308	GEICO Common Stock	4,116	10,516
324,580	Kaiser Aluminum and Chemical Corp.	11,218	9,981
226,900	Knight-Ridder Newspapers	7,534	8,736
170,800	Ogilvy & Mather International	2,762	6,960
1,305,800	Kaiser Industries, Inc.	778	6,039
	Total	$ 71,893	$ 139,081
	All other common stocks	34,996	41,992
	Total common stocks	$ 106,889	$ 181,073

Note: Dollar amounts are in thousands.
Source: 1977 Berkshire Hathaway Annual Report.

Appendix B

Table B.2 Berkshire Hathaway 1978 Common Stock Portfolio

Number of Shares	Company	Cost	Market Value
934,000	The Washington Post Company	$ 10,628	$ 43,445
1,986,953	GEICO Convertible Preferred	19,417	28,314
953,750	SAFECO Corporation	23,867	26,467
592,650	Interpublic Group of Companies	4,531	19,039
1,066,934	Kaiser Aluminum and Chemical Corp.	18,085	18,671
453,800	Knight-Ridder Newspapers	7,534	10,267
1,294,308	GEICO Common Stock	4,116	9,060
246,450	American Broadcasting Companies	6,082	8,626
	Total	$ 94,260	$ 163,889
	All other common stocks	39,506	57,040
	Total common stocks	$ 133,766	$ 220,929

Note: Dollar amounts are in thousands.
Source: 1978 Berkshire Hathaway Annual Report.

Table B.3 Berkshire Hathaway 1979 Common Stock Portfolio

Number of Shares	Company	Cost	Market Value
5,730,114	GEICO Corp. (common stock)	$ 28,288	$ 68,045
1,868,000	The Washington Post Company	10,628	39,241
1,007,500	Handy & Harman	21,825	38,537
953,750	SAFECO Corporation	23,867	35,527
711,180	Interpublic Group of Companies	4,531	23,736
1,211,834	Kaiser Aluminum and Chemical Corp.	20,629	23,328
771,900	F.W. Woolworth Company	15,515	19,394
328,700	General Foods, Inc.	11,437	11,053
246,450	American Broadcasting Companies	6,082	9,673
289,700	Affiliated Publications	2,821	8,800
391,400	Ogilvy & Mather International	3,709	7,828
282,500	Media General, Inc.	4,545	7,345
112,545	Amerada Hess	2,861	5,487
	Total	$ 156,738	$ 297,994
	All other common stocks	28,675	36,686
	Total common stocks	$ 185,413	$ 334,680

Note: Dollar amounts are in thousands.
Source: 1979 Berkshire Hathaway Annual Report.

Table B.4 Berkshire Hathaway 1980 Common Stock Portfolio

Number of Shares	Company	Cost	Market Value
7,200,000	GEICO Corporation	$ 47,138	$ 105,300
1,983,812	General Foods	62,507	59,889
2,015,000	Handy & Harman	21,825	58,435
1,250,525	SAFECO Corporation	32,063	45,177
1,868,600	The Washington Post Company	10,628	42,277
464,317	Aluminum Company of America	25,577	27,685
1,211,834	Kaiser Aluminum and Chemical Corp.	20,629	27,569
711,180	Interpublic Group of Companies	4,531	22,135
667,124	F.W. Woolworth Company	13,583	16,511
370,088	Pinkerton's, Inc.	12,144	16,489
475,217	Cleveland-Cliffs Iron Company	12,942	15,894
434,550	Affiliated Publications, Inc.	2,821	12,222
245,700	R.J. Reynolds Industries	8,702	11,228
391,400	Ogilvy & Mather International	3,709	9,981
282,500	Media General	4,545	8,334
247,039	National Detroit Corporation	5,930	6,299
151,104	The Times Mirror Company	4,447	6,271
881,500	National Student Marketing	5,128	5,895
	Total	$ 298,848	$ 497,591
	All other common stocks	26,313	32,096
	Total common stocks	$ 325,161	$ 529,687

Note: Dollar amounts are in thousands.
Source: 1980 Berkshire Hathaway Annual Report.

Table B.5 Berkshire Hathaway 1981 Common Stock Portfolio

Number of Shares	Company	Cost	Market Value
7,200,000	GEICO Corporation	$ 47,138	$ 199,800
1,764,824	R.J. Reynolds Industries	76,668	83,127
2,101,244	General Foods	66,277	66,714
1,868,600	The Washington Post Company	10,628	58,160
2,015,000	Handy & Harman	21,825	36,270
785,225	SAFECO Corporation	21,329	31,016

(Continued)

Table B.5 (Continued)

Number of Shares	Company	Cost	Market Value
711,180	Interpublic Group of Companies	4,531	23,202
370,088	Pinkerton's, Inc.	12,144	19,675
703,634	Aluminum Company of America	19,359	18,031
420,441	Arcata Corporation	14,076	15,136
475,217	Cleveland-Cliffs Iron Company	12,942	14,362
451,650	Affiliated Publications, Inc.	3,297	14,362
441,522	GATX Corporation	17,147	13,466
391,400	Ogilvy & Mather International	3,709	12,329
282,500	Media General	4,545	11,088
	Total	$ 335,615	$ 616,490
	All other common stocks	16,131	22,739
	Total common stocks	$ 351,746	$ 639,229

Note: Dollar amounts are in thousands.
Source: 1981 Berkshire Hathaway Annual Report.

Table B.6 Berkshire Hathaway 1982 Common Stock Portfolio

Number of Shares	Company	Cost	Market Value
7,200,000	GEICO Corporation	$ 47,138	$ 309,600
3,107,675	R.J. Reynolds Industries	142,343	158,715
1,868,600	The Washington Post Company	10,628	103,240
2,101,244	General Foods	66,277	83,680
1,531,391	Time, Inc.	45,273	79,824
908,800	Crum & Forster	47,144	48,962
2,379,200	Handy & Harman	27,318	46,692
711,180	Interpublic Group of Companies	4,531	34,314
460,650	Affiliated Publications, Inc.	3,516	16,929
391,400	Ogilvy & Mather International	3,709	17,319
282,500	Media General	4,545	12,289
	Total	$ 402,422	$ 911,564
	All other common stocks	21,611	34,058
	Total common stocks	$ 424,033	$ 945,622

Note: Dollar amounts are in thousands.
Source: 1982 Berkshire Hathaway Annual Report.

Table B.7 Berkshire Hathaway 1983 Common Stock Portfolio

Number of Shares	Company	Cost	Market Value
6,850,000	GEICO Corporation	$ 47,138	$ 398,156
5,618,661	R.J. Reynolds Industries	268,918	314,334
4,451,544	General Foods	163,786	228,698
1,868,600	The Washington Post Company	10,628	136,875
901,788	Time, Inc.	27,732	56,860
2,379,200	Handy & Harman	27,318	42,231
636,310	Interpublic Group of Companies	4,056	33,088
690,975	Affiliated Publications, Inc.	3,516	26,603
250,400	Ogilvy & Mather International	2,580	12,833
197,200	Media General	3,191	11,191
	Total	$ 558,863	$ 1,260,869
	All other common stocks	7,485	18,044
	Total common stocks	$ 566,348	$ 1,278,913

Note: Dollar amounts are in thousands.
Source: 1983 Berkshire Hathaway Annual Report.

Table B.8 Berkshire Hathaway 1984 Common Stock Portfolio

Number of Shares	Company	Cost	Market Value
6,850,000	GEICO Corporation	$ 47,138	$ 397,300
4,047,191	General Foods	149,870	226,137
3,895,710	Exxon Corporation	173,401	175,307
1,868,600	The Washington Post Company	10,628	149,955
2,553,488	Time, Inc.	89,237	109,162
740,400	American Broadcasting Companies	44,416	46,738
2,379,200	Handy & Harman	27,318	38,662
690,975	Affiliated Publications, Inc.	3,516	32,908
818,872	Interpublic Group of Companies	2,570	28,149
555,949	Northwest Industries	26,581	27,242
	Total	$ 573,340	$ 1,231,560
	All other common stocks	11,634	37,326
	Total common stocks	$ 584,974	$ 1,268,886

Note: Dollar amounts are in thousands.
Source: 1984 Berkshire Hathaway Annual Report.

Table B.9 Berkshire Hathaway 1985 Common Stock Portfolio

Number of Shares	Company	Cost	Market Value
6,850,000	GEICO Corporation	$ 45,713	$ 595,950
1,727,765	The Washington Post Company	9,731	205,172
900,800	American Broadcasting Companies	54,435	108,997
2,350,922	Beatrice Companies, Inc.	106,811	108,142
1,036,461	Affiliated Publications, Inc.	3,516	55,710
2,553,488	Time, Inc.	20,385	52,669
2,379,200	Handy & Harman	27,318	43,718
	Total	$ 267,909	$ 1,170,358
	All other common stocks	7,201	27,963
	Total common stocks	$ 275,110	$ 1,198,321

Note: Dollar amounts are in thousands.
Source: 1985 Berkshire Hathaway Annual Report.

Table B.10 Berkshire Hathaway 1986 Common Stock Portfolio

Number of Shares	Company	Cost	Market Value
2,990,000	Capital Cities/ABC, Inc.	$ 515,775	$ 801,694
6,850,000	GEICO Corporation	45,713	674,725
1,727,765	The Washington Post Company	9,731	269,531
2,379,200	Handy & Harman	27,318	46,989
489,300	Lear Siegler, Inc.	44,064	44,587
	Total	$ 642,601	$ 1,837,526
	All other common stocks	12,763	36,507
	Total common stocks	$ 655,364	$ 1,874,033

Note: Dollar amounts are in thousands.
Source: 1986 Berkshire Hathaway Annual Report.

Table B.11 Berkshire Hathaway 1987 Common Stock Portfolio

Number of Shares	Company	Cost	Market Value
3,000,000	Capital Cities/ABC, Inc.	$ 517,500	$ 1,035,000
6,850,000	GEICO Corporation	45,713	756,925
1,727,765	The Washington Post Company	9,731	323,092
	Total common stocks	$ 572,944	$ 2,115,017

Note: Dollar amounts are in thousands.
Source: 1987 Berkshire Hathaway Annual Report.

Table B.12 Berkshire Hathaway 1988 Common Stock Portfolio

Number of Shares	Company	Cost	Market Value
3,000,000	Capital Cities/ABC, Inc.	$ 517,500	$ 1,086,750
6,850,000	GEICO Corporation	45,713	849,400
14,172,500	The Coca-Cola Company	592,540	632,448
1,727,765	The Washington Post Company	9,731	364,126
2,400,000	Federal Home Loan Mortgage Corp.	71,729	121,200
	Total common stocks	$ 1,237,213	$ 3,053,924

Note: Dollar amounts are in thousands.
Source: 1988 Berkshire Hathaway Annual Report.

Table B.13 Berkshire Hathaway 1989 Common Stock Portfolio

Number of Shares	Company	Cost	Market Value
23,350,000	The Coca-Cola Company	$ 1,023,920	$ 1,803,787
3,000,000	Capital Cities/ABC, Inc.	517,500	1,692,375
6,850,000	GEICO Corporation	45,713	1,044,625
1,727,765	The Washington Post Company	9,731	486,366
2,400,000	Federal Home Loan Mortgage Corp.	71,729	161,100
	Total common stocks	$ 1,668,593	$ 5,188,253

Note: Dollar amounts are in thousands.
Source: 1989 Berkshire Hathaway Annual Report.

Table B.14 Berkshire Hathaway 1990 Common Stock Portfolio

Number of Shares	Company	Cost	Market Value
46,700,000	The Coca-Cola Company	$ 1,023,920	$ 2,171,550
3,000,000	Capital Cities/ABC, Inc.	517,500	1,377,375
6,850,000	GEICO Corporation	45,713	1,110,556
1,727,765	The Washington Post Company	9,731	342,097
2,400,000	Federal Home Loan Mortgage Corp.	71,729	117,000
	Total common stocks	$ 1,958,024	$ 5,407,953

Note: Dollar amounts are in thousands.
Source: 1990 Berkshire Hathaway Annual Report.

Appendix B

Table B.15 Berkshire Hathaway 1991 Common Stock Portfolio

Number of Shares	Company	Cost	Market Value
46,700,000	The Coca-Cola Company	$ 1,023,920	$ 3,747,675
6,850,000	GEICO Corporation	45,713	1,363,150
24,000,000	The Gillette Company	600,000	1,347,000
3,000,000	Capital Cities/ABC, Inc.	517,500	1,300,500
2,495,200	Federal Home Loan Mortgage Corp.	77,245	343,090
1,727,765	The Washington Post Company	9,731	336,050
31,247,000	Guinness plc	264,782	296,755
5,000,000	Wells Fargo & Company	289,431	290,000
	Total common stocks	$ 2,828,322	$ 9,024,220

Note: Dollar amounts are in thousands.
Source: 1991 Berkshire Hathaway Annual Report.

Table B.16 Berkshire Hathaway 1992 Common Stock Portfolio

Number of Shares	Company	Cost	Market Value
93,400,000	The Coca-Cola Company	$ 1,023,920	$ 3,911,125
34,250,000	GEICO Corporation	45,713	2,226,250
3,000,000	Capital Cities/ABC, Inc.	517,500	1,523,500
24,000,000	The Gillette Company	600,000	1,365,000
16,196,700	Federal Home Loan Mortgage Corp.	414,527	783,515
6,358,418	Wells Fargo & Company	380,983	485,624
4,350,000	General Dynamics	312,438	450,769
1,727,765	The Washington Post Company	9,731	396,954
38,335,000	Guinness plc	333,019	299,581
	Total common stocks	$ 3,637,831	$ 11,442,318

Note: Dollar amounts are in thousands.
Source: 1992 Berkshire Hathaway Annual Report.

Table B.17 Berkshire Hathaway 1993 Common Stock Portfolio

Number of Shares	Company	Cost	Market Value
93,400,000	The Coca-Cola Company	$ 1,023,920	$ 4,167,975
34,250,000	GEICO Corporation	45,713	1,759,594
24,000,000	The Gillette Company	600,000	1,431,000
2,000,000	Capital Cities/ABC, Inc.	345,000	1,239,000
6,791,218	Wells Fargo & Company	423,680	878,614
13,654,600	Federal Home Loan Mortgage Corp.	307,505	681,023
1,727,765	The Washington Post Company	9,731	440,148
4,350,000	General Dynamics	94,938	401,287
38,335,000	Guinness plc	333,019	270,822
	Total common stocks	$ 3,183,506	$ 11,269,463

Note: Dollar amounts are in thousands.
Source: 1993 Berkshire Hathaway Annual Report.

Table B.18 Berkshire Hathaway 1994 Common Stock Portfolio

Number of Shares	Company	Cost	Market Value
93,400,000	The Coca-Cola Company	$ 1,023,920	$ 5,150,000
24,000,000	The Gillette Company	600,000	1,797,000
20,000,000	Capital Cities/ABC, Inc.	345,000	1,705,000
34,250,000	GEICO Corporation	45,713	1,678,250
6,791,218	Wells Fargo & Company	423,680	984,272
27,759,941	American Express Company	723,919	818,918
13,654,600	Federal Home Loan Mortgage Corp.	270,468	644,441
1,727,765	The Washington Post Company	9,731	418,983
19,453,300	PNC Bank Corporation	503,046	410,951
6,854,500	Gannett Co., Inc.	335,216	365,002
	Total common stocks	$ 4,280,693	$ 13,972,817

Note: Dollar amounts are in thousands.
Source: 1994 Berkshire Hathaway Annual Report.

Appendix B

Table B.19 Berkshire Hathaway 1995 Common Stock Portfolio

Number of Shares	Company	Cost	Market Value
49,456,900	American Express Company	$ 1,392.70	$ 2,046.30
20,000,000	Capital Cities/ABC, Inc.	345.00	2,467.50
100,000,000	The Coca-Cola Company	1,298.90	7,425.00
12,502,500	Federal Home Loan Mortgage Corp.	260.10	1,044.00
34,250,000	GEICO Corporation	45.70	2,393.20
48,000,000	The Gillette Company	600.00	2,502.00
6,791,218	Wells Fargo & Company	423.70	1,466.90
	Total common stocks	$ 4,366.10	$ 19,344.90

Note: Dollar amounts are in millions.
Source: 1995 Berkshire Hathaway Annual Report.

Table B.20 Berkshire Hathaway 1996 Common Stock Portfolio

Number of Shares	Company	Cost	Market Value
49,456,900	American Express Company	$ 1,392.70	$ 2,794.30
200,000,000	The Coca-Cola Company	1,298.90	10,525.00
24,614,214	The Walt Disney Company	577.00	1,716.80
64,246,000	Federal Home Loan Mortgage Corp.	333.40	1,772.80
48,000,000	The Gillette Company	600.00	3,732.00
30,156,600	McDonald's Corporation	1,265.30	1,368.40
1,727,765	The Washington Post Company	10.60	579.00
7,291,418	Wells Fargo & Company	497.80	1,966.90
	Total common stocks	$ 5,975.70	$ 24,455.20

Note: Dollar amounts are in millions.
Source: 1996 Berkshire Hathaway Annual Report.

Table B.21 Berkshire Hathaway 1997 Common Stock Portfolio

Number of Shares	Company	Cost	Market Value
49,456,900	American Express Company	$ 1,392.70	$ 4,414.00
200,000,000	The Coca-Cola Company	1,298.90	13,337.50
21,563,414	The Walt Disney Company	381.20	2,134.80
63,977,600	Freddie Mac	329.40	2,683.10
48,000,000	The Gillette Company	600.00	4,821.00
23,733,198	Travelers Group Inc.	604.40	1,278.60
1,727,765	The Washington Post Company	10.60	840.60
6,690,218	Wells Fargo & Company	412.60	2,270.90
	Total common stocks	$ 5,029.80	$ 31,780.50

Note: Dollar amounts are in millions.
Source: 1997 Berkshire Hathaway Annual Report.

Table B.22 Berkshire Hathaway 1998 Common Stock Portfolio

Number of Shares	Company	Cost*	Market Value
50,536,900	American Express Company	$ 1,470	$ 5,180
200,000,000	The Coca-Cola Company	1,299	13,400
51,202,242	The Walt Disney Company	281	1,536
60,298,000	Freddie Mac	308	3,885
96,000,000	The Gillette Company	600	4,590
1,727,765	The Washington Post Company	11	999
63,595,180	Wells Fargo & Company	392	2,540
	Others	2,683	5,135
	Total common stocks	$ 7,044	$ 37,265

*Represents tax-basis cost, which, in aggregate, is $1.5 billion less than GAAP cost.
Note: Dollar amounts are in millions.
Source: 1998 Berkshire Hathaway Annual Report.

Appendix B

Table B.23 Berkshire Hathaway 1999 Common Stock Portfolio

Number of Shares	Company	Cost*	Market Value
50,536,900	American Express Company	$ 1,470	$ 8,402
200,000,000	The Coca-Cola Company	1,299	11,650
59,559,300	The Walt Disney Company	281	1,536
60,298,000	Freddie Mac	294	2,803
96,000,000	The Gillette Company	600	3,954
1,727,765	The Washington Post Company	11	960
59,136,680	Wells Fargo & Company	349	2,391
	Others	4,180	6,848
	Total common stocks	$ 8,203	$ 37,008

*Represents tax-basis cost, which, in aggregate, is $691 million less than GAAP cost.
Note: Dollar amounts are in millions.
Source: 1999 Berkshire Hathaway Annual Report.

Table B.24 Berkshire Hathaway 2000 Common Stock Portfolio

Number of Shares	Company	Cost	Market Value
151,610,700	American Express Company	$ 1,470	$ 8,329
200,000,000	The Coca-Cola Company	1,299	12,188
96,000,000	The Gillette Company	600	3,468
1,727,765	The Washington Post Company	11	1,066
55,071,380	Wells Fargo & Company	319	3,067
	Others	6,703	9,501
	Total common stocks	$ 10,402	$ 37,619

Note: Dollar amounts are in millions.
Source: 2000 Berkshire Hathaway Annual Report.

Table B.25 Berkshire Hathaway 2001 Common Stock Portfolio

Number of Shares	Company	Cost	Market Value
151,610,700	American Express Company	$ 1,470	$ 5,410
200,000,000	The Coca-Cola Company	1,299	9,430
96,000,000	The Gillette Company	600	3,206
15,999,200	H&R Block, Inc.	255	715
24,000,000	Moody's Corporation	499	957
1,727,765	The Washington Post Company	11	916
53,265,080	Wells Fargo & Company	306	2,315
	Others	4,103	5,726
	Total common stocks	$ 8,543	$ 28,675

Note: Dollar amounts are in millions.
Source: 2001 Berkshire Hathaway Annual Report.

Table B.26 Berkshire Hathaway 2002 Common Stock Portfolio

Number of Shares	Company	Cost	Market Value
151,610,700	American Express Company	$ 1,470	$ 5,359
200,000,000	The Coca-Cola Company	1,299	8,768
15,999,200	H&R Block, Inc.	255	643
24,000,000	Moody's Corporation	499	991
1,727,765	The Washington Post Company	11	1,275
53,265,080	Wells Fargo & Company	306	2,497
	Others	4,621	5,383
	Total common stocks	$ 9,146	$ 28,363

Note: Dollar amounts are in millions.
Source: 2002 Berkshire Hathaway Annual Report.

Appendix B

Table B.27 Berkshire Hathaway 2003 Common Stock Portfolio

Number of Shares	Company	Cost	Market Value
151,610,700	American Express Company	$ 1,470	$ 7,312
200,000,000	The Coca-Cola Company	1,299	10,150
96,000,000	The Gillette Company	600	3,526
14,610,900	H&R Block, Inc.	227	809
15,476,500	HCA Inc.	492	665
6,708,760	M&T Bank Corporation	103	659
24,000,000	Moody's Corporation	499	1,453
2,338,961,000	PetroChina Company Limited	488	1,340
1,727,765	The Washington Post Company	11	1,367
56,448,380	Wells Fargo & Company	463	3,324
	Others	2,863	4,682
	Total common stocks	$ 8,515	$ 35,287

Note: Dollar amounts are in millions.
Source: 2003 Berkshire Hathaway Annual Report.

Table B.28 Berkshire Hathaway 2004 Common Stock Portfolio

Number of Shares	Company	Cost	Market Value
151,610,700	American Express Company	$ 1,470	$ 8,546
200,000,000	The Coca-Cola Company	1,299	8,328
96,000,000	The Gillette Company	600	4,299
14,350,600	H&R Block, Inc.	233	703
6,708,760	M&T Bank Corporation	103	723
24,000,000	Moody's Corporation	499	2,084
2,338,961,000	PetroChina "H" Shares (or equivalents)	488	1,249
1,727,765	The Washington Post Company	11	1,698
56,448,380	Wells Fargo & Company	463	3,508
1,724,200	White Mountain Insurance	369	1,114
	Others	3,351	5,465
	Total common stocks	$ 9,056	$ 37,717

Note: Dollar amounts are in millions.
Source: 2004 Berkshire Hathaway Annual Report.

Table B.29 Berkshire Hathaway 2005 Common Stock Portfolio

Number of Shares	Company	Cost	Market Value
151,610,700	American Express Company	$ 1,287	$ 7,802
30,322,137	Ameriprise Financial, Inc.	183	1,243
43,854,200	Anheuser-Busch, Inc.	2,133	1,844
200,000,000	The Coca-Cola Company	1,299	8,062
6,708,760	M&T Bank Corporation	103	732
48,000,000	Moody's Corporation	499	2,084
2,338,961,000	PetroChina "H" Shares (or equivalents)	488	1,915
100,000,000	The Procter & Gamble Company	940	5,788
19,944,300	Wal-Mart Stores, Inc.	944	933
1,727,765	The Washington Post Company	11	1,322
95,092,200	Wells Fargo & Company	2,754	5,975
1,724,200	White Mountain Insurance	369	963
	Others	4,937	7,154
	Total common stocks	$ 15,947	$ 46,721

Note: Dollar amounts are in millions.
Source: 2005 Berkshire Hathaway Annual Report.

Table B.30 Berkshire Hathaway 2006 Common Stock Portfolio

Number of Shares	Company	Cost	Market Value
151,610,700	American Express Company	$ 1,287	$ 9,198
36,417,400	Anheuser-Busch, Inc.	1,761	1,792
200,000,000	The Coca-Cola Company	1,299	9,650
17,938,100	ConocoPhillips	1,066	1,291
21,334,900	Johnson & Johnson	1,250	1,409
6,708,760	M&T Bank Corporation	103	820
48,000,000	Moody's Corporation	499	3,315
2,338,961,000	PetroChina "H" Shares (or equivalents)	488	3,313
3,486,006	POSCO	572	1,158
100,000,000	The Procter & Gamble Company	940	6,427
299,707,000	Tesco plc	1,340	1,820
31,033,800	U.S. Bancorp	969	1,123

(Continued)

Table B.30 (Continued)

Number of Shares	Company	Cost	Market Value
17,072,192	USG Corp.	536	936
19,944,300	Wal-Mart Stores, Inc.	942	921
1,727,765	The Washington Post Company	11	1,288
218,169,300	Wells Fargo & Company	3,697	7,758
1,724,200	White Mountain Insurance	369	999
	Others	5,866	8,315
	Total common stocks	$ 22,995	$ 61,533

Note: Dollar amounts are in millions.
Source: 2006 Berkshire Hathaway Annual Report.

Table B.31 Berkshire Hathaway 2007 Common Stock Portfolio

Number of Shares	Company	Cost	Market Value
151,610,700	American Express Company	$ 1,287	$ 7,887
35,563,200	Anheuser-Busch, Inc.	1,718	1,861
60,828,818	Burlington Northern Santa Fe	4,731	5,063
200,000,000	The Coca-Cola Company	1,299	12,274
17,508,700	ConocoPhillips	1,039	1,546
64,271,948	Johnson & Johnson	3,943	4,287
124,393,800	Kraft Foods, Inc.	4,152	4,059
48,000,000	Moody's Corporation	499	1,714
3,486,006	POSCO	572	2,136
101,472,000	The Procter & Gamble Company	1,030	7,450
17,170,953	Sanofi-Aventis	1,466	1,575
227,307,000	Tesco plc	1,326	2,156
75,176,026	U.S. Bancorp	2,417	2,386
17,072,192	USG Corp.	536	611
19,944,300	Wal-Mart Stores, Inc.	942	948
1,727,765	The Washington Post Company	11	1,367
303,407,068	Wells Fargo & Company	6,677	9,160
1,724,200	White Mountain Insurance	369	886
	Others	5,238	7,633
	Total common stocks	$ 39,252	$ 74,999

Note: Dollar amounts are in millions.
Source: 2007 Berkshire Hathaway Annual Report.

Table B.32 Berkshire Hathaway 2008 Common Stock Portfolio

Number of Shares	Company	Cost	Market Value
151,610,700	American Express Company	$ 1,287	$ 2,812
200,000,000	The Coca-Cola Company	1,299	9,054
84,896,273	ConocoPhillips	7,008	4,398
30,009,591	Johnson & Johnson	1,847	1,795
130,272,500	Kraft Foods, Inc.	4,330	3,498
3,947,554	POSCO	768	1,191
91,941,010	The Procter & Gamble Company	643	5,684
22,111,966	Sanofi-Aventis	1,827	1,404
11,262,000	Swiss Re	733	530
227,307,000	Tesco plc	1,326	1,193
75,145,426	U.S. Bancorp	2,337	1,879
19,944,300	Wal-Mart Stores, Inc.	942	1,118
1,727,765	The Washington Post Company	11	674
304,392,068	Wells Fargo & Company	6,702	8,973
	Others	6,035	4,870
	Total common stocks	$ 37,135	$ 49,073

Note: Dollar amounts are in millions.
Source: 2008 Berkshire Hathaway Annual Report.

Table B.33 Berkshire Hathaway 2009 Common Stock Portfolio

Number of Shares	Company	Cost	Market Value
151,610,700	American Express Company	$ 1,287	$ 6,143
225,000,000	BYD Company, Ltd.	232	1,986
200,000,000	The Coca-Cola Company	1,299	11,400
37,711,330	ConocoPhillips	2,741	1,926
28,530,467	Johnson & Johnson	1,724	1,838
130,272,500	Kraft Foods, Inc.	4,330	3,541
3,947,554	POSCO	768	2,092
83,128,411	The Procter & Gamble Company	533	5,040
25,108,967	Sanofi-Aventis	2,027	1,979
234,247,373	Tesco plc	1,367	1,620
76,633,426	U.S. Bancorp	2,371	1,725

(Continued)

Table B.33 (Continued)

Number of Shares	Company	Cost	Market Value
39,037,142	Wal-Mart Stores, Inc.	1,893	2,087
334,235,585	Wells Fargo & Company	7,394	9,021
	Others	6,680	8,636
	Total common stocks	$ 34,646	$ 59,034

Note: Dollar amounts are in millions.
Source: 2009 Berkshire Hathaway Annual Report.

Table B.34 Berkshire Hathaway 2010 Common Stock Portfolio

Number of Shares	Company	Cost	Market Value
151,610,700	American Express Company	$ 1,287	$ 6,507
225,000,000	BYD Company, Ltd.	232	1,182
200,000,000	The Coca-Cola Company	1,299	13,154
29,109,637	ConocoPhillips	2,028	1,982
45,022,563	Johnson & Johnson	2,749	2,785
97,214,684	Kraft Foods, Inc.	3,207	3,063
19,259,600	Munich Re	2,896	2,924
3,947,554	POSCO	768	1,706
72,391,036	The Procter & Gamble Company	464	4,657
25,848,838	Sanofi-Aventis	2,060	1,656
242,163,773	Tesco plc	1,414	1,608
78,060,769	U.S. Bancorp	2,401	2,105
39,037,142	Wal-Mart Stores, Inc.	1,893	2,105
358,936,125	Wells Fargo & Company	8,015	11,123
	Others	3,020	4,956
	Total common stocks	$ 33,733	$ 61,513

Note: Dollar amounts are in millions.
Source: 2010 Berkshire Hathaway Annual Report.

Table B.35 Berkshire Hathaway 2011 Common Stock Portfolio

Number of Shares	Company	Cost	Market Value
151,610,700	American Express Company	$ 1,287	$ 7,151
200,000,000	The Coca-Cola Company	1,299	13,994
29,100,937	ConocoPhillips	2,027	2,121
63,905,931	International Business Machines Corp.	10,856	11,751
31,416,127	Johnson & Johnson	1,880	2,060
79,034,713	Kraft Foods, Inc.	2,589	2,953
20,060,390	Munich Re	2,990	2,464
3,947,555	POSCO	768	1,301
72,391,036	The Procter & Gamble Company	464	4,829
25,848,838	Sanofi	2,055	1,900
291,577,428	Tesco plc	1,719	1,827
78,060,769	U.S. Bancorp	2,401	2,112
39,037,142	Wal-Mart Stores, Inc.	1,893	2,333
400,015,828	Wells Fargo & Company	9,086	11,024
	Others	6,895	9,171
	Total common stocks	$ 48,209	$ 76,991

Note: Dollar amounts are in millions.
Source: 2011 Berkshire Hathaway Annual Report.

Table B.36 Berkshire Hathaway 2012 Common Stock Portfolio

Number of Shares	Company	Cost	Market Value
151,610,700	American Express Company	$ 1,287	$ 8,715
400,000,000	The Coca-Cola Company	1,299	14,500
24,123,911	ConocoPhillips	1,219	1,399
22,999,600	DirecTV	1,057	1,154
68,115,484	International Business Machines Corp.	11,680	13,048
28,415,250	Moody's Corporation	287	1,430
20,060,390	Munich Re	2,990	3,599
20,668,118	Phillips 66	660	1,097
3,947,555	POSCO	768	1,295
52,477,678	The Procter & Gamble Company	336	3,563
25,848,838	Sanofi	2,073	2,438

(Continued)

Appendix B

Table B.36 (Continued)

Number of Shares	Company	Cost	Market Value
415,510,889	Tesco plc	2,350	2,268
78,060,769	U.S. Bancorp	2,401	2,493
54,823,433	Wal-Mart Stores, Inc.	2,837	3,741
456,170,061	Wells Fargo & Company	10,906	15,592
	Others	7,646	11,330
	Total common stocks	$ 49,796	$ 87,662

Note: Dollar amounts are in millions.
Source: 2012 Berkshire Hathaway Annual Report.

Table B.37 Berkshire Hathaway 2013 Common Stock Portfolio

Number of Shares	Company	Cost	Market Value
151,610,700	American Express Company	$ 1,287	$ 13,756
400,000,000	The Coca-Cola Company	1,299	16,524
22,238,900	DIRECTV	1,017	1,536
41,129,643	Exxon Mobil Corp.	3,737	4,162
13,062,594	The Goldman Sachs Group, Inc.	750	2,315
68,121,984	International Business Machines Corp.	11,681	12,778
24,669,778	Moody's Corporation	248	1,936
20,060,390	Munich Re	2,990	4,415
20,668,118	Phillips 66	660	1,594
52,477,678	The Procter & Gamble Company	336	4,272
22,169,930	Sanofi	1,747	2,354
301,046,076	Tesco plc	1,699	1,666
96,117,069	U.S. Bancorp	3,002	3,883
56,805,984	Wal-Mart Stores, Inc.	2,976	4,470
483,470,853	Wells Fargo & Company	11,871	21,950
	Others	11,281	19,984
	Total Common Stocks	$56,581	$117,505

Note: Dollar amounts are in millions.
Source: 2013 Berkshire Hathaway Annual Report.

Table B.38 Berkshire Hathaway 2014 Common Stock Portfolio

Number of Shares	Company	Cost	Market Value
151,610,700	American Express Company	$ 1,287	$ 14,106
400,000,000	The Coca-Cola Company	1,299	16,888
18,513,482	Da Vita HealthCare Partners, Inc.	843	1,402
15,430,586	Deere & Company	1,253	1,365
24,617,939	DIRECTV	1,454	2,134
13,062,594	The Goldman Sachs Group, Inc.	750	2,532
76,971,817	International Business Machines Corp.	13,157	12,349
24,669,778	Moody's Corporation	248	2,364
20,060,390	Munich Re	2,990	4,023
52,477,678	The Procter & Gamble Company	336	4,683
22,169,930	Sanofi	1,721	2,032
96,890,665	U.S. Bancorp	3,033	4,335
43,387,980	USG Corporation	836	1,214
67,707,544	Wal-Mart Stores, Inc.	3,798	5,815
483,470,853	Wells Fargo & Company	11,871	26,504
	Others	10,180	15,704
	Total Common Stocks	$55,056	$117,470

Note: Dollar amounts are in millions.
Source: 2014 Berkshire Hathaway Annual Report.

Table B.39 Berkshire Hathaway 2015 Common Stock Portfolio

Number of Shares	Company	Cost	Market Value
151,610,700	American Express Company	$ 1,287	$ 10,545
46,577,138	AT&T	1,283	1,603
7,463,157	Charter Communications, Inc.	1,202	1,367
400,000,000	The Coca-Cola Company	1,299	17,184
18,513,482	Da Vita HealthCare Partners, Inc.	843	1,291
22,164,450	Deere & Company	1,773	1,690
24,617,939	DIRECTV	1,454	2,134
11,390,582	The Goldman Sachs Group, Inc.	654	2,053
81,033,450	International Business Machines Corp.	13,791	11,152

(Continued)

Table B.39 (Continued)

Number of Shares	Company	Cost	Market Value
24,669,778	Moody's Corporation	248	2,475
55,384,926	Phillips 66	4,357	4,530
52,477,678	The Procter & Gamble Company	336	4,683
22,169,930	Sanofi	1,701	1,896
101,859,335	U.S. Bancorp	3,239	4,346
63,507,544	Wal-Mart Stores, Inc.	3,593	3,893
500,000,000	Wells Fargo & Company	12,730	27,180
	Others	10,276	16,450
	Total Common Stocks	$58,612	$112,338

Note: Dollar amounts are in millions.
Source: 2015 Berkshire Hathaway Annual Report.

Table B.40 Berkshire Hathaway 2016 Common Stock Portfolio

Number of Shares	Company	Cost	Market Value
151,610,700	American Express Company	$ 1,287	$ 11,231
61,242,652	Apple Inc.	$6,747	7,093
6,789,054	Charter Communications, Inc.	1,210	1,955
400,000,000	The Coca-Cola Company	1,299	16,584
54,934,718	Delta Airlines Inc.	2,299	2,702
11,390,582	The Goldman Sachs Group, Inc.	654	2,727
81,232,303	International Business Machines Corp.	13,815	13,484
24,669,778	Moody's Corporation	248	2,326
74,587,892	Phillips 66	5,841	6,445
22,169,930	Sanofi	1,692	1,791
43,203,775	Southwest Airlines Co.	1,757	2,153
101,859,335	U.S. Bancorp	3,239	5,233
26,620,184	United Continental Holdings Inc.	1,477	1,940
43,387,980	USG Corp.	836	1,253
500,000,000	Wells Fargo & Company	12,730	27,255
	Others	10,697	17,560
	Total Common Stocks	$65,828	$122,032

Note: Dollar amounts are in millions.
Source: 2016 Berkshire Hathaway Annual Report.

Table B.41 Berkshire Hathaway 2017 Common Stock Portfolio

Number of Shares	Company	Cost	Market Value
151,610,700	American Express Company	$ 1,287	$ 15,056
166,713,209	Apple Inc.	20,961	28,213
700,000,000	Bank of America Corporation	5,007	20,664
53,307,534	The Bank of New York Mellon Corporation	2,230	2,871
225,000,000	BYD Company Ltd.	232	1,961
6,789,054	Charter Communications, Inc.	1,210	2,281
400,000,000	The Coca-Cola Company	1,299	18,352
53,110,395	Delta Airlines Inc.	2,219	2,974
44,527,147	General Motors Company	1,343	1,825
11,390,582	The Goldman Sachs Group, Inc.	654	2,902
24,669,778	Moody's Corporation	248	3,642
74,587,892	Phillips 66	5,841	7,545
47,659,456	Southwest Airlines Co.	1,997	3,119
103,855,045	U.S. Bancorp	3,343	5,565
482,544,468	Wells Fargo & Company	11,837	29,276
	Others	14,968	24,294
	Total Common Stocks	$74,676	$170,540

Note: Dollar amounts are in millions.
Source: 2017 Berkshire Hathaway Annual Report.

Table B.42 Berkshire Hathaway 2018 Common Stock Portfolio

Number of Shares	Company	Cost	Market Value
151,610,700	American Express Company	$ 1,287	$ 14,452
255,300,329	Apple Inc.	36,044	40,271
918,919,000	Bank of America Corporation	11,650	22,642
84,488,751	The Bank of New York Mellon Corporation	3,860	3,977
6,789,054	Charter Communications, Inc.	1,210	1,935
400,000,000	The Coca-Cola Company	1,299	18,940
65,535,000	Delta Airlines Inc.	2,860	3,270
18,784,698	The Goldman Sachs Group, Inc.	2,380	3,138
50,661,394	JPMorgan Chase & Co.	5,605	4,946
24,669,778	Moody's Corporation	248	3,455

(*Continued*)

Appendix B

Table B.42 (Continued)

Number of Shares	Company	Cost	Market Value
47,890,899	Southwest Airlines Co.	2,005	2,226
21,938,642	United Continental Holdings Inc.	1,195	1,837
146,346,999	U.S. Bancorp	5,548	6,688
43,387,980	USG Corporation	836	1,851
449,349,102	Wells Fargo & Company	10,639	20,706
	Others	16,201	22,423
	Total Common Stocks	$102,867	$172,757

Note: Dollar amounts are in millions.
Source: 2018 Berkshire Hathaway Annual Report.

Table B.43 Berkshire Hathaway 2019 Common Stock Portfolio

Number of Shares	Company	Cost	Market Value
151,610,700	American Express Company	$ 1,287	$ 18,874
250,866,566	Apple Inc.	35,287	73,667
947,760,000	Bank of America Corporation	12,560	33,380
81,488,751	The Bank of New York Mellon Corporation	3,696	4,101
5,426,609	Charter Communications, Inc.	944	2,632
400,000,000	The Coca-Cola Company	1,299	22,140
70,910,456	Delta Airlines Inc.	3,125	4,147
12,435,814	The Goldman Sachs Group, Inc.	890	2,859
60,059,932	JPMorgan Chase & Co.	6,556	8,372
24,669,778	Moody's Corporation	248	5,857
46,692,713	Southwest Airlines Co.	1,940	2,520
21,938,642	United Continental Holdings Inc.	1,195	1,933
149,497,786	U.S. Bancorp	5,706	8,864
10,239,160	Visa Inc.	349	1,924
345,688,918	Wells Fargo & Company	7,040	18,598
	Others	28,215	38,159
	Total Common Stocks	$110,340	$248,027

Note: Dollar amounts are in millions.
Source: 2019 Berkshire Hathaway Annual Report.

Table B.44 Berkshire Hathaway 2020 Common Stock Portfolio

Number of Shares	Company	Cost	Market Value
25,533,082	AbbVie, Inc.	$ 2,333	$ 2,736
151,610,700	American Express Company	1,287	18,331
907,559,761	Apple Inc.	31,089	120,424
1,032,852,006	Bank of America Corporation	14,631	31,306
66,835,615	The Bank of New York Mellon Corporation	2,918	2,837
225,000,000	BYD Co. Ltd.	232	5,897
5,213,461	Charter Communications, Inc.	904	3,449
48,498,965	Chevron Corporation	4,024	4,096
400,000,000	The Coca-Cola Company	1,299	21,936
52,975,000	General Motors Company	1,616	2,206
81,304,200	Itochu Corporation	1,862	2,336
28,697,435	Merck & Co., Inc.	2,390	2,347
24,669,778	Moody's Corporation	248	7,160
148,176,166	U.S. Bancorp	5,638	6,904
146,716,496	Verizon Communications Inc.	8,691	8,620
	Others	29,458	40,850
	Total Common Stocks	$108,620	$281,170

Note: Dollar amounts are in millions.
Source: 2020 Berkshire Hathaway Annual Report.

Table B.45 Berkshire Hathaway 2021 Common Stock Portfolio

Number of Shares	Company	Cost	Market Value
151,610,700	American Express Company	$ 1,287	$ 24,804
907,559,761	Apple Inc.	31,089	161,155
1,032,852,006	Bank of America Corp	14,631	45,952
66,835,615	The Bank of New York Mellon Corp.	2,918	3,882
225,000,000	BYD Co. Ltd.	232	7,693
3,828,941	Charter Communications, Inc.	643	2,496
38,245,036	Chevron Corporation	3,420	4,488
400,000,000	The Coca-Cola Company	1,299	23,684
52,975,000	General Motors Company	1,616	3,106

(Continued)

Table B.45 (Continued)

Number of Shares	Company	Cost	Market Value
89,241,000	ITOCHU Corporation	2,099	2,728
81,714,800	Mitsubishi Corporation	2,102	2,593
93,776,200	Mitsui & Co., Ltd.	1,621	2,219
24,669,778	Moody's Corporation	248	9,636
143,456,055	U.S. Bancorp	5,384	8,058
158,824,575	Verizon Communications Inc.	9,387	8,253
	Others	26,629	39,972
	Total Common Stocks	$104,605	$350,719

Note: Dollar amounts are in millions.

Source: 2021 Berkshire Hathaway Annual Report.

Notes

Chapter One
World's Greatest Investor

1. Cited by Carol Loomis, "Inside Story of Warren Buffett," *Fortune* (April 11, 1998). According to NASDAQ, a four-sigma event is to be expected about every 31,560 days, or about 1 trading day in 126 years. And a five-sigma event is to be expected every 3,483,046 days, or about 1 day every 13,932 years.
2. John Templeton managed the Templeton Growth Fund for 38 years starting in 1954. William H. Kidd managed Central Securities Corp, a closed-end fund from 1974 to 2022, 48 years. Phil Carret founded the Pioneer Fund in 1928 and managed the portfolio for 55 years.
3. George Johnson, *Fire in the Mind: Science, Faith and the Search for Order* (New York: Vintage Books, 1996), 104.
4. Stephen Jay Gould, "The Streak of Streaks," *Triumph and Tragedy in Mudville: A Lifelong Passion for Baseball* (New York: W.W. Norton & Company, 2004), 173.
5. Roger Lowenstein, *Buffett: The Making of an American Capitalist* (New York: Random House, 1995), 10.
6. Lowenstein, 20.
7. Alice Schroeder, *The Snowball: Warren Buffett and the Business of Life* (New York: Bantam Books, 2008), 63.
8. F. C. Minaker, *One Thousand Ways to Make $1,000: Practical Suggestions, Based on Actual Experience, for Starting a Business of Your Own and Making Money in Your Spare Time* (Chicago: Dartnell Corporation, 1936), 14.
9. Schroeder, 64.
10. Minaker, 15.
11. Ibid.
12. Ibid.
13. Ibid., 17.
14. Andrew Kilpatrick, *Of Permanent Value: The Story of Warren Buffett: 2015 Golden Anniversary Edition* (Birmingham, AL, AKPE Publishing, 2015), 39.
15. Ibid., 40.
16. Schroeder, 129.
17. John Train, *The Money Masters* (New York: Penguin Books, 1981), 11.
18. Schroeder, 129.
19. Lowenstein, 26.

280 Notes

20. Schroeder, 146. Note: Schroeder references this apt analogy to Plato's cave, which was originally made by Patrick Byrne.
21. Lowenstein, 120.
22. Train, 11.
23. John Brooks, *The Go-Go Years* (New York: Weybright & Talley), 1973.
24. Jeremy C. Miller, *Warren Buffett's Ground Rules* (New York: HarperCollins, 2016), xii.
25. Train, 12.
26. Ibid.
27. Miller, 250.
28. Lowenstein, 120.
29. 2014 Berkshire Hathaway Annual Report, 25.
30. Ibid., 30.
31. In his letters to his partners, Buffett devoted time helping his partners better understand investing. The "Joys of Compounding" appeared in a Buffett Partnership Letter as cited by Jeremy C. Miller, *Warren Buffett's Ground Rules* (New York: Harper Collins, 2016), 18-21.

Chapter Two

The Education of Warren Buffett

1. John R. Minahan and Thusiith I. Mahanama, "Investment Philosophy and Manager Evaluation, Again," *The Journal of Investing* (Spring 2017), 26–32.
2. Alice Schroeder, *The Snowball: Warren Buffett and the Business of Life* (New York: Bantam Dell, 2008), 643.
3. David McCullough, *The Pioneers: The Heroic Story of the Settlers Who Brought the American Ideal West* (New York: Simon & Schuster, 2019), 12.
4. Greg Ip, "The Era of Fed Power Is Over: Prepare for a More Perilous Road Ahead," *Wall Street Journal* (January 15, 2020).
5. Roger Lowenstein, *Buffett: The Making of an American Capitalist* (New York: Random House, 1995), 11.
6. Steve Jordon, *The Oracle & Omaha* (Omaha: Omaha World Herald, 2013), 19.
7. Michael Dirda, *Bound to Please: An Extraordinary One-Volume Literary Education* (New York: W. W. Norton, 2004), 118.
8. Lowenstein, 26.
9. Jordon, 33.
10. Ralph Waldo Emerson, *Self-Reliance*, Vol I, Collected Essays, Richard Whelan, ed. (Harmony Publishing, First Edition, 1991).
11. As told to me by Steve Jordon on September 25, 2019, who in turn had the conversation with Warren Buffett.
12. Lowenstein, 26.
13. *Becoming Warren Buffett*, HBO Documentary, February 11, 2017.
14. Andy Kilpatrick, *Of Permanent Value: The Story of Warren Buffett*, rev. ed. (Birmingham, AL: AKPE, 2000), 81.

15. Jordon, September 25, 2019.
16. Irving Kahn and Robert Milne, *Benjamin Graham: The Father of Financial Analysis*, Occasional Paper Number 5 (Charlottesville, VA: The Financial Analysts Research Foundation, 1977).
17. Brian Thomas, ed., *Columbia Business School: A Century of Ideas* (New York: Columbia University Press, 2016). The background information on Benjamin Graham's history at Columbia University was referenced from this work.
18. Ibid., 32.
19. Ibid., 33.
20. Louis Rich, "Sagacity and Securities," *The New York Times* (December 2, 1934), 13.
21. Benjamin Graham and David Dodd, *Security Analysis*, 3rd ed. (New York: McGraw-Hill, 1951), 38.
22. Benjamin Graham, *The Intelligent Investor* 4th rev. ed. (New York: Harper & Row, 1973), 1–3.
23. 1997 Berkshire Hathaway Annual Report, 13.
24. 1989 Berkshire Hathaway Annual Report, 20.
25. Graham, 277.
26. 1990 Berkshire Hathaway Annual Report, 14.
27. 1987 Berkshire Hathaway Annual Report, 11–12.
28. 1987 Berkshire Hathaway Annual Report, 12.
29. Lowenstein, 36.
30. Ibid., 44.
31. A popular Warren Buffett witticism.
32. Stuart Lavietes, "Philip A. Fisher, 96, Is Dead: Wrote Key Investment Book, *The New York Times* (April 19, 2004).
33. Warren Buffett, "What We Can Learn from Philip Fisher," *Forbes* (October 19, 1987), 40.
34. John Train, *The Money Masters* (New York: Penguin Books, 1981), 60.
35. Fisher's 15 Point System can be found in his book, *Common Stocks and Uncommon Profits* (New York: Harper & Brothers, 1958).
36. Ibid., 11.
37. Ibid., 16.
38. Ibid., 33.
39. Philip Fisher, *Developing an Investment Philosophy*, Monograph Number 10 (Charlottesville, VA: Financial Analysts Research Foundation), 1.
40. Fisher, *Common Stocks and Uncommon Profits*, 13.
41. Train, 64
42. Fisher, *Developing an Investment Philosophy*, 9.
43. "The Money Men—How Omaha Beats Wall Street," *Forbes* (November 1, 1969), 82.
44. L. J. Davis, "Buffett Takes Stock," *The New York Magazine* (April 1, 1990), 61.
45. 1983 Berkshire Hathaway Annual Report, 5.
46. Ibid.
47. Ibid.

48. James W. Michaels, "Are You Doing Things Your Rivals Haven't Yet Figured Out?", *Forbes* (September 23, 1996), 222.
49. 2014 Berkshire Hathaway Annual Report, 26.
50. Kilpatrick, 89.
51. Warren Buffett, "The Superinvestors of Graham-and-Doddsville," *Hermes* (Fall 1984).
52. Remarks made at the 1997 Berkshire Annual Meeting; quoted in Jane Lowe's biography of Charlie Munger, *Damn Right!* (New York: John Wiley & Sons, 2000).
53. 2014 Berkshire Hathaway Annual Report, 27.
54. The reference was made by Lou Simpson, noted in Janet Lowe's book *Damn Right*, 77.
55. Robert Lenzner and Robert Dindiller, "The Not So Silent Partner," *Forbes* (January 22, 1996), 78.
56. See Peter Bevelin, *Seeking Wisdom from Darwin to Munger* (Malmo: Sweden: Post Scriptum AB, 2003); Tren Griffin, *Charlie Munger: The Complete Investor* (New York: Columbia Business School Publishing, 2015); Lowe, *Damn Right!*
57. Robert G. Hagstrom, *Investing: The Last Liberal Art* (New York: Columbia Business School Publishing, 2015).
58. Charles T. Munger, *Poor Charlie's Almanack: The Wit and Wisdom of Charles T. Munger* (Virginia Beach, VA: PCA Publications, 2005), 393–394.
59. Munger, 398.
60. Munger, 430–433.
61. Munger, 443, 444.
62. Lowenstein, xv.
63. 2015 Berkshire Hathaway Annual Meeting.
64. A. C. Grayling, *History of Philosophy* (London: Viking, 2009), 256.
65. Robert Lenzner, "Warren's Idea of Heaven," *Forbes* (October 18, 1993).
66. Griffin, 40.
67. Jason Zweig and Nicole Friedman, "Charlie Munger Unplugged," *Wall Street Journal* (May 3, 2019).
68. Remarks at the *Daily Journal* Annual Conference, February 11, 2020; reported by Alex Griese in Whitney Tilson's blog.
69. Griffin, 40.
70. Whitney Tilson blog.

Chapter Three

Business-Driven Investing

1. Benjamin Graham, *The Intelligent Investor*, 4th ed. (New York: Harper & Row, 1973), 286.
2. Robert G. Hagstrom, *The Warren Buffett Way* (New York: John Wiley & Sons, 1994), 97.
3. Graham, 286.

4. Ibid., 102.
5. 1987 Berkshire Hathaway Annual Report, 14.
6. Ibid.
7. Robert Lenzner, "Warren Buffett's Idea of Heaven: 'I Don't Have to Work with People I Don't Like," *Forbes* (October 18, 1993).
8. Robert Lenzner, "Warren Buffett's Idea of Heaven: I Don't Have to Work with People I Don't Like," *Forbes* (October 18, 1993).
9. 1987 Berkshire Hathaway Annual Report, 7.
10. 1989 Berkshire Hathaway Annual Report, 22.
11. 1995 Berkshire Hathaway annual meeting as quoted in Andrew Kilpatrick, *Of Permanent Value: The Story of Warren Buffett,* rev. ed. (Birmingham, AL: AKPE, 2004), 1356.
12. *St. Petersburg Times* (December, 15, 1999) as quoted in Kilpatrick, 1356.
13. *Fortune* (November 22, 1999) as quoted in Kilpatrick, 1356.
14. Lenzner.
15. Kilpatrick, 1344.
16. 1989 Berkshire Hathaway Annual Report.
17. Carol Loomis, "The Inside Story of Warren Buffett," *Fortune* (April 11, 1988).
18. 1988 Berkshire Hathaway Annual Report, 5.
19. 1986 Berkshire Hathaway Annual Report, 5.
20. Kilpatrick, 89.
21. 1989 Berkshire Hathaway Annual Report, 22.
22. Linda Grant, "The $4 Billion Regular Guy," *Los Angeles Times* (magazine section) (April 17, 1991), 36.
23. Lenzner.
24. 1985 Berkshire Hathaway Annual Report, 9.
25. 1979 Berkshire Hathaway Annual Report, 1.
26. Ibid., 2.
27. 1987 Berkshire Hathaway Annual Report, 20.
28. 1984 Berkshire Hathaway Annual Report, 15.
29. 1986 Berkshire Hathaway Annual Report, 25.
30. Carol Loomis, *Tap Dancing to Work: Warren Buffett and Practically Everything, 1996–2012* (New York: Time, Inc., 2012).
31. 1990 Berkshire Hathaway Annual Report, 16.
32. 1992 Berkshire Hathaway Annual Report, 9.
33. Ibid.
34. Ibid.
35. Ibid.
36. Ibid.
37. Jim Rasmussen, "Buffett Talks Strategy with Students," *Omaha World-Herald* (January 2, 1994), 26.
38. Paul Sonkin and Paul Johnson, *Pitch the Perfect Investment: The Essential Guide to Winning on Wall Street* (Hoboken, NJ: John Wiley & Sons, 2017), 69.
39. John C. Bogle, "The (Non) Lessons of History—and the (Real) Lessons of Returns and Costs." Remarks before The American Philosophical Society, Philadelphia, PA, November 10, 2012.

Notes

40. Sonkin and Johnson, 63–64.
41. 1994 Berkshire Hathaway Annual Report, 2.
42. Benjamin Graham and David Dodd, *Security Analysis* (1934), as quoted in Sonkin and Johnson, 130.
43. Seth A. Klarman, *Margin of Safety: Risk Averse Value Investing Strategies for the Thoughtful Investor* (New York: Harper Collins, 1991), as quoted in Sonkin and Johnson.
44. 1999 Berkshire Hathaway Annual Report, 5.
45. Kilpatrick, 800.
46. A popular Buffett witticism. The exact John Maynard Keynes quote is "It is better to be roughly right than precisely wrong."
47. A popular Warren Buffett witticism.
48. A popular Warren Buffett witticism.

Chapter Four

Common Stock Purchases

1. 1985 Berkshire Hathaway Annual Report, 8.
2. 2014 Berkshire Hathaway Annual Report, 8–9.
3. For an excellent review of the story of the *Washington Post* see the Pulitzer Prize–winning *Personal History* by Katharine Graham (New York: Alfred A. Knopf, 1997).
4. Mary Rowland, "Mastermind of a Media Empire," *Working Women* (November 11, 1989), 115.
5. 1991 Washington Post Company Annual Report, 2.
6. 1984 Berkshire Hathaway Annual Report, 9.
7. 1985 Berkshire Hathaway Annual Report, 17.
8. Chalmers M. Roberts, *The Washington Post: The First 100 Years* (Boston: Houghton Mifflin, 1977), 499.
9. William Thorndike Jr., *The Outsiders: Eight Unconventional CEOs and Their Radically Rational Blueprint for Success* (Boston: Harvard Business Review Press, 2012), 110.
10. 1991 Berkshire Hathaway Annual Report, 4.
11. Carol Loomis, "An Accident Report on GEICO," *Fortune* (June 1976), 120.
12. Although the 1973–1974 bear market contributed to part of GEICO's earlier fall, its decline in 1975 and 1976 was all of its own making. In 1975, the Standard & Poor's 500 Index began at 70.23 and ended the year at 90.9. The next year, the stock market was equally strong. In 1976, interest rates fell and the stock market rose. GEICO's share price decline in 1975 and 1976 had nothing to do with the financial markets.
13. 1980 Berkshire Hathaway Annual Report, 7.
14. Ibid.
15. Ibid.

16. Ibid, 7–8.
17. Beth Brophy, "After the Fall and Rise," *Forbes* (February 2, 1981), 86.
18. Lynn Dodds, "Handling the Naysayers," *Financial World* (August 17, 1985), 42.
19. Solveig Jansson, "GEICO Sticks to Its Last," *Institutional Investor* (July 1986), 130.
20. 1991 GEICO Annual Report, 5.
21. David Vise, "GEICO's Top Market Strategist Churning Out Profits," *Washington Post* (May 11, 1987).
22. 1990 GEICO Annual Report, 5.
23. Berkshire Hathaway Compilation of Annual Reports 1977–1983, 58
24. 1995 Berkshire Hathaway Annual Report, 6.
25. Compilation of Berkshire Hathaway Annual Reports 1977–1983, 33.
26. 2010 Berkshire Hathaway Annual Report, 9.
27. Ibid.
28. Andrew Kilpatrick, *Warren Buffett: The Good Guy of Wall Street* (New York: Donald Fine, 1992), 102.
29. Anthony Bianco, "Why Warren Buffett Is Breaking His Own Rules," *BusinessWeek* (April 15, 1985), 34.
30. 1991 Berkshire Hathaway Annual Report, 8.
31. Bianco, 34.
32. Dennis Kneale, "Murphy & Burke," *Wall Street Journal* (February 2, 1990), 1.
33. 1992 Capital Cities/ABC Inc. Annual Report.
34. "A Star Is Born," *BusinessWeek*, 77.
35. Anthony Baldo, "CEO of the Year Daniel B. Burke," *Financial World* (April 2, 1991), 38.
36. William N. Thorndike, *The Outsiders: Eight Unconventional CEOs and Their Radically Rational Blueprint for Success* (Boston: Harvard Business Review Press, 2012), 13–16.
37. "Tom Murphy's Pleasant Cash Problem," *Forbes* (October 1, 1976). Cited in Thorndike, 15.
38. 1985 Berkshire Hathaway Annual Report, 20.
39. Kilpatrick, 123.
40. Ibid.
41. Mark Pendegrast, *For God, Country, and Coca-Cola* (New York: Charles Scribner & Sons, 1993).
42. Art Harris, "The Man Who Changed the Real Thing." *Washington Post* (July 22, 1985), B1.
43. "Strategy for the 1980s," The Coca-Cola Company.
44. Ibid.
45. Roger Lowenstein, *Buffett: The Making of an American Capitalist* (New York: Random House, 1995), 323.
46. Carlota Perez, *Technological Revolutions: The Dynamics of Bubbles and Golden Ages* (Cheltenham, UK: Edward Elgar, 2002).
47. Dominic Rushe, "Warren Buffett Buys $10b IBM Stake," *The Guardian* (November 14, 2011).

286 Notes

48. Akin, Oyedele, "Here's How Apple Shares Do Right After the New iPhone Launches." *Business Insider* (May 24, 2017).
49. Andrew Kilpatrick, *Of Permanent Value: The Story of Warren Buffett, 2020 Elephant Edition* (Birmingham, AL: AKPE Publishing, Inc., 2020), 14–15.
50. Paul Johnson, "Seminar in Value Investing," Columbia University Graduate School of Business, EMBA, Apple: Case Study: 3A (May 2020).
51. Andrew J. Mead, *The Complete Financial History of Berkshire Hathaway* (Petersfield, UK: Harriman House Ltd., 2021.), 679.
52. Professor Todd Finkle's recollection as cited in his book, *Warren Buffett: Investor and Entrepreneur* (New York: Columbia Business School Publishing, 2023), 100.
53. Ibid., 102–103.
54. Michael J. Mauboussin and Dan Callahan, "The Impact of Intangibles on Base Rates" (Consilient Observer), Morgan Stanley Investment Management, Counter Global Insights (June 23, 2021).
55. Ibid.
56. Michael Mauboussin and Dan Callahan, "ROIC and Intangible Assets: A Look at How Adjustments for Intangibles Affect ROIC" (Consilient Observer), Morgan Stanley Investment Management, Counterpoint Global Insights (November 9, 2022).
57. Michael Mauboussin and Dan Callahan, "What Does an EV/EBITDA Multiple Mean?" Blue Mountain Capital Management (September 13, 2018).
58. Michael Mauboussin and Dan Callahan, "What Does a Price-Earnings Multiple Mean? An Analytical Bridge Between P/Es and Solid Economics," Credit-Suisse (January 29, 2014).
59. Ibid.
60. "Apple CEO and Fuqua Alum Tim Cook Talks Leadership at Duke" (February 21, 2014). http://www.fuqua.duke.edu/news_events/feature_stories/tim-cook-talks-leadership/.
61. As of August 10, 2023.
62. Mead, 680.
63. W. Brian Arthur, "Increasing Returns and the New World of Business," *Financial Management* (July–August 1996).
64. Patrick McGee, "Apple Profits Rise as Services Arm Surpasses 1b Users," *Financial Times* (August 3, 2023).
65. Malcom Owen, "Apple Extends Share Buybacks by Another $90 Billion" (May 4, 2023). https://appleinsider.com/articles/23/05/04apple-extends-share-buybacks-by-another-90b.
66. Kilpatrick, 953.
67. Ibid.
68. Author's notes from the 2019 Berkshire Hathaway Annual Meeting.
69. 1980 Berkshire Hathaway Annual Report, 1–2.
70. Ibid.
71. Ibid.
72. Ibid.

73. As quoted in the 2019 Berkshire Hathaway Annual Report, 4.
74. Ibid.
75. Ibid.
76. 2019 Berkshire Hathaway Annual Report, 10.
77. 2020 Berkshire Hathaway Annual Report, 3.
78. Ibid.

Chapter Five
Managing a Portfolio of Businesses

1. Author conversation with Warren Buffett (August 1998).
2. S&P Dow Jones Indices, "SPIVA U.S. Scorecard" (Year-end 2022), 9.
3. 1993 Berkshire Hathaway Annual Report, 15.
4. 1991 Berkshire Hathaway Annual Report, 11.
5. 2021 Berkshire Hathaway Annual Report, 3.
6. 1991 Berkshire Hathaway Annual Report, 11.
7. Ibid.
8. 1993 Berkshire Hathaway Annual Report, 11.
9. Mark Hulbert, "Be a Tiger Not a Hen." *Forbes* (May 25, 1992), 298.
10. 1991 Berkshire Hathaway Annual Report, 11.
11. Interview with Philip Fisher (September 15, 1998).
12. Philip Fisher, *Common Stocks and Uncommon Profits* (New York: John Wiley & Sons, Inc., 1996), 108.
13. Interview with Philip Fisher (September 15, 1998).
14. Interview with Kenneth Fisher (September 15, 1998).
15. 1978 Berkshire Hathaway Annual Report, 6.
16. Author conversation with Warren Buffett (August 1998).
17. 1993 Berkshire Hathaway Annual Report, 9.
18. 1990 Berkshire Hathaway Annual Report, 15.
19. The heading "Superinvestors of Buffettville" is a nod to Warren Buffett's speech given to the Columbia University Business School, on May 17, 1984, at a seminar marking the 50th anniversary of the publication of Benjamin Graham and David Dodd's *Security Analysis*. The title of Buffett's talk was "The Superinvestors of Graham-and-Doddsville."
20. Jess H. Chua and Richard S. Woodward, "J. M. Keynes's Investment Performance: A Note." *The Journal of Finance* XXXVIII, no. 1 (March 1983).
21. Ibid.
22. Ibid.
23. Warren Buffett, "The Superinvestors of Graham-and-Doddsville," *Hermes* (Fall 1984).
24. Ibid.
25. Ibid.
26. 1996 Sequoia Fund Annual Report.

27. 1986 Berkshire Hathaway Annual Report, 15.
28. 1995 Berkshire Hathaway Annual Report, 10.
29. The research described here was part of larger research study I conducted with Joan Lamm-Tennant, vice president, General-Re Corporation, Stamford, CT.
30. Joseph Nocera, "Who's Got the Answers?" *Fortune* (November 24, 1997), 329.
31. Ibid.
32. Andrew Mauboussin and Samuel Arbesman, "Differentiating Skill and Luck in Financial Markets with Streaks" (February 3, 2011). http://ssrn.com/abstract=1664031.
33. Eugene Shahan, "Are Short-Term Performance and Value Investing Mutually Exclusive?" *Hermes* (Spring 1986). Note: Shahan's article was a follow-up to Warren Buffett's commentary written for *Hermes* in 1984 titled "The Superinvestors of Graham-and-Doddsville."
34. March 21, 1996, Sequoia Fund Quarterly Report.
35. Mark Cahart, "On Persistence in Mutual Fund Performance," *The Journal of Finance* LII, no. 1 (March 1997); Burton G. Malkiel, "Returns from Investing in Equity Mutual Funds 1971 to 1991," *The Journal of Finance* L, no. 2 (June 1995).
36. Darryll Hendricks, Jayendu Patel, and Richard Zeckhauser, "Hot Hands in Mutual Fund: Short-Run Persistence of Relative Performance, 1974–1988, *The Journal of Finance* XLVIII, no. 1 (March 1993).
37. Amit Goyal and Sunil Wahal, "The Selection and Termination of Investment Management Firms by Plan Sponsors," *The Journal of Finance* 63, no. 4 (2008), 1805–1847.
38. Edward J. Russo and Paul J. H. Shoemaker, *Winning Decisions: Getting It Right the First Time* (New York: Double day, 2002).
39. Robert Rubin, Harvard Commencement Address (2001).
40. Widely referenced quote by Warren Buffett.
41. 1987 Berkshire Hathaway Annual Report, 14.
42. Ibid.
43. Ibid.
44. 1991 Berkshire Hathaway Annual Report, 2–3.
45. Ibid., 3.
46. *Outstanding Investor Digest* (August 10, 1995), 10.
47. Ibid.
48. 1996 Berkshire Hathaway Annual Report, 11.
49. Ibid.
50. Carole Gould, "The Price of Turnover," *New York Times* (November 21, 1997).
51. Robert Jeffrey and Robert Arnott, "Is Your Alpha Big Enough to Cover Your Taxes?" *Journal of Portfolio Management* (Spring 1993).
52. Ibid.
53. Ibid.
54. Robert G. Hagstrom, *The Warren Buffett Portfolio: Mastering the Power of the Focus Investment Strategy* (New York: John Wiley & Sons, 1999).
55. K. J. Martijn Cremers and Antii Petajisto, "How Active Is Your Fund Manager? A New Measure That Predicts Performance," *Review of Financial Studies* 22, no. 9 (September 2009), 3329–3365.

56. K. J. Martijn Cremers and Ankur Pareek, "Patient Capital Outperformance: The Investment Skill of High Active Share Managers Who Trade Infrequently," *Journal of Financial Economics* 122 (August 24, 2016), 288–305.
57. *Outstanding Investor Digest* (May 5, 1995), 61.
58. *Outstanding Investor Digest* (May 5, 1998).

Chapter Six
It's Not That Active Management Doesn't Work

1. Author's notes from the 1997 Berkshire Hathaway Annual Shareholder Meeting.
2. Peter Bernstein, *Capital Ideas: The Improbable Origins of Wall Street* (New York: The Free Press, 1992), 44.
3. Ibid., 37.
4. Ibid., 46.
5. Ibid., 47.
6. John Burr Williams, *The Theory of Investment Value* (Boston: Harvard University Press, 1938), preface.
7. Harry Markowitz, "Portfolio Selection," *Journal of Finance* 7, no.1 (March 1952), 77–91.
8. Ibid., 77.
9. Ibid., 89.
10. 1975 Berkshire Hathaway Annual Report, 3.
11. *Outstanding Investor Digest* (April 8, 1990), 18.
12. 1993 Berkshire Hathaway Annual Report, 13.
13. Ibid., 10.
14. 1993 Berkshire Hathaway Annual Report, 11.
15. 2014 Berkshire Hathaway Annual Report, 9.
16. 1996 Berkshire Hathaway Annual Report, 3.
17. 2014 Berkshire Hathaway Annual Report, 18.
18. Markowitz, 89.
19. A popular Warren Buffett witticism.
20. *Outstanding Investor Digest* (August 8, 1996), 29.
21. Bernstein, 44.
22. Ibid., 14.
23. Peter Schjeldahl, *Let's See: Writing on Art from The New Yorker* (New York: Thames & Hudson, 2008), 11.
24. "The Superinvestors of Graham-and-Doddsville" appeared in the 1984 fall edition of *Hermes*.
25. The track records of the individuals and firms mentioned in Warren Buffet's speech, "The Superinvestors of Graham-and-Doddsville," included Warren Buffett, Pacific Partners, Stan Perlmeter, Sequoia Fund, Walter Schloss, Tweedy, Browne, and Charlie Munger.
26. 1988 Berkshire Hathaway Annual Report, 18.

27. Ibid., 17.
28. Jason Zweig, "From a Skeptic: A Lesson on Beating the Market," *Wall Street Journal* (December 22, 2018).
29. Ibid.
30. 1998 Berkshire Hathaway Annual Report, 18.
31. Benjamin Graham, *The Intelligent Investor*, in the 1987 Berkshire Hathaway Annual Report, 12.
32. John Maynard Keynes, *The General Theory of Employment, Interest, and Money* (New York: Harcourt Brace & Company, 1964), 156.
33. Ibid.
34. Ibid., 154.
35. *Outstanding Investor Digest* (August 8, 1997), 14.
36. 2000 Berkshire Hathaway Annual Report, 14; 2013 Berkshire Hathaway Annual Report, 18.
37. 1985 Berkshire Hathaway Annual Report, 2.
38. Ibid.
39. Keynes, 155.
40. Keynes, 157–158.
41. Graham, 95–96.
42. Ibid., 105, 106.
43. Ibid.
44. Robert Lenzner, "Warren Buffett's Idea of Heaven: I Don't Have to Work with People I Don't Like," *Forbes* (October 18, 1993), 43.
45. Carol Loomis, "Inside Story of Warren Buffett," *Fortune* (April 11, 1988), 34.
46. *Outstanding Investor Digest* (March 13, 1998), 63.
47. *Outstanding Investor Digest* (August 10, 1995), 21.
48. Ibid.

Chapter Seven

Money Mind

1. 2017 Berkshire Hathaway shareholder meeting.
2. 2017 Berkshire Hathaway Annual Meeting.
3. Andrew Kilpatrick, *Of Permanent Value: The Story of Warren Buffett, 2020 Elephant Edition* (Birmingham, AL: AKPE Publishing, 2020), 151.
4. Warren Buffett, *Back to School: Question and Answer Session with Business Students* (Hawthorne, CA: BN Publishing. 2008), 19.
5. Arnold LeUnes and Jack Nation, *Sports Psychology: An Introduction* (Wadsworth, CA: Pacific Grove, 2002) as quoted in *Pragmatism and the Philosophy of Sport*, eds. Richard Lally, Douglas Anderson, and John Kagg (Latham, MD: Lexington Books, 2013), 21.
6. It was John Dewey, US philosopher, psychologist, and educational reformer who introduced the concept of "shared experience" in his 1938 book, *Experience and Education* (New York: Macmillan Company, 1939).

7. Daniel Pecaut and Corey Wren, *University of Berkshire: 30 Years of Lessons Learned from Warren Buffett & Charlie Munger at the Annual Shareholder Meetings* (Sioux City, IA: Daniel Pecaut & Corey Wren, 2017).
8. Robert Armstrom, Eric Platt, and Oliver Ralph, "Warren Buffett: I'm Having More Fun Than Any 88-Year-Old in the World," *Financial Times* (April 25, 2019).
9. Linda Simon, *Genuine Reality: A Life of William James* (New York: Harcourt Brace & Company, 1998), 264.
10. Simon, 267.
11. John Kaag, *Sick Souls, Healthy Minds: How William James Can Save Your Life* (Princeton, NJ: Princeton University Press, 2020), 153.
12. Ibid., 155.
13. Robert G. Hagstrom, *The Warren Buffett Way: Investment Strategies of the World's Greatest Investor* (New York: John Wiley & Sons, 1994), 256.
14. Carol Loomis, *Tap Dancing to Work: Warren Buffett on Practically Everything, 1996–2012* (New York: Penguin, 2012), xviii.
15. Kilpatrick, 3.
16. Peter Schjeldahl, *Hot Cold, Heavy, Light, 100 Art Writings, 1988–2016* (New York: Abrams Press, 2019), 32.
17. Lance Esplund, *The Art of Looking: How to Read and Modern Contemporary Art* (New York: Basic Books, 2018), 231.
18. Kaag, 169.
19. Steve Jordon, *The Oracle of Omaha: How Warren Buffett and His Hometown Shape Each Other* (Marceline, MO: Wadsworth, 2013), 211.
20. Michael Mauboussin and Dan Callahan, "Why Corporate Longevity Matters: What Index Turnover Tells Us About Corporate Results," *Credit-Suisse Global Financial Strategies* (April, 16, 2014).
21. Ibid.
22. Carla Perez, *Technological Revolutions: The Dynamics of Bubbles and Golden Ages* (Cheltenham, UK: Edward Elgar, 2002), 11.
23. 2014 Berkshire Hathaway Annual Report, 29.
24. 2022 Berkshire Hathaway Annual Report, 7.
25. 2021 Berkshire Hathaway Annual Report, 5.
26. 2023 Berkshire Hathaway Annual Meeting.
27. 2014 Berkshire Hathaway Annual Report, 31.
28. 2022 Berkshire Hathaway Annual Report, 7
29. 2018 Berkshire Hathaway Annual Report, 13.
30. 2016 Berkshire Hathaway Annual Report, 6.
31. Ibid.
32. 2015 Berkshire Hathaway Annual Report, 8.
33. Kilpatrick, 1269.
34. Quotes from Susan Decker and Carol Loomis are from the 2018 Berkshire Hathaway Shareholder Meeting.
35. Nicole Friedman, "Buffett Says Exit Won't Halt Success," *Wall Street Journal* (May 5, 2018).

Acknowledgments

First, and foremost, I want to express my deep appreciation to Warren Buffett—not only for his teachings but for allowing me to use his copyrighted material from the Berkshire Hathaway Annual Reports. It is next to impossible to improve on what Warren has written. The readers of this book are fortunate to be able to read his words rather than be subjected to a second-best paraphrase.

I have never hesitated to confess that the success of *The Warren Buffett Way* is first and foremost a testament to Warren, to both his warm-hearted nature, which makes him the most popular role model in investing, and his unparalleled success, which makes him the world's greatest investor. It's quite a combination. My thanks also goes to Debbie Bosanek for her kindness and the willingness to keep the communication flowing, these past 30 years, even though I am sure there were 100 other things that demanded her attention that day.

I would also like to thank Charlie Munger for his contributions to the broad study of investing. His insights on the "psychology of misjudgment" and the "latticework of mental models" are extremely important and should be studied by all. Next to studying Warren, the journey of discovering the major mental models by following Charlie's art of achieving worldly wisdom has been one the most fulfilling accomplishments of my career. There is no doubt I am a better investor through being able to think in multidisciplinary terms. Charlie's motivation inspires me each and every day.

Soon after *The Warren Buffett Way* was published I received a letter from Phil Fisher, then 87 years old. This led to multiyear correspondence discussing different investment topics. Those early letters encouraged me that I was indeed on the right path. I will always be grateful for our friendship, although sadly it was all too brief.

I was honored by both Peter Lynch and Howard Marks, two legendary investors, for writing forewords to the book. I am also deeply grateful to Bill Miller for also writing a foreword. In the development of my investment skills, no one has been more important in moving me from the theoretical to the practical than Bill. He is a friend and intellectual coach. He introduced me to the Santa Fe Institute, the study of complex adaptive systems, and the deep well that is philosophical thought. Bill's intellectual generosity these past 40 years has meant more to me than I can say.

Over the years, I have had countless opportunities to talk about Warren Buffett, and investing, with many bright individuals. Whether they realized it or not, they gave me important additional insights that ultimately found their way into this book. With gratitude, I would like to thank Peter Bernstein, Jack Bogle, David Braverman, Charles Ellis, Ken Fisher, Burton Gray, Ed Haldeman, Ajit Jain, Paul Johnson, Michael Mauboussin, Lisa Rapuano, John Rothchild, Bill Ruane, and Lou Simpson.

I have been fortunate to be included in a community of Berkshire writers and, as such, I am also the beneficiary of those who have studied Warren, Charlie, and Berkshire Hathaway. Special thanks goes to Andy Kilpatrick. I consider him to be the official historian of Berkshire. And to this, we can add Adam Mead's book *The Complete Financial History of Berkshire Hathaway*. I am indebted to Larry Cunningham for his masterful work organizing Warren's writings along with his other insightful books, with thanks also to Stephanie Cuba. Let me also thank Bob Miles not only for his fine books but also for his continued support to the study of all things Berkshire. And a special thanks to Carol Loomis, whose legacy of financial writing is unmatched. Two years before Warren started his partnership, Carol began her career as a research associate at *Fortune* rising to become senior editor-at-large, a *New York Times* best-selling author, and one of the great American financial journalists. And as many of you know, she has been editing Warren Buffett's Letters to Shareholders since 1977.

Carol's earliest words of encouragement meant more to me than I can express.

Other writers who have added to my thinking on Warren Buffett, Charlie Munger, and Berkshire Hathaway that I wish to acknowledge and thank include Peter Bevlin, Ronald Chan, David Clark, Todd Finkle, Tren Griffin, Steve Jordon, Janet Lowe, Roger Lowenstein, Jeremy Miller, F. C. Minaker, Daniel Peacut, Laura Rittenhouse, Alice Schroeder, Will Thorndike, and Corey Wren.

I owe special thanks to Bob Coleman, who was the first of the Berkshire faithful to reach out to me three decades ago. Bob has an insatiable curiosity about investing and it has been a great benefit for me to be a part of his conversations. Importantly, Bob introduced me to Tom Russo, who added to my understanding of global investing. Thank you, Tom. From there, the floodgates opened. I would also like to thank Chuck Akre, Jamie Clark, Chris Davis, Tom Gayner, Mason Hawkins, and Wally Weitz.

I am grateful to John Wiley & Sons, Inc. for not only publishing *The Warren Buffett Way, 30th Anniversary Edition*, but for their unwavering support and tireless dedication to the book. Everyone at Wiley is a true professional. Let me begin by thanking Kevin Harreld, acquisitions editor; Susan Cerra, managing editor; Gus A. Miklos, development editor; and Susan Geraghty, copyeditor.

In 1993, I was introduced to Myles Thompson, then the publisher and editor at John Wiley & Sons, and told him about my idea of writing a book on Warren Buffett. Myles championed what eventually became *The Warren Buffett Way* when it was only halfway written. It is my everlasting good fortune that he was willing to take a chance on a first-time writer with no impressive credentials. Had Myles turned me down, my life would have turned out much different and not likely better. Thanks for everything, Myles.

I cannot adequately express my deep gratitude to Laurie Harper. She is the perfect agent. Laurie is smart, kind, and loyal. She navigates the publishing world with integrity, honesty, good humor, and grace. I could not be in better hands. And a word of appreciation, too, to the late Michael Cohn for taking a chance on a first-time writer.

Last, but certainly not least, I owe Maggie Stuckey, my editor and writing partner, more than I can express for her decades of help turning a first-time writer into an adequate author. Although we are separated by a continent, I am always amazed at how Maggie is able to connect intimately to the material. She works tirelessly from one chapter to the next, always searching for the best way to structure the material and articulate, in simple language, the work I have forwarded to her. Maggie Stuckey is the best in the business, and I am fortunate that she has chosen to share her talents with me, the author, and you, the reader.

For all that is good and right about this book, you may thank the people I have mentioned. For any errors or omissions, I alone am responsible.

ROBERT G. HAGSTROM
NOVEMBER 2023

About the Author

Robert Hagstrom is one of the best-known authors of investment books for general audiences. He has written seven books, including the *New York Times* bestseller *The Warren Buffett Way* now a Wiley Investment Classic in its 30th anniversary edition. The book is an international bestseller translated into 18 foreign languages. Robert also wrote *The Warren Buffett Portfolio: Mastering the Power of the Focus Investment Strategy*, the first book to analyze concentrated, low-turnover portfolio management. In addition, he is the author of *Warren Buffett: Inside the Ultimate Money Mind*, a philosophical look at the temperament and mindset of the world's greatest investor.

In addition to the Buffett shelf, Robert has also written other investment books that cover a wide range of topics, including *The NASCAR Way: The Business That Drives the Sport* and *The Detective and the Investor: Uncovering Investment Techniques from the Legendary Sleuths*. Robert is also the author of *Investing: The Last Liberal Art*, now in its second edition. In it, he honors the multidisciplinary approach to investing that follows Charlie Munger's art of achieving worldly wisdom.

Robert has been an investment professional for 40 years. He was the portfolio manager of the institutional growth equity strategy at Legg Mason Capital Management. Robert received honorable mention recognition in Morningstar's Domestic Stock Fund Manager of the Year in 2007. Afterwards, he became the chief investment officer of EquityCompass Investment Management and the senior portfolio manager of the Global Leaders Portfolio.

Robert earned his bachelor and master of arts degrees from Villanova University. He is a chartered financial analyst and a member of the CFA Institute and the CFA Society of Philadelphia.

Index

Page numbers followed by *f* and *t* refer to figures and tables, respectively.

Abel, Greg 249
Academic research 216–217
Accounting controls 45
Active management
    164–166, 203–233
  after-tax returns with 198
  and Efficient Market
    Hypothesis 218–225
  focus investing as 166. *See also*
    Focus investing
  index investing vs. 164–166
  and investment vs. speculation 225–229
  in the investment
    zone 231–233
  and investor behavior
    230–231
  and Modern Portfolio
    Theory 204–218
Active share 200–202
After-tax returns 198–200
Alleghany Corporation 95
Allied Crude Vegetable Oil
    Company 18
Aluminum Company of America
    (Alcoa) 44
Amazon 158, 159

Amazon Web
    Services (AWS) 158
American Broadcasting
    Company (ABC)
    121, 125–127
American Express 18,
    112–113, 169
American Tailwind 246–248
Angel, Doc 20
Annual reports 75, 78–79
Apple, Inc. 96, 140–159
  as Berkshire giant 245
  Berkshire's assets in 169
  determining value of
    147–152
  ecosystem of 154–155
  favorable long-term prospects
    for 154–159
  intangible investments of
    149
  products and services of
    143–146, 154, 156–157
  rational management
    at 152–154
  return on equity at 145–146
  as simple and understandable 143–145

Index

"Are Short-Term Performance and Value Investing Mutually Exclusive?" (Shahan) 186–187
Arnott, Robert 198–200
Assets, tangible and intangible 147–150
Asset-heavy businesses 81–82
Austin, Jeanne 133–134
Austin, Paul 133–134
Average annual return 181–185, 182f, 183f

Bacon, Francis 56, 60, 62
Bayes, Thomas 56
Beeman, Richard 55
Behavioral finance 57
"The Behavior of Stock Prices" (Fama) 219
Berkshire Cotton Manufacturing 20, 244
Berkshire Hathaway 20
  1965–2022 performance vs. S&P 500, 3, 251t–252t
  1977–2021 common stock portfolios 253t–278t. *See also* Common stock purchases
  as American institution 245–250
  American Tailwind for 246–248
  annual reports of 75

annual shareholder meetings at 235–236, 240
Blue Chip Stamps merged with 51
Buffett on permanence of 244
Buffett Partnership's shares in 3, 20, 21
Buffett's control of 3, 20–23
Buffett's familiarity with holdings of 68
concentrated holdings of 169–170
as conglomerate 22
culture of 249
"four giants" of 245–246
insurance stocks owned by 111, 160
look-through earnings of 193, 194
market value of 23
Money Mind at 235–236
Munger's design of 50
Munger's role at 63
performance measurement at 194–195
present transition at 249
profit margins of 83–84
reference library at 10
Samuelson's shares in 223
See's Candies bought by 52–53
as shared experience 239–240
succession at 235–236

value of retained earnings at 159–161
whole companies and common stocks owned by 91, 161–162, 246
Berkshire Hathaway Energy (BHE) 245
Berkshire Hathaway Letters to Shareholders 240
Bernoulli, Jacob 23
Bernstein, Peter 216, 217
Beta factor 211, 213
Bezos, Jeff 106, 158
Bloom, Harold 30
Blue Chip Stamps 51, 52
Bradlee, Ben 97, 98
Brown, Nathan 8
Buffett (Lowenstein) 6–7, 30
Buffett, Ernest 5
Buffett, Hannah Titus 4
Buffett, Howard 249
Buffett, Howard Homan 5, 6 14, 26–32, 110
Buffett, John 4
Buffett, Leila Stahl 5
Buffett, Sidney Homan 4–5, 27
Buffett, Warren 1–26
  as artist 242–245
  background and family of 4–7
  Berkshire Hathaway acquired/grown by 20–23
  Buffett Limited Partnership of 16–20
  career of 2–3, 14–16

  character of 248–249
  on compounding 22–23
  education of 11–13
  on great companies 71
  greatest achievement of 249
  influences on 7–15. *See also* Influences on Buffett
  investment philosophy of 25–26, 67, 236–237. *See also specific topics*
  on patterns 4
  as sportsman 238–239
  as teacher 239–242
  as Washington Post director 97, 99
Buffett-Falk & Company 14
Buffett Limited Partnership 2–3, 16–20
  1957–1969 returns of 3, 17–19, 173
  buying stocks for 91
  focus investing by 173–174, 174*t*
  and salad oil scandal 18, 112
  stock-picking method at 23
Burke, Dan 79, 83 120–122, 125–130
Burlington Northern Santa Fe (BNSF), xviii, xx, 245
Business-driven investing 65–92. *See also* Focus investing
  advantage of 224–225
  biggest challenge in 229
  business tenets 67–71

302 Index

Business-driven investing (*Continued*)
  financial tenets 67, 79–84
  intelligent 91–92
  management tenets 67, 71–79
  Modern Portfolio Theory vs. 212–215, 217, 224
  purposeful detachment from stock market in 232–233
  value tenets 67, 85–91
Business tenets 67–71. *See also individual tenets*
Buy and hold strategy 185–186
Buy at attractive prices 90–91
  Coca-Cola Company 138–140
  Washington Post Company 102
Byrne, John J. "Jack," 110–116, 126

Cahart, Mark 190
Candid management 74–75
  Coca-Cola Company 135–136
  GEICO 113–114
Capital:
  allocation of 72–73, 77, 153
  cost of 87, 88, 152
  opportunity cost of 88
  return on invested capital 150–152
Capital Cities (Cap Cities) 103, 120–121, 125–127
Capital Cities/ABC 96, 120–130
  consistent operating history of 122
  determining value of 123–127
  favorable long-term prospects for 122–123
  institutional imperative for 128–130
  one-dollar premise for 127
  rational management at 127–128
  as simple and understandable 122
Capital expenditures 82
Capital gains and losses 81, 246
Capital gains taxes 198–199
Carnegie, Andrew 158, 161
Cash flow(s) 82, 87
  of technology companies 141
  of Washington Post Company 104
CBS 129
Chace, Ken 93
Change:
  economic 244–245
  and irrational business decisions, *see* The institutional imperative
  unwillingness to accept 76–77
Charles Munger Partnership 51, 174–176, 175t
Chest Fund, King's College 170–173, 172t, 187, 187t, 188t
Cialdini, Robert 58
Cigar butt theory 21
Circle of competence 48–50, 69
Closet indexers 201

Coca-Cola Amatil 131
The Coca-Cola Company 53,
    96, 130–140
  Berkshire's assets in 169
  bought at attractive
    price 138–140
  candid management
    at 135–136
  determining value of 137–138
  favorable long-term prospects
    for 132–134
  market value of 133,
    134, 137–140
  owner earnings at 136–138
  profit margins of 134
  rational management at 136
  return on equity at 134–135
  share price of 139
  as simple and under-
    standable 131
Coca-Cola Enterprises 131
Combs, Todd 142–143, 249
Commodity businesses
    70–71, 113
Common stock purchases 91,
    93–162, 246
  1977–2021, 253t–278t
  Apple, Inc. 140–159
  Buffett's approach to
    231–232. *See also*
    Business-driven investing
  as business ownership 66
  Capital Cities/ABC
    120–130
  The Coca-Cola
    Company 130–140

concentrated 169
failed investments 37–38
in the future, Buffett on 92
GEICO Corporation
    107–120
IBM 141–143
retained earnings of 159–160
value of retained earnings
    in 159–162
Washington Post
    Company 96–107
*Common Stocks and Uncommon
    Profits* (Fisher) 41–42, 168
*Common Stocks as Long Term
    Investments* (Smith) 161
Compounding 9, 21–23
  of Apple returns 154
  of GEICO returns 117
  of intrinsic value 224
  of retained earnings 161
  with See's Candies 53
  of Washington Post Company
    returns 105, 107
Concentrated holdings
    169–170, 179, 215. *See also*
    Focus investing
Conglomerates 22
Consistent operating history 69
  Capital Cities/ABC 122
  GEICO 111–113
  Washington Post
    Company 100
Consumer electronics
    143–144
Cook, Tim 147, 152, 153, 158
Corporate longevity 244

Cost(s):
  of capital 87, 88, 152
  of doing business 45, 46
  switching 156
  transaction 197
Cost controls 83
Covariance 209–210
Cowles, Alfred 205–206
Cremers, K. J. Martijn 200–202
Cuniff, Rick 14, 176, 177
Cunningham, Lawrence 249

Daly, Don 6
Darwin, Charles 56
David, Edwin 50–51
Davidson, Lorimer 108–110
De Angelis, Tino 18
Debt levels 81, 103, 130
Decentralization 126
Decker, Susan 249
Descartes, René 56, 60
Determine the value 85–89
  Apple, Inc. 147–152
  Capital Cities/ABC 123–127
  Coca-Cola Company 137–138
  GEICO 118–120
  Washington Post Company 101–102
Diminishing returns 155. *See also* Increasing Returns Economics
Discounted cash flow model 87, 147
Discount rate 87, 88, 98
Disequilibrium 55–56

Diversification 2, 117, 165, 168, 214–215
Dividends 73. *See also specific companies*
Dividend discount models 87, 147
"Dividend Policy, Growth, and the Valuation of Shares" (Miller and Modigliani) 150
Dividend yield 86
Dodd, David 35
  book by 2, 12, 35, 108, 209
  Buffett's study with 2, 12
  intellectual village of 221
Dow Jones Industrial Average:
  in 1955, 15
  1957–1969 Buffett Limited Partnership's returns vs. 3, 17–19, 173, 174*t*
  1962–1975 Charles Munger Partnership's returns vs. 174–176, 175*t*
  in 1973, 98
DuPont 44

Earnings per share (EPS) 80
Economic benchmark 195
Economic change 244–245
Ecosystems 154–155
Education 54–55
"Efficient Capital Markets" (Fama) 220
Efficient Market Hypothesis/Efficient Market Theory (EMT) 218–225

Index

Einstein, Albert 9
Emerson, Ralph
    Waldo 30–32, 57
Empiricism 59–62
*An Enquiry Concerning Human
    Understanding* (Hume) 61
*An Enquiry Concerning Principles
    of Morals* (Hume) 61
Equilibrium 55–56
Equity risk premium 87–88
Error volatility 201
Esplund, Lance 243
Expenses 83, 198
Extraordinary items 81

Failure 57, 74–75, 77. *See also*
    The institutional imperative
Falk, Carl 7, 14
Fama, Eugene 218–220
Favorable long-term prospects 70–71
    Apple, Inc. 154–159
    Capital Cities/ABC 122–123
    Coca-Cola Company 132–134
    GEICO 113
    Washington Post
        Company 100–101
Fermat, Pierre de 56
"15 Point System," 42–44
Financial performance
    reports 74
Financial tenets 67, 79–84.
    See also individual tenets
Finkle, Todd 147
Fisher, Philip 41–50,
    83, 168–169

Fisher & Company 42
Float 95, 245
Focus investing 164, 166–185
    average annual return with
        181–185, 182*f*, 183*f*
    Buffett Partnership, Ltd.
        173–174, 174*t*
    Charles Munger Partnership
        174–176, 175*t*
    concentrated holdings
        in 169–170
    as high-active share
        investing 200–202
    holding period in 196–197
    John Maynard Keynes
        170–173, 172*t*
    look-through earnings
        in 193–194
    portfolio management
        vs. 166–170
    Sequoia Fund 176–178, 178*t*
    Lou Simpson at GEICO
        179–181, 180*t*
    underperforming periods in
        187–189, 187*t*, 188*t*
Ford, Henry 161
Franchises 70, 106, 156
Franklin, Benjamin 53–55
"From a Skeptic" (Zweig) 223
Future value creation 150–151

GEICO Corporation
    96, 107–120
    Berkshire's assets in 169
    candid management
        at 113–114

GEICO Corporation (*Continued*)
  consistent operating history of 111–113
  determining value of 118–120
  favorable long-term prospects for 113
  institutional imperative for 115–117
  profit margins of 118
  rational management at 115
  return on equity at 118
  as simple and understandable 110–111
  Simpson's focus investing at 179–181, 180*t*
GEICO Insurance 95
General Re 95
The General Theory of Employment, Interest, and Money (Keynes) 225–226
Gerstner, Lou 141–142
Gidden, Norman 109
Goethe, Johann Wolfgang von 243
Goizueta, Robert 79, 132, 134, 135, 139
Goldenson, Leonard 121
Goodwill 119–120, 137
Goodwin, Leo 107–108
Google 159
Government Employees Insurance Company (GEICO) 14, 107–108. *See also* GEICO Corporation
Goyal, Amit 190–191
Graham, Benjamin 33–41, 105
  background of 33, 229
  books by 2, 12, 35, 36, 38, 39, 65, 108, 209
  Buffett influenced by 14, 15, 33–41, 49
  Buffett's departure from method of 22–23
  Buffett's study with 2, 12–13
  on businesslike investing 65–66
  career of 33–35
  cigar butt theory of 21
  as director of GEICO 110
  GEICO stock bought by 108
  Graham-Newman Corporation 13–15
  intellectual village of 221
  on intrinsic value 89
  investing rules of 37–38
  on investor behavior 227
  on margin of safety 36–39, 90
  on the market 38–40, 193, 224
  Munger's similarities to 53
  as rationalist 61
  on security analysis 34–35
  on speculative habits 225, 230
  on stock market correction 14
  on temperament 230, 237
  on timing and pricing 229
  value principles of 16–17
Graham, Don 99
Graham, Katharine 97–99, 102–104
Graham, Philip 96–97
Graham-Newman Corporation 2, 13–15, 34, 221

Grayling, A. C. 61
Great company, Buffett's definition of a 71
Great Depression 6–7
Growth investing, value investing vs. 86

Hathaway Manufacturing 20
Hendricks, Darryll 190
High active-share investing 200–202. *See also* Focus investing
Holding period 196–197, 213
Hough, Marcian "Ted," 140
"How Active Is Your Fund Manager?" (Cremers and Petajisto) 200–202
Huggins, Chuck 52
Hume, David 56, 61, 62, 205

IBM 98, 141–143
Increasing returns economics 154–155
Independent thinking 116
Index investing 164–166, 203
Influence (Cialdini) 58
Influences on Buffett 25–63
  Howard Homan Buffett 26–32
  Philip Fisher 41–50
  Benjamin Graham 33–41, 49
  in his early life and career 7–15
  Charlie Munger 50–63
Information technology (IT) industry 142

The institutional imperative 75–78
  Capital Cities/ABC 128–130
  GEICO 115–117
  Insurance companies 76, 94–95, 111, 115, 118, 160. *See also specific companies*
Intangible investing 147–150
The Intelligent Investor (Graham) 2, 12, 36, 38, 39, 65, 209, 229
Intrinsic value 36–39
  calculating 88–89
  determining 150. *See also* Determine the value
  of newspapers 106
  and price 90, 139–140, 212
Investing:
  as the best game 238–239
  business-driven, *see* Business-driven investing
  change in Buffett's thinking on 49–50
  circle of competence for 48–50, 69
  Fisher's approach to 41–50
  focus, *see* Focus investing
  Graham's rules for 37–38
  growth vs. value 86
  high active-share 200–202
  in high-return businesses run for shareholders 116
  history of 204
  index 164–166, 203
  intangible vs. tangible 147–150

Index

Investing: (*Continued*)
 intelligent 91–92
 long-term 117
 mindset for, *see* Money Mind
 patterns in 3–4
 philosophy of 25–26
 rational 61–62
 speculating vs. 225–229
 standard approach to 224
 temperament in 1, 26, 230
 theories of 1–2
 value 38–41, 85–86
The investment zone 231–233
Investor behavior 227–231
"Is Your Alpha Big Enough to Cover Its Taxes?" (Jeffrey and Arnott) 198–200

Jain, Ajit 249
James, William 57, 241–242, 244
J.C. Penney 8
Jeffrey, Robert 198–200
Jensen, Michael 220
Jobs, Steve 143, 144, 152–153
Jordon, Steve 244
Judgment Under Uncertainty (Kahneman and Tversky) 57–58

Kahn, Irving 33
Kahneman, Daniel 57–58
Kant, Immanuel 56, 60–62
Keough, Donald 79, 138–139
Keppel, Frederick 33
Ketchum, Marshall 206
Keynes, John Maynard 161, 168
 on escaping old ideas 49
 focus investing by 170–173, 172t, 179, 180
 performance percentage over time 187, 187t, 188t
 on speculation 225–226, 228
Klarman, Seth 89
Knapp, Tom 14
Knowledge 239
Kreeger, David 108, 109

Larson, Harry 8–9
Leverage 81
Libertarianism 29–30
Locke, John 29
Lock-in 155–156
Long-term prospects, *see* Favorable long-term prospects
Look-through earnings 193–194
Loomis, Carol 72, 242, 249
Lowenstein, Roger 6–7, 15, 30, 41, 59

Maestri, Lucas 157, 158
Malkiel, Burton 190
Management:
 of Cap Cities 130
 decentralization of 126
 Fisher on 46–48
 influences on behavior of 77

of portfolios, *see* Portfolio management
Management tenets 67, 71–79. *See also individual tenets*
Mandelbrot, Benoit 219
Managers:
   performance evaluations of 191
   who behave like owners 71–72
Margin of safety 36–39, 89–91. *See also* Buy at attractive prices; Determine the value
Margin of Safety (Klarman) 89
Markowitz, Harry Max 205–211, 214–215
Marschak, Jacob 206
Mauboussin, Michael 147–151
Media businesses 105–106, 122–123. *See also individual businesses*
Mental errors 58–59
Meyer, Eugene 96, 97
Microsoft 144
Miller, Merton 150–151
Minaker, Frances Mary Cowan 7–11, 14, 16
Mindless imitation 77. *See also* The institutional imperative
Mindset for investing 205. *See also* Money Mind
Mistakes 75, 90
Moats 70
Modern Portfolio Theory (MPT) 2, 204–218
   Buffett's ideas vs. 211–212, 215
   business-driven investing vs. 212–215, 217
   Efficient Market Hypothesis in 218
   investment risk leg of 207–214
   portfolio diversification in 214–215, 224
   rethinking 215–218
   risk and return in 205, 207–212
   variance as risk measure in 208–210
   volatility in 210–212, 224
Modigliani, Franco 150–151
Monen, Dan 16
Money Mind 235–250
   at Berkshire Hathaway 245–250
   of Buffett 238–245
   and succession at Berkshire Hathaway 235–236
Morningstar 197
Munger, Charlie 10
   background of 50–51
   on Berkshire investing style 203
   on the Berkshire system 202
   Buffett influenced by 50–63
   Buffett on 50
   Buffett's relationship with 63
   on Buffett's valuation calculations 147
   Charles Munger Partnership 51, 174–176, 175*t*

on economic benchmark 195
focus investing by 174–176,
    175t, 179, 180
on gaining knowledge 233
investment philosophy of
    51–52, 61–63
on measuring against
    alternatives 88
on not buying Amazon 158
on not buying Google 159
performance percentage over
    time 187, 187t, 188, 188t
as polymath 53–55
as thought leader 241
on tracking error 202
on value of studying
    mistakes 75
videos of 240
worldly wisdom of 55–63
Municipal bonds 20
Murphy, Tom 79, 83,
    96, 120–130

National Fire & Marine
    Insurance Company 94–95
National Indemnity Company
    76, 94–95, 245
Net present value (NPV)
    206–207, 214
Network effects 155–156
Net worth 13
Newman, Jerome "Jerry," 15, 34
Newspapers 96–100, 105–106.
    See also Washington
    Post Company
Newsweek magazine 97, 100, 103

Newton, Isaac 55
Nocera, Joseph 185–186

Omaha, Nebraska 4–5, 27
Omaha Sun 100
The one-dollar premise 84
    Capital Cities/ABC 127
    Washington Post
        Company 106–107
*One Thousand Ways
    to Make $1,000*
    (Minaker) 7–11, 16
Operating history of company,
    see Consistent operat-
    ing history
Opportunity cost 88
The Oracle of Omaha
    (Jordon) 244
The Outsiders
    (Thorndike) 105, 129
Owner earnings 81–83
    Coca-Cola Company 136–138
    during inflationary
        periods 102

Paine, Thomas 29–30
Paley, Bill 129
Palmisano, Sam 141, 142
Pareek, Ankur 201–202
Pascal, Blaise 56
Patel, Jayendau 190
Path dependence 156
"Patient Capital
    Outperformance"
    (Cremers and
    Pareek) 201–202

Patterns 3–4
Penney, James C. 8
Performance measurement
   185–200, 187*t*–189*t*
  after-tax returns 198–200
  alternative benchmarks
    for 192–195
  Berkshire's measuring
    stick 194–195
  five-year averages vs. yearly
    results 79
  and holding period 196–197
  look-through earn-
    ings 193–194
  return on equity 80–81
  short-term (price) 186–192,
    187*t*–189*t*, 224
  transaction costs 197
  value of management
    reflected in 78
Persistence 190
Person, Chuck 16
Petajisto, Antii 200–202
Phillips, Don 186
Philosophy 56–57
Plato 248
Poor Charlie's Almanack
    (Munger) 54, 58
Portfolio management 163–202
  active 164–166. *See also* Active
    management
  diversification in 2, 165
  Fisher on 48
  focus investing vs. 166–185
  high active-share invest-
    ing 200–202

performance measurement
   185–200, 187*t*–189*t*
  turnover in 170, 197–200
"Portfolio Selection"
    (Markowitz) 207, 210, 214
Positive feedback 155
Pragmatism 57
Price(s):
  buy at attractive prices tenet
    90–91, 102, 138–140
  GEICO's guideline
    for 116–117
  and market efficiency 219
  as measure of perfor-
    mance 186–192
  and mob-like investor behav-
    ior 227–228
  and net worth of company 13
  over long term 4
  and risk 2, 205–210, 212
  on stock market 84, 85
  stock market as base fac-
    tor for 210
  and timer horizon 213
Price-earnings ratio 86
Price-to-book value 86
Price-to-earnings ratio 151, 152
Price variance 208–210
Price volatility 88, 210–212, 214
Pricing flexibility 70
Principia Mathematica
    (Newton) 55
Probability theory 56, 220–221
Profitability:
  Buffett on 83
  comparing 118

of intangible investments 149
significance of 45–46
Profit margins 83–84
Coca-Cola Company 134
GEICO 118
Washington Post
Company 103–104
Proposals Relating to the Education of Youth in Pensilvania (Franklin) 54–55
Psychology 57–59
and long-term prospects 155–156
of the market 225–227
"The Psychology of Human Misjudgment" (Munger) 58–59

Rational investing 61–62
Rationalism 59–62
Rationality 59–62, 76
Rational management 72–74
Apple, Inc. 152–154
Capital Cities/ABC 127–128
Coca-Cola Company 136
GEICO 115
Washington Post
Company 104
Recessions 27–28
Reinvested earnings 72–73
The Republic (Plato) 248
Repurchases of stock 74, 104
by Apple 148, 153–154
by Capital Cities/ABC 127–128
by GEICO 115
by IBM 142
Retained earnings 72, 84, 105, 159–162, 193
Return on equity 80–81
Apple, Inc. 145–146
Coca-Cola Company 134–135
with focus investing 181–185, 182*f*, 183*f*
GEICO 118
Washington Post
Company 102–103
Return on invested capital (ROIC) 150–152
Rhea, Cleaves 107–108
Rich, Louis 35
Ringwalt, Jack 76, 111
Risk:
Buffett on 212–214
and diversification 2, 215
downside price 90
and earnings 88
in Modern Portfolio
Theory 205–213
and share price 212
variance as measure
of 208–210
volatility as measure
of 210–212
Risk-free rate 87, 88
Risk tolerance 1, 204–205, 218
Rockefeller, John 158, 161
Rothbard, Murray 29
Ruane, Bill 13, 14, 19

focus investing by 176–178, 178t, 179, 180
performance percentage over time 187, 187t, 188, 188t
Ruane, Cuniff and Company 177, 178
Rubin, Robert 191–192
Russell 3000, 149

Salad oil scandal 18, 112
Sales 44–45, 152
Samuelson, Paul 218, 223
Schloss, Walter 14
Schroeder, Alice 15
Schumpeter, Joseph 244
Scott, Ridley 143
Scuttlebutt investigation 47–48
Security analysis 34–35
Security Analysis (Graham and Dodd) 2, 12, 35, 108, 209
See, Mary 52
See's Candies 52–53, 162
Self-reliance 30–31, 40
"Self-Reliance" (Emerson) 30–31
Sequoia Fund 19
  focus investing by 176–178, 178t
  performance percentage over time 187, 187t, 188, 188t
Shahan, V. Eugene 186–187
Shareholders, returning money to 73–74, 104

Shareholder value 84, 116. *See also* The one-dollar premise
Sharpe, William 210–211
Short-term performance 186–192, 187t–189t, 224
Simple and understandable 68–69
  Apple, Inc. 143–145
  Capital Cities/ABC 122
  Coca-Cola Company 131
  GEICO 110–111
  Washington Post Company 99–100
"A Simplified Model of Portfolio Analysis" (Sharpe) 210
Simpson, Lou 115–117
  focus investing by 179–181, 180t
  performance percentage over time 187, 187t, 188, 188t
Smith, Edgar Lawrence 160–161
Smith, Frank 120
The Snowball (Schroeder) 15
Social-proof tendency 58
Speculation 35, 217, 225–229
Standard approach to investing 224
Standard & Poor's (S&P) 500 Index:
  1965–2022 Berkshire Hathaway performance vs. 3, 251t–252t
  Apple compared to 147

Standard & Poor's (S&P)
(*Continued*)
  average ROIC of 152
  Coca-Cola compared
    to 133, 140
  focus investing compared to
    181–185, 182*f*, 183*f*
  GEICO compared to 117, 180*t*
  as measuring stick 195
  pretax margins of *Washington
    Post* compared to 102
  Sequoia Fund com-
    pared to 178*t*
  Washington Post Company
    compared to 102, 107
Steady-state value 150. *See also*
  Determine the value
Stock exchanges 204
Stock market:
  1973–1974 bear market
    216–217
  as base factor for price 210
  behavior of 1–2
  Buffett's view of 66
  company values reflected
    in 84. *See also* The
    one-dollar premise
  different views of 25–26
  Efficient Market
    Hypothesis 218–225
  focus on news from 230
  Graham on 38–40, 193, 224
  and investor behavior
    227–231
  prices in 84
  purposeful detachment
    from 232–233
  suspension of trading on 192
  timing and pricing in 229
  values in, and return on
    equity 80–81
  as voting machine vs.
    weighing machine 193
  "The Superinvestors of
    Graham-and-Doddsville"
    (Buffett) 220–221
Switching costs 156

Taff, Conrad 223
Talk to Students (James)
  241–242
Tangible investments 147–149
Tap Dancing to Work
  (Loomis) 242
Taxes 198–200
Technology companies
  140–141, 155–156
Temperament 1, 26, 230, 237
Tenets of *The Warren Buffett Way*
  67, 236–237. *See also individual tenets*
  business tenets 68–71
  buy at attractive prices
    102, 138–140
  candid management 113–
    114, 135–136
  consistent operating history
    100, 111–113, 122

determine the value 101–102,
    118–120, 123–127,
    137–138, 147–152
favorable long-term prospects
    100–101, 113, 122–123,
    132–134, 154–159
financial tenets 79–84
the institutional imperative
    115–117, 128–130
management tenets 71–79
one-dollar premise
    106–107, 127
owner earnings 136–137
profit margins 103–
    104, 118, 134
rational management
    104, 115, 127–128,
    136, 152–154
return on equity 102–103,
    118, 134–135, 145–146
simple and understandable
    99–100, 110–111, 122,
    131, 143–145
and temperament 237
value tenets 85–91
Textiles 20–21, 93–94
The Theory of Investment Value
    (Williams) 86–87,
    206–207, 225
Thinking 58–62, 116
Thomas, Lowell 120
Thoreau, Henry David 30
Thorndike, William 105,
    129

Times-Herald 96, 100, 103
Transaction costs 197
*A Treatise of Human
    Nature* (Hume) 61
Turnarounds 69, 94, 111–113
Turner, Mellisa 132
Tversky, Amos 57–58

Understandable businesses, *see*
    Simple and understandable
UnitedHealth Group 153
Unrealized gain 199

Value:
    determining 85–89. *See also*
        Determine the value
    future value creation
        150–151
    intrinsic, *see* Intrinsic value
    with network effects 155
    price vs. 85
    of retained earnings 159–162
    Williams' definition of 86–87
Value investing 38–41, 85–86
Value tenets 67, 85–91. *See also
    individual tenets*
Variance 208–210
Volatility 2, 39–40, 210–212,
    214

Wahal, Sunhil 190–191
Wanamaker, John 8
Wanamaker & Brown 8
Washington Post 96–98, 106

Washington Post
    Company 96–107
  Berkshire's assets in 169
  bought at attractive price 102
  consistent operating history of 100
  determining value of 101–102
  favorable long-term prospects for 100–101
  one-dollar premise for 106–107
  profit margins of 103–104
  rational management at 104
  return on equity at 102–103
  as simple and understandable 99–100

Wayne, Ronald 143
Weschler, Ted 142–143, 249
Williams, John Burr 86–87, 147, 150, 206–207, 225
Wisdom of the crowd's effect 56
Wittgenstein, Ludwig 56–57
Woodruff, Robert 134
Wozniak, Steve 143

Zeckhauser, Richard 190
Zweig, Jason 223